HUME

Modern Studies in Philosophy is a series of anthologies presenting contemporary interpretations and evaluations of the works of major philosophers. The editors have selected articles designed to show the systematic structure of the thought of these philosophers, and to reveal the relevance of their views to the problems of current interest. These volumes are intended to be contributions to contemporary debates as well as to the history of philosophy; they not only trace the origins of many problems important to modern philosophy, but also introduce major philosophers as interlocutors in current discussions.

Modern Studies in Philosophy is prepared under the general editorship of Dr. Amelie Rorty, Douglass College, Rutgers University.

V. C. CHAPPELL, who holds a Ph.D. from Yale University, is Associate Professor of Philosophy at the University of Chicago, with which he has been associated since 1957. He is an active contributor to philosophical journals, and has edited several volumes, including *The Philosophy of Mind, The Philosophy of David Hume,* and *Ordinary Language: Essays in Philosophical Method.*

MODERN STUDIES IN PHILOSOPHY

HUME

EDITED BY V. C. CHAPPELL

UNIVERSITY OF NOTRE DAME PRESS

NOTRE DAME   LONDON

First Hardbound Edition: 1968

University of Notre Dame Press

Notre Dame, Indiana 46556

Printed by special arrangement with Doubleday & Company, Inc.

Anchor Books Edition: 1966
Doubleday & Company, Inc.
Garden City, New York

Manufactured in the United States of America

CONTENTS

HUME

INTRODUCTION

Current opinion is generally favorable to Hume. True, his philosophy is more studied than accepted by contemporary thinkers. But it *is* studied, and cited, and contended with—almost as if its author were still among us and not two centuries dead. And yet, this "current opinion" goes back no more than thirty years. As recently as 1925, a distinguished Hume-scholar could write that Hume "is no longer a living figure." Professor Hendel has himself remarked the change since then. "Nowadays," he wrote in 1962, "we all think very differently. Hume is no pale ghost of the past."[1] Before 1925 Hume had been a favorite object of attack of the Absolute Idealists, then dominant in Anglo-American philosophy. As such, he was very much a living figure; but interest in him as such faded when Idealism itself began to wane.

What then accounts for the revival of interest in Hume? One factor certainly is the growth of so-called Analytic Philosophy in Britain and America since 1930. Analytic Philosophy is less a set of doctrines than an attitude of mind, a philosophical spirit or temper. And the spirit of modern analysis is very much the

[1] Charles W. Hendel, *Studies in the Philosophy of David Hume*, new ed. (Indianapolis, Ind., 1963), p. xxi.

spirit of Hume. There is the same distrust of grand
hypotheses, the same respect for hard fact and careful
argument, above all the same modesty regarding the
power of philosophy itself. There are of course great
differences between Russell and Moore, Carnap and
Ryle, Quine and Austin, Wittgenstein early and Wittgenstein late—and differences between all of these and
Hume. Most importantly, the modern analysts observe
the line between philosophy and psychology, between
conceptual matters and matters of fact. Unlike Hume,
they know how to be empiricists without making all
questions empirical. But the analytic temper is as
strong in Hume's work as in theirs. Even so, we might
wonder why Hume should have been revived at this
time: there have always been analysts in the history of
philosophy. The answer is that this philosophic age is
more thoroughly analytic than any other ever has
been, and that Hume is the most thoroughly analytic
philosopher ever to have written before the present
century. Given even a minimal interest in one's philosophical forebears, a philosopher in this age could
hardly fail to find in Hume a kindred spirit.

But there is another reason for Hume's recent
emergence from philosophical ghosthood. This is the
quantity of first-rate scholarship on Hume produced
since 1925. First, a new edition of his letters, published
by Greig in 1932. Then Kemp Smith's edition of the
Dialogues in 1935, followed by Jessop's *Bibliography*
and the newly rediscovered *Abstract* in 1938. Then
Kemp Smith's monumental study, *The Philosophy of
David Hume*, in 1941. Finally, in 1954, another volume
of letters, edited by Klibansky and Mossner, and Moss-

ner's definitive biography, *The Life of David Hume*.[2]
The effect of all this work has been to make Hume
and Hume's philosophy accessible to even casual students. With so much known about him, no wonder
that Hume again appeared a living figure.

These two factors—the Humean ·temper of recent
philosophy and the amount known about Hume's
mind and thought—have worked together in producing the contemporary interest in Hume. Hence that
interest is, for the most part, neither purely philosophical nor purely scholarly. Philosophers take off
from Hume in their search for conceptual truths, but
they are also careful to establish just what it is that
Hume maintained. Conversely, scholars examine the
texts in order to determine Hume's meaning, but they
are often prompted to do so by some philosophical per-
plexity. The contemporary scholars of Hume are at
any rate more philosophically sophisticated than their
predecessors were, just as the contemporary philosophical critics of Hume are more attentive and faith-

[2] The works referred to are:
The Letters of David Hume, ed. J. Y. T. Greig, 2 vols. Oxford,
    1932.
Hume's Dialogues concerning Natural Religion, ed. Norman
    Kemp Smith. Oxford, 1935. 2nd ed. London, 1947.
T. E. Jessop, *A Bibliography of David Hume and of Scottish
    Philosophy from Francis Hutcheson to Lord Balfour.* Lon-
    don and Hull, 1938.
Hume, *An Abstract of A Treatise of Human Nature,* ed. J. M.
    Keynes and P. Sraffa. Cambridge, 1938.
Norman Kemp Smith, *The Philosophy of David Hume.* Lon-
    don, 1941.
New Letters of David Hume, ed. Raymond Klibansky and Ernest
    C. Mossner. Oxford, 1954.
Ernest Campbell Mossner, *The Life of David Hume.* London,
    1954.

ful to the letter of their subject's statements. The result is progress in both scholarship and philosophy.

All of the papers which make up this volume exemplify, in varying degrees, this two-sided interest. There are twenty-one papers altogether, all written since 1950. Three of these—the second papers by Robinson and Flew and the paper by Nathan—have not been previously published; the others are reprinted from various journals by permission of their authors and of the appropriate editors. (Information concerning the original publication of the reprinted papers, together with formal acknowledgment of permission to reprint them, is given in a note at the beginning of each such paper.) I have tried to choose papers of high quality and such as to represent the range of Hume's own philosophical interests; also, papers with some distinctive interpretive and/or critical thesis as opposed to mere expositions. Despite the relatively large number of papers included, I have had to pass over several good pieces. These are all listed in (though they by no means exhaust) the "Articles" section of the Bibliography printed at the end of the volume.

I have arranged the twenty-one papers as follows. First, three papers on Hume's philosophy in general; then fifteen papers on more specific topics, in the order in which these topics are treated in the *Treatise*; finally, three papers on Hume's philosophy of religion, which is not dealt with in the *Treatise*. Some of the papers in the second group are more specific than others; those of Wolff and Hayek are the least specific, being concerned with a central feature of Hume's whole philosophy of mind and with Hume's political and legal philosophy in general, respectively. This second group also contains two connected series of papers, in which the later members are responses to the earlier: those of Robinson, Richards, and Robinson again on "cause," and those of MacIntyre, Atkinson, Flew, Hunter, Flew again, and Hudson on "is" and "ought."

The reprinted papers appear as originally published, except for a few changes of spelling, punctuation, and footnote form. References to papers included in this volume are all to the pages of this volume, while references to Hume's works are all either to the Green and Grose edition of *The Philosophical Works* or to the Selby-Bigge editions of the *Treatise* and *Enquiries* and the second Kemp Smith edition of the *Dialogues*. This has also necessitated some editorial revision of the papers' original versions.

PHILOSOPHY AND BIOGRAPHY:
THE CASE OF DAVID HUME

ERNEST CAMPBELL MOSSNER

Interpretation of a philosophical text, as indeed of all texts, must derive primarily from the text itself, the written words which express certain relations of ideas. Yet especially in the case of earlier philosophers, the reader may be assisted by secondary information, various types of historical knowledge, such as the precise meaning of key words at the time written, the intellectual climate of the age, the biography of the author. Biography may not only provide information about sources and motives but can provide information that compels a reconstruction of character based upon the interpretation of a text. And knowledge of character, in turn, may be of great utility in the comprehension of textual passages which are ambiguous because of oblique presentation or of the possible presence of irony. When it becomes desirable to deal with the biography and the character of a philosopher in order to gain fuller understanding of his meaning, it is requisite that the biographical data employed be true and that the character inferred be consistent with them.

The necessity of emphasizing these truisms may be

From *The Philosophical Review*, Vol. LIX (1950). Reprinted by permission of the author and *The Philosophical Review*.

illustrated in the case of the two traditions of exegesis concerning David Hume, in one of which he is portrayed as a devoted inquirer into truth and in the other, as a charlatan in philosophy. In the first tradition, Hume's ideas, however possibly fallacious or inconsistent, are taken as his best effort to deal with specified intellectual issues and are consequently given serious consideration. In the second tradition, his ideas are taken as an attempt to do something other than strictly to inquire into truth and are consequently subject to summary, and even contemptuous, dismissal. It is the present purpose to investigate this second tradition and to prove that it is based upon distortion of psychology and misrepresentation of fact.

I

The questioning of Hume's motives, of his intellectual and moral integrity, began with some of his contemporaries in the second half of the eighteenth century. Dr. John Brown, for instance, described Hume as a writer "of our own Times, bent upon *Popularity* and *Gain*. . . ." Dr. William Warburton wrote to Hume's publisher, Andrew Millar: "You have often told me of this man's moral virtues. He may have many, for aught I know; but let me observe to you, there are vices of the *mind* as well as of the *body*: and I think a wickeder mind, and more obstinately bent on public mischief, I never knew." Dr. James Beattie regarded him as spawning in an unnatural manner "the vile effusion of a hard and stupid heart, that mistakes its own restlessness for the activity of genius, and its own captiousness for sagacity of understanding. . . ." James Boswell speculated that "vanity, as a fascinating mistress, seized upon his fondness, and never quitted her dominion over him." Dr. Samuel Johnson called Hume a blockhead and a rogue and asserted flatly that he lied.[1]

Noteworthy instances in the nineteenth century include John Stuart Mill, who, though generally regarded as a distinguished follower of Hume, restated the same thesis in severe language:

> Hume possessed powers of a very high order; but regard for truth formed no part of his character. He reasoned with surprising acuteness; but the object of his reasonings was, not to obtain truth, but to show that it is unattainable. His mind, too, was completely enslaved by a taste for literature; not those kinds of literature which teach mankind to know the causes of their happiness and misery, that they may seek the one and avoid the other; but that literature which without regard for truth or utility, seeks only to excite emotion.[2]

And T. H. Huxley, also in the tradition of Hume, was in general agreement:

> . . . Hume exhibits no small share of the craving

<hr />

[1] John Brown, *Estimate of the Manners and Principles of the Times* (London, 1757), Sect. VI, p. 57; William Warburton, *A Selection from Unpublished Works*, ed. Francis Kilvert (London, 1841), pp. 309–10; James Beattie, *Essay on Truth*, 4th ed. (London, 1773), p. 482; James Boswell, *The Hypochondriack*, ed. Margaret Bailey (Stanford, Calif., 1928), II, 157; Samuel Johnson in Boswell, *Private Papers* (New York, 1928–34), I, 128, and XIII, 23.

[2] J. S. Mill, review of Brodie's *History of the British Empire*, in *Westminster Review*, II (1824), 34.

after mere notoriety and vulgar success, as distinct from the pardonable, if not honourable, ambition for solid and enduring fame, which would have harmonized better with his philosophy. Indeed, it appears to be by no means improbable that this peculiarity of Hume's moral constitution was the cause of his gradually forsaking philosophical studies, after the publication of the third part . . . of the Treatise, in 1740, and turning to those political and historical topics which were likely to yield, and did in fact yield, a much greater return of that sort of success which his soul loved.[3]

In the twentieth century the charge of unworthy motives has continued to be leveled against Hume, two instances of which in the past decade are to be noticed here. In 1939, the Danish scholar Vinding Kruse wrote:

Hume was a far more complex, versatile, and ambitious character than, for instance, Kant or Spinoza. He combined two glaring contrasts: he was not only, like these, a great solitary thinker, knowing but one purpose, the realization of truth; he was, indeed, a man with many irons in the fire, a man with divers aims. And among these aims the realization of truth was not the most important; for Hume was possessed by literary ambition to such an extent that he set aside all considerations, even the consideration of truth, in order to win the favour of the public. For instance, it is well known that in his later life Hume time after time suppressed his most radical ideas in order to be better appreciated by the public, and it is characteristic that in his autobiography he describes the "ruling passion" of his life not as a Spinoza would have done,

[3] T. H. Huxley, *Hume* (London, 1879), pp. 10–11.

as the urge of philosophical cognition, but love of literary fame.

And this literary ambition was not of the nature which was content with the immortality usually accorded to great thinkers by a late posterity; but, practical and concrete as he was, he craved first and foremost the admiration of his contemporaries. And therefore he was consistently led to regard the judgement of the public as his supreme court, his only guide in his literary work.[4]

The latest instance comes from Professor John H. Randall, Jr.; and, since it is perhaps the most extensive treatment since that of Beattie and also the most far-reaching in its implications, it will require fuller presentation.[5] The customary antithesis between Spinoza and Hume as to personality and thought is repeated. "Hume . . . set as his goal precisely those usual surroundings of social life, the pleasures of the senses, riches, and fame [which had been rejected by Spinoza]. He was never melancholy but 'of an open, social, and cheerful humour'; he was satisfied when he had made a competence; and he delighted all his life in setting forth opinions diametrically opposite to those of his fellow men."

Professor Randall presses the charge, developing it along somewhat new lines:

Hume wrote for two purposes: to make money,

[4] Vinding Kruse, *Hume's Philosophy in his Principal Work, A Treatise of Human Nature, and in his Essays*, tr. P. T. Federspiel (London, 1939), p. 8.

[5] John H. Randall, Jr., "David Hume: Radical Empiricist and Pragmatist," in *Freedom and Experience: Essays Presented to Horace M. Kallen*, ed. Sidney Hook and Milton R. Konvitz (Ithaca and New York, 1947), pp. 289–312.

and to gain a literary reputation. He acknowledged, "My ruling passion is the love of literary fame." As a youth he studied Locke and Berkeley, and Cicero and the ancient Academic skeptics; in their thought he saw the chance to reach startling conclusions and become a shocking success. Berkeley had attacked Newtonian science for serious reasons; he was a crusader, interested in a sound and consistent science. Hume subtly criticized it primarily to attract attention to the Scotsman David Hume. He hated Newton and Locke as Englishmen, besides; for next to priests Englishmen were his most cordial hatred. . . .

He was early seized with a passion for literature. . . . Since he couldn't shock men by a new theory of science, he would try politics and religion. . . .

Philosophy was after all a rather narrow field; so he turned to history and wrote a good Tory history of the Stuarts because the Whigs were in power. . . .

And yet—David Hume is beyond all question the ablest British philosopher; though his interest in philosophy was largely to startle Englishmen into recognizing the Scottish writer David Hume, and he remained a good sound Tory at heart. . . . He was extremely acute, and malicious throughout. Just because he had no real interest in either science or religion, no deep feeling for the values involved, he was able to be utterly consistent in the pricking of metaphysical bubbles, both scientific and theological. . . .

This intellectual personality of Hume's makes clear why his thought is so elusive, why it is so difficult to emerge from his subtle dialectic with definite conclusions. He was wholly uninterested in building up a consistent position of his own, either a new theory of science or a new natural theology. Though the former is certainly implied in his thought, he was always ready to sacrifice it to the literary display of his dialectical skill. . . . He was interested, not in establishing a method and conclusions of his own but in com-

menting on the methods and conclusions of others.
. . . Hume's whole attitude is: I don't for a minute
believe it, any more than you do. But refute it if you
can; I won't.
Hume employs this skepticism, not as a position
to be defended, but as a literary device.[6]

Those eighteenth-century writers who professed to
believe that Hume was a charlatan in philosophy also
believed—and with admirable consistency—that his
philosophy was inconsequential. The nineteenth-century writers made somewhat more generous concessions. It is, however, Professor Randall's paradox of
the philosopher of unworthy motives ("to make
money, and to gain a literary reputation") who is "beyond all question the ablest British philosopher" that
staggers psychology and that demands scrutiny. The
present investigation will be mainly confined to biographical materials; but, first, it will be helpful to point
out certain psychological weaknesses in that curiously
unresolved paradox of the intellectual charlatan who
was Britain's ablest philosopher.

II

The psychological weaknesses inherent in Professor
Randall's paradox may be conveniently put in the form
of generalized questions which require answers prior
to specific biographical evidence. First, would a rational
man of modest circumstances who was desirous of mak-

[6] John H. Randall, Jr., "David Hume: Radical Empiricist and
Pragmatist," pp. 293–94, 296–97.

ing money by writing devote the first ten years of his career to the study and publication of abstract philosophy? Second, would a man writing on philosophy, or on any other subject for that matter, desire *not* to gain a reputation? Third, would a writer wishing to attain a "shocking" success cut out of his manuscript before publication the single section most likely to provide him with that shock? Fourth, is not the risking of possible personal safety and of almost certain obloquy to be taken as a presumption of sincerity rather than of insincerity?

These points have previously been raised by one or another of the defenders of Hume's integrity. Such defenders, who were not necessarily followers of Hume's philosophy, include the biographers, John Hill Burton and J. Y. T. Greig, and also Leslie Stephen, Charles W. Hendel, Jr., and, more recently, Norman Kemp Smith. The above objections would have to be faced in the case of a writer of whatever name. In the case of David Hume they must be answered, not only in terms of general human nature, but also in the concrete data of his biography.

III

The single document which has been most consistently employed to build up the case for Hume's unworthy motives is his autobiography. Now a full autobiography is a boon to the biographer; a brief one, a curse. Of the latter class is David Hume's *My Own*

Life.[7] Its seven pages have confused the general reader
and troubled the biographer. The biographer's trou-
bles are both factual and semantic. By way of illus-
trating the difficulties of fact:

> In 1752, the Faculty of Advocates chose me their
> Librarian, an Office from which I received little or no
> Emolument, but which gave me the Command of a
> large Library. I then formed the Plan of writing the
> History of England; but being frightened with the
> Notion of continuing a Narrative, through a Period
> of 1700 Years, I commenced with the Accession of
> the House of Stuart. . . .

This account seems straightforward and unambiguous,
but actually it is not. Many of Hume's manuscript
memoranda of reading which seem to belong to the
1737–1740 period refer to historical works, both ancient
and modern.[8] And in the "Advertisement" to the
Treatise of 1739, Hume announced that, after dealing
with the Understanding and the Passions, he intended
to proceed "to the examination of Morals, Politics, and
Criticism; which will complete this Treatise of Human Nature."[9] Politics, in the eighteenth century, included political practice as well as theory; so here already in 1739 is intimation that Hume was prepared,
in due course, to proceed to the writing of history.

[7] The text used here is that in *The Letters of David Hume*, ed.
J. Y. T. Greig, 2 vols. (Oxford, 1932), I, 1–7. No further page
references will be given for this short work.
[8] See E. C. Mossner, "Hume's Early Memoranda, 1729–1740:
The Complete Text," *Journal of the History of Ideas*, IX (1948),
492–517. The notes in question are reprinted, pp. 503–17, and
are discussed, pp. 495–96.
[9] Hume, *The Philosophical Works*, ed. T. H. Green and T. H.
Grose, 4 vols. (London, 1874–75), I, 303.

Definitive evidence that he did do so at an early date is to be found in a series of four manuscripts dating from 1745 through 1749, the first of which is a 64-page narrative epitome of British history from the Roman Invasion through the reign of Henry II, together with a few remarks about that of Henry VIII.[10]

The simple statement in *My Own Life*, that "I then [1752] formed the Plan of writing the History of England . . . ," must consequently be expanded by the biographer to read somewhat as follows:

> The Advocates' Library appointment in 1752 at last gave me the opportunity for which I had been waiting ever since originally planning my career many years ago, that is, to write the history of England. But previous experiments in writing that history from the remote beginnings convinced me that it would be preferable to start with the latest age before the contemporary, that of the accession of the House of Stuart, and to work backwards.

The seven-page autobiography of a man of sixty-five who has lived a full and varied life is inevitably a work of high compression and cannot deal with all the *if's*, *and's*, and *but's* which lie behind the simplest statement of fact.

The most significant passages in *My Own Life*, from the point of view of indicating Hume's possible unworthy motives as philosopher, are those dealing with literary ambition and with the life of letters in general. These selections deserve careful study, to facilitate which the key words are here italicized:

[10] For a full description, see E. C. Mossner, "An Apology for David Hume, Historian," *PMLA*, LVI (1941), 675–76.

But this Narrative shall contain little more than the History of my Writings; as indeed, *almost all my Life has been spent in literary Pursuits and Occupations.*

I passed through the ordinary Course of Education with Success; and was seized very early with *a passion for Literature which has been the ruling Passion of my Life,* and the great Source of my Enjoyments.

My studious Disposition, my Sobriety, and my Industry gave my Family a Notion that the Law was a proper Profession for me: But *I found an unsurmountable Aversion to every thing but the pursuits of Philosophy and general Learning;* and while they fancyed I was poring over Voet and Vinnius, Cicero and Virgil were the Authors which I was secretly devouring.

I resolved to make a very rigid Frugality supply my Deficiency of Fortune, to maintain unimpaired my Independency, and *to regard every object as contemptible, except the Improvement of my Talents in Literature.*

I had always entertained a Notion, that *my want of Success, in publishing the Treatise of human Nature, had proceeded more from the manner than the matter;* and that I had been guilty of a very usual Indiscretion, in going to the Press too early.

In 1751, I removed from the Countrey to *the Town; the true Scene for a man of Letters.*

Even *my Love of literary Fame, my ruling Passion,* never soured my humour, notwithstanding my frequent Disappointments.

These passages from *My Own Life* are fraught with difficulties stemming from confusion over the meanings of words. At the outset, it is obvious that Hume regarded himself as a man of letters and that his life was dedicated to literature. Right here, perhaps, the modern philosopher will balk. "I thought," he may comment, "that we were dealing with a philosopher and not with a *mere* literary man." Yet it should seem clear that Hume did not restrict literature to fine letters. To Hume (and to the eighteenth century in general) literature included "Philosophy and general Learning." Consequently, by his "Talents in Literature," Hume implied his ability to think and to present his thoughts in writing on nearly all intellectual subjects. It is further to be remarked that Moral Philosophy as studied at the Scottish universities in the eighteenth century was devoted to man and his multifarious activities, including—to employ modern terminology—metaphysics, psychology, ethics, political theory and history, social institutions, rhetoric, literary criticism and history, and aesthetics.

In the second excerpt from *My Own Life* above, Hume refers to "a passion for Literature which has been the ruling Passion of my Life . . ."; and in the last, he refers to "my Love of literary Fame, my ruling Passion. . . ." Here again, the modern philosopher is wont to bring these two passages together, rightly enough to be sure, and to inquire: "Is this not an inadvertent admission on the part of Hume that *fame*, rather than *literature* (even in the extended eighteenth-century sense), was his real objective? And is not Hume thereby convicted in his own words of having affected singularity of opinion for the sole purpose of attracting attention to himself?" These questions are crucial and will be given full consideration;

but the only legitimate answers must start with the meanings that Hume attached to key words and phrasings.

The diction employed by Hume is partly the diction of popular psychology, especially Pope's in the *Essay on Man* (a work that he read on its first appearance), and partly his own in the *Treatise of Human Nature*. Some of the confusion lies in the fact that in the *Treatise* Hume took over diction from earlier systems and gave approbation to terms that had previously been employed with disapprobation, and conversely, as in the cases of *pride* and *humility*. It is meet, therefore, to turn to the *Treatise* itself, especially, to several sections of Book II, "Of Pride and Humility," "Of the Love of Fame," "Of Curiosity, or the Love of Truth," to which may be added, "Of Greatness of Mind," from Book III. Yet happily a passage at the close of Book I provides an epitome of the whole subject and is of especial significance in that Hume is not generalizing but is writing strictly of himself. The salient parts are italicized here:

At the time, therefore, that I am tir'd with amusement and company, and have indulg'd a reverie in my chamber, or in a solitary walk by a river-side, I feel my mind all collected within itself, and am naturally inclin'd to carry my view into all those subjects, about which I have met with so many disputes in the course of my reading and conversation. *I cannot forbear having a curiosity to be acquainted with the principles of moral good and evil, the nature and foundation of government, and the cause of those several passions and inclinations, which actuate and govern me.* I am uneasy to think I approve of one object, and disapprove of another; call one thing beautiful, and another deform'd; decide concerning truth and falshood, reason and folly, without knowing upon what principles I proceed. *I am concern'd for the condition of the learned world*, which lies under such a deplorable ignorance in all these particulars. *I feel an ambition to arise in me of contributing to the instruction of mankind, and of acquiring a name by my inventions and discoveries.* These sentiments spring up naturally in my present disposition; and shou'd I endeavour to banish them, by attaching myself to any other business or diversion, I feel I shou'd be a loser in point of pleasure; and *this is the origin of my philosophy*.[11]

Here, then, is Hume's own analysis of why he was compelled to write philosophy. The passage may be paraphrased, somewhat as follows, in order to clarify the ambiguities of the psychological diction employed in *My Own Life*:

I cannot help (*ruling passion*) but inquire into fundamental ideas of philosophy, psychology, ethics, and society (*passion for literature or curiosity, or the love of truth*). In the learned world, I am unable to find satisfactory answers to the problems which I am compelled to face. I feel that I must, therefore, present my own conclusions to that learned world in the hope (passion of *sympathy*) of instructing and bettering it. The personal satisfaction (*love of fame*) which I would get from the consideration and, particularly, from the approbation of the learned world, drives me on through all the intellectual difficulties and physical exertions necessary to the completion of my research. It is thus psychologically impossible for me *not* to be a philosopher, an inquirer into truth.

[11] Hume, *The Philosophical Works*, I, 550. The italics are mine, Hume's own being omitted.

IV

It is now fitting for the biographer to review the major facts of Hume's career in order to determine, apart from the account in *My Own Life*,[12] whether he was, indeed, motivated primarily by the desire to make money. In this brief review, which is so crucial to the problem at hand, all statements of fact are to be fully documented so that the unbeliever may be able to verify them for himself.

Born as the second son of a country-gentry family which was, in his own words, "good" but "not rich," David Hume's inheritance brought him little more than £40 a year of income.[13] In 1750, at the age of thirty-nine, he was able to exult that this sum had been boosted to £50; and in 1768, after a highly successful career, he commented in retrospect: "Had I been born to a small Estate in Scotland of a hundred a year, I shoud have remained at home all my Life, planted and improved my Fields, read my Book, and wrote Philosophy. . . ."[14] This statement points to the conclusion that Hume would never have permitted his passion for learning and his pursuit of truth to be thwarted under any circumstances, but that his insecure financial situation, to a considerable extent, determined his

[12] All unidentified quotations in the present section are taken from *My Own Life.*

[13] The estimate is Greig's (*The Letters of David Hume*, I, 23, n. 4) and is corroborated by manuscript materials which I have inspected.

[14] *Ibid.*, II, 188.

actual mode of living. After passing through Edinburgh University "with success," he was prevailed upon by his family to choose a career which would provide him with a respectable living; and, in the tradition of the Humes of Ninewells, he chose that of law. Yet his heart was not in the law. Neglecting it from the start, he threw it up as "nauseous"[15] in 1729 when he believed that he had made a momentous philosophical discovery.

This precipitous decision at the age of eighteen meant that David Hume was deliberately flouting potential security and resigning himself, for a minimum of ten years, to certain insecurity. It was probably this decision also that inspired his mother's famous remark —a remark, unfortunately, that has no documentary basis—that "our Davie's a fine good-natured crater, but uncommon wake-minded."[16] The good Lady Ninewells may easily be forgiven for her seeming obtuseness. During those ten years of study, her son devoted himself to reading and to writing, being at one time, 1733–1734, on the verge of a nervous breakdown from overapplication. The several months' trial in 1734 of a business career at Bristol was never really for the purpose of a business career and of business rewards. The trial was for the recovery of mental health as Hume informed a physician[17] in London at that time: "For this reason I resolved to seek out a more active

[15] *Ibid.*, I, 13.
[16] John Hill Burton, *Life and Correspondence of David Hume*, 2 vols. (Edinburgh, 1846), I, 294 n.
[17] Probably Dr. Arbuthnot. See E. C. Mossner, "Hume's Epistle to Dr. Arbuthnot, 1734: The Biographical Significance," *Huntington Library Quarterly*, VII (1944), 135–52.

Life, & tho' I cou'd not quit my Pretensions in Learning, but with my last Breath, to lay them aside for
some time, in order the more effectually to resume
them."[18]

The following three years, 1734–1737, were spent in
France largely in the composition of the *Treatise*,
during which period Hume presumably used up, not
only current income, but most of his savings, and perhaps some borrowings. Back in London in the late
summer of 1737, he had two immediate purposes: to
prepare the manuscript for the press and to secure
good terms for publication. Revision of the manuscript
resulted in the excision of the section "Of Miracles,"
for prudential and diplomatic reasons: "I am afraid
[it] will give too much offence," wrote Hume to Henry
Home (later Lord Kames) at Edinburgh, "even as the
world is disposed at present. . . . I am at present cas-
trating my work, that is, cutting off its nobler parts;
that is, endeavouring it shall give as little offence as
possible, before which, I could not pretend to put it
into the Doctor's hands."[19] The last reference is to
Doctor, later Bishop, Joseph Butler, famous author of
the *Analogy of Religion* (1736) and of the *Fifteen
Sermons Preached at the Rolls Chapel* (1726). No
distortion of interpretation can ever succeed in making
this action of Hume's argue an overweening desire
to be a "shocking" success. Concerning publication,
Hume ultimately signed what might seem to be an
adequate contract for an unknown writer, but which
was actually one that he came to regret because it

18 Hume, *Letters*, I, 17.
19 *Ibid.*, I, 24–25.

restricted him from bringing out a second and corrected edition.[20]

In a letter from London of February 13, 1739, written shortly after publication of the first two volumes of the *Treatise*, Hume advised Henry Home: "In looking over your Letters I find one of a twelve-month's Date, wherein you desire me to send down a great many Copys to Scotland. You propos'd no doubt to take the Pains of recommending them, & pushing the Sale. But to tell the Truth there is so little to be gain'd that way in such Works as these, that I wou'd not have you take the Trouble."[21]

This passage, which did not appear in any of the printed editions of Hume's letters before 1954, is substantial evidence that mere sales were not what he wanted. The letter continues with a passage, which did appear in print before 1954, and which gives specific indication of what he really wanted: "If you know anybody that is a Judge, you wou'd do me a sensible Pleasure in engaging him to a serious Perusal of the Book. Tis so rare to meet with one, that will take Pains on a Book, that does not come recommended by some great Name or Authority, that, I confess, I am as fond of meeting with such a one, as if I were sure of his Approbation."

Hume's comment in *My Own Life* on the reception of the *Treatise* is well known, so well known as to provide further trouble for the biographer: "It fell *dead-born from the Press*; without reaching such dis-

[20] *Ibid.*, I, 36–37.
[21] *New Letters of David Hume*, ed. R. Klibansky and E. C. Mossner (Oxford, 1954), p. 4.

tinction as even to excite a Murmur among the Zealots." Yet the *such* and the *even* of the sentence should
indicate that Hume's basic aim was not "to excite a
Murmur among the Zealots." The implication is that
in the desire to have the foremost philosophical minds
react favorably, or even unfavorably, to his system, he
was bitterly disappointed; and, to rub it in, the work
was not noticed even by the zealots. By an historical
accident, tragic from Hume's point of view, there were
few eminent philosophers available to deal with the
Treatise at the time of publication and, indeed, for
many years later. In Britain, Berkeley had retired into
the Neoplatonism of his *Siris;* Butler had apparently
abandoned philosophical studies after the appearance
of the *Analogy;* Hartley seemingly never knew the
Treatise; Kames and Reid studied that work from the
outset, to be sure, but it took the one twelve years to
formulate his public reply and the other, a full quarter
of a century. The sole exception was Hutcheson, with
whom, as will soon be made evident, Hume formed a
personal acquaintance. On the Continent, Leibniz and
Malebranche were dead, and Kant was but a boy.
There is no evidence that either Wolff or Condillac
was aware of the *Treatise,* and only questionable evidence in the case of Maupertuis. The contemporary
philosophical tide was definitely at an ebb.

Yet if the *Treatise* failed to attract the attention of
distinguished philosophical minds, or even to excite
the religious zealots, it was not completely overlooked.
The hostile and scurrilous review in the *History of the
Works of the Learned* is notorious; and notices and
reviews in three French and two German periodicals

have recently been brought to light.[22] None of these reviews, however, indicated the slightest comprehension of Hume's proposed intellectual revolution, and their very obtuseness could only have intensified his disappointment. Yet one zealot did produce, in an English periodical of 1740, a hitherto unknown, "short Answer to a long Book lately published."[23] As philosophy, however, its murmur was barely audible.

With no career, or even prospect of a career in mind, Hume returned to Scotland early in 1739, where he could live most reasonably with his mother and brother and where he could prosecute the studies for which he had already sacrificed so much. Abstract and unintelligible, the critics were calling his book. He now determined to show them that his philosophy had important practical applications and that it could be presented in such a manner as to be comprehensible to all educated men. The *Essays, Moral and Political*, Hume's first venture at practical application, was moderately well received but reached only three editions between 1741 and 1748. To the third volume of the *Treatise*, he also devoted much effort; it was published in 1740 with the advice and the patronage of Scotland's foremost moral philosopher, Professor Francis Hutcheson of Glasgow University. But it, too, met with little notice beyond a few casual and uninformed reviews.

The *Treatise*, however, was not dead. It had, rather,

[22] See E. C. Mossner, "The Continental Reception of Hume's Treatise, 1739–1741," *Mind*, LVI (1947), 31–43.
[23] See E. C. Mossner, "The First Answer to Hume's *Treatise*: An Unnoticed Item of 1740," *Journal of the History of Ideas*, XII (1951), 291–94.

a perverse sort of vitality. When, in 1744–1745, David Hume was proposed by the Lord Provost of Edinburgh, his friend John Coutts, as a candidate for the Professorship of Moral Philosophy at Edinburgh University, the *Treatise* was sufficiently alive to be used against his candidacy by Principal William Wishart. The inimical and biased treatment at the hands of Wishart drove Hume to compose A *Letter from a Gentleman to his Friend at Edinburgh; containing some Observations on a Specimen of the Principles Concerning Religion and Morality, said to be maintained in a Book lately published intituled, A Treatise of Human Nature, &c.*, which was sent to the press at Edinburgh by Henry Home in May, 1745.[24] This anonymous tract, the very name of which was hitherto unknown and no copy of which has yet come to light, may possibly prove to be as fruitful in the understanding of Hume's motives and of the *Treatise* itself as *An Abstract of a Treatise of Human Nature* (1740), which was discovered little more than a decade ago.[25]

Shortly before the failure of the professorial candidacy, Hume had accepted his first money-making position—the Bristol clerkship may be discounted—that of tutor to the mad Marquess of Annandale. The position came to him, as did all positions that he ever held, fortuitously. The wealthy young nobleman had been "charmed" by some of Hume's essays.[26] Never eager

[24] The part played by the two men in this affair is revealed in another letter of Hume's, published for the first time in *New Letters*, pp. 14–18.

[25] Reprinted with an introduction by J. M. Keynes and P. Sraffa (Cambridge, 1938).

[26] See *Letters of David Hume*, ed. Thomas Murray (Edinburgh, 1841), pp. 72–73.

to be a tutor because of the constrained life, Hume accepted this offer because of the good salary and the hope of an annuity after some years' service. His devotion to the life of the inquirer and the man of letters dictated this acceptance, as it was to dictate acceptance in 1746 of General St. Clair's offer of a secretaryship on the proposed military expedition to Canada, which ended, oddly enough, in an incursion on the coast of France. A relation of Hume's by marriage, the General had immediately been taken with his personality at a chance meeting in London. In 1748 Hume accepted the position of aide-de-camp to St. Clair on a secret military embassy to the Courts of Vienna and Turin. During this period of miscellaneous employment, 1745–1749, Hume made his first attempt at writing English history and completed the revision of Book I of the *Treatise* into the *Philosophical Essays concerning Human Understanding*, later entitled the *Enquiry concerning Human Understanding*, which appeared at London in 1748, while he was still in Italy. Though containing the incendiary "Of Miracles," the work attracted little attention, and certainly no shock, until 1751. In 1751–1752 Hume's academic aspirations were dashed once again, this time at Glasgow University, where he stood candidate to succeed Hutcheson. Any resemblance between Hume's two efforts to win a professorship and to make money are quite beyond the comprehension of this twentieth-century professor!

In 1752 Hume was able to publish a volume of *Political Discourses*, the result of several years' labor. This, he acknowledges in *My Own Life*, was "the only work of mine, that was successful on the first Publica-

tion: It was well received abroad and at home." But
the *Enquiry concerning the Principles of Morals* of
1751, the revision of Book III of the *Treatise*, had
come "unnoticed and unobserved into the World." The
unexpected offer in 1752 of the Keepership of the Ad-
vocates' Library at Edinburgh presented Hume, as has
already been seen, with the long-wished-for collection
of books and with sufficient time in which to prosecute
the colossal undertaking of writing the *History of England*. Insofar as that was Tory history, it could hardly
have been designed as a money-maker during a Whig
age, nor could it have been aimed at government
patronage at a time when all posts were in the hands
of Whig ministers. It was simply English history as
interpreted by David Hume, man of letters; and the
work was totally unsuccessful until the appearance of
the later volumes on earlier and less controversial
periods. When Hume became more Tory at that time,
he was but reflecting the contemporary political situation. Like many Scottish Whigs, he was driven to the
opposing party in order to combat the anti-Scottish
drive in England; his political principles, however, remained basically unchanged.[27]

There is no need to proceed in further detail with
Hume's career. Lord Hertford's proffer in 1763 of the
secretaryship of the English Embassy at Paris came
from a man personally unknown to Hume. The Under-
Secretaryship of State in 1767 came from Hertford's
brother, General Conway. The external features of

[27] See E. C. Mossner, "Was Hume a Tory Historian? Facts
and Reconsiderations," *Journal of the History of Ideas*, II
(1941), 449–51.

Hume's career were all named by chance and were all accepted by him out of the desire for a competency so as to be able to devote himself to the real career which he had never deserted since early youth, the life of letters. The present review may fittingly end, as it began, with Hume's own reading of his career: "Had I been born to a small estate in Scotland of a hundred a year, I shoud have remained at home all my Life, planted and improved my Fields, read my Book, and Wrote Philosophy. . . ." The plan of the career of man of letters he never altered; but the necessity of providing for a decent livelihood induced him to become, in turn, a tutor, a secretary, an aide-de-camp, a librarian, a diplomat, a statesman. When Hume finally retired to Scotland in 1769, he was well off financially and was able to devote his few remaining years to sociability and to final revisions of his publications. He died, according to Lord Monboddo's witticism, confessing, not his sins, but his Scotticisms. In the strictest interpretation, Hume died true to his ideals.

V

Hume's second motivation in the view of Professor Randall, "to gain a literary reputation," is not entirely disjunct from that of making money. Yet it warrants separate treatment because it involves the subsidiary charge of Hume's desertion of philosophy: "Since he couldn't shock men by a new theory of science, he would try politics and religion. . . . Philosophy was after all a rather narrow field so he turned to his-

tory. . . ." To assert that Hume deserted philosophy
for more popular fields is blindly to disregard the evidence. It is time to insist that Hume never deserted
philosophy.

The *Treatise*, as it stands, is not a complete system
of the sciences; yet it was originally designed as a complete system. Implied in the "Advertisement" to the
Treatise, Hume's program was fully stated in *An Abstract of a Treatise of Human Nature*. The most important sentence is here italicized:

> Beside the satisfaction of being acquainted with what
> most nearly concerns us, it may be safely affirmed,
> that almost all the sciences are comprehended in the
> science of human nature, and are dependent on it.
> The sole end of logic is to explain the principles and
> Operations of our reasoning faculty, and the nature
> of our ideas; morals and criticism regard our tastes
> and sentiments; and politics consider men as united
> in society, and dependent on each other. *This treatise
> therefore of human nature seems intended for a sys-
> tem of the sciences.* The author has finished what
> regards logic, and has laid the foundation of the other
> parts in his account of the passions.[28]

Hume's intention to continue the *Treatise* so as to
form "a system of the sciences" was frustrated by the
fact that the work was ignored by those minds that
were in any way competent to deal with it and misunderstood by those that were not. Eager to correct his
errors, Hume was understandably chagrined at being
ignored. As early as March, 1740, he stated his sentiments concerning the reception of his work in a letter
to Hutcheson:

[28] Hume, *Abstract*, p. 7.

I wish I cou'd discover more fully the particulars wherein I have fail'd. I admire so much the Candour I have observed in Mr. Locke, Yourself, & a very few more, that I woud be extremely ambitious of imitating it, by frankly confessing my Errors: If I do not imitate it, it must proceed neither from my being free from Errors, nor from want of Inclination; but from my real unaffected ignorance.[29]

And in 1754 Hume further confessed to Professor John Stewart of Edinburgh University, "I am willing to be instructed by the Public: tho' human Life is so short that I despair of ever seeing the decision."[30] Stung with the charge of unintelligibility, he took the blame entirely to himself. "Where a man of Sense mistakes my Meaning," he informed Stewart, "I own I am angry: But it is only at myself: For having exprest my Meaning so ill as to have given Occasion to the Mistake."

Since no first-rate mind had taken the pains to point out the mistakes of reasoning of the *Treatise*, Hume was driven to conclude that its major mistake was literary, that is, that it lay in the manner of presentation. This manner was described to Stewart in penitential language: "Above all, the positive Air, which prevails in that Book, & which may be imputed to the Ardor of Youth, so much displeases me, that I have not Patience to review it." Different organization and different style might have a different effect and were certainly worth the attempt. That the matter, however, as differentiated from the manner, was to remain the same, except for minor corrections, was made perfectly

[29] Hume, *Letters*, I, 39.
[30] *Ibid.*, I, 187.

clear in the same letter to Stewart: "But what Success
the same Doctrines, better illustrated & exprest, may
meet with, *Ad huc sub judice lis est.*"

Though the doctrines of the *Treatise* remained essentially unaltered in the two *Enquiries*, Hume deliberately omitted some part of the more technical philosophical analysis of the *Treatise*. This decision was
presumably made because he had already presented
that analysis, only to have it ignored, and because the
omission gave him the better opportunity to restate
his conclusions in simpler form and to emphasize their
applications. Always alert to the social consequences
of thought, Hume restored "Of Miracles" to its original context and, in subsequent publications, applied
the principles of his "science of human nature" to the
fields of economics, government, history, and religion.
The relation of the two *Enquiries* to the *Treatise*, a
subject that cannot be further explored here, is essentially one of simplification of form and of style.[31]

Hume's cultivation of style in the post-*Treatise* period has curiously irritated some modern philosophers.
Little need be said on that subject, however, except
perhaps to suggest that it is the rare philosopher who
is also an artist. Plato was one; so was Berkeley; so is
Santayana. The company is select but good, and
Hume's place in it is unlikely to be disputed. Clearly it
is no act of indecorum for a philosopher to attempt
to present his thoughts in a comely manner, nor does

[31] The full relation has been recently studied by Norman
Kemp Smith, *The Philosophy of David Hume: A Critical Study
of its Origins and Central Doctrines* (London, 1941), pp. 519–
50.

there seem to be any legitimate reason to question his intellectual integrity therefor.

VI

The validity of the tradition of David Hume as the devoted inquirer into truth, no matter what the possible limits and defects of his inquiry, is firmly established in biographical fact. It is also well to recall that, within his lifetime, Hume was known by intimate friends and by congenial controversialists as *le bon David*. This is a matter of the interpretation of character and is relevant to the present thesis because the charge against Hume in the opposing tradition rests, as I have argued, on the misreading of character. In 1777 Adam Smith, who was closest to Hume in intellect and in spirit, gave the world the most famous portrait of *le bon David*, a portrait that the researches of the biographer have been able to substantiate but little to augment.[32] "Thus died," wrote Smith,

> our most excellent, and never-to-be-forgotten friend; concerning whose philosophical opinions men will no doubt judge variously, every one approving or condemning them according as they happen to coincide, or disagree with his own; but concerning whose character and conduct there can scarce be a difference of opinion. . . . Upon the whole, I have always considered him, both in his lifetime, and since his death, as approaching as nearly to the idea of a perfectly

[32] See E. C. Mossner, *The Forgotten Hume: Le bon David* (New York, 1943). The following quotations from Smith and Keith are to be found in that book, pp. 208–9, 212.

wise and virtuous man, as perhaps the nature of human frailty will admit.

To Adam Smith there was no disparity between Hume the inquirer into truth and *le bon David*, between the philosopher and the man. The identity is still not impugned by any known matters of fact, nor perhaps has it ever been more felicitously phrased than by Earl Marischal Keith, who wrote to Hume after the unhappy quarrel with Rousseau: "To the highflyers you are . . . a sad whig, to the whigs an hidden Jacobite, and to reasonable men *le bon David*, a Lover of truth."

SOME MISUNDERSTANDINGS OF HUME

T. E. JESSOP

Hume has been treated by some as a scoundrel, and by others as a hero. He would have repudiated both designations, and rightly. What this diverse treatment signifies is that there was something in him that demanded notice, something so marked that it evoked a strong partisanship of either antipathy or admiration. In his lifetime he was a hero only in France, not, however, as a philosopher, but as the author primarily of the *Political Discourses*, and secondarily of a *History of Great Britain* written from a new point of view: Paris fêted him in the salons and at the Court. In Britain he was stigmatized as a sceptic and an atheist, his philosophical opinions being judged chiefly by the canons of religious orthodoxy, though Reid, unlike Beattie, did recognize that the Hume to be answered was a man of philosophical acumen, and therefore to be argued with, not prophetically thundered at. His *History* continued to be read, and his *Essays, Moral and Political*, but the original cloud that gathered round his philosophical writings remained. It was probably Kant's confession of indebtedness that made

From *Revue Internationale de Philosophie*, No. 20 (1952). Reprinted by permission of the author and the *Revue Internationale de Philosophie*.

students of various schools and countries aware that
Hume was a thinker to be reckoned with. When the
influence of Kant and Hegel made its belated impression in Britain, Hume became again a major butt of
attack, with the significant difference that his chief
idealistic critic, T. H. Green, collaborated in the republication of Hume's works.[1] As an undergraduate I
was required to read Hume in order to refute him.
Since then the pendulum has swung back to something like our traditional empiricism, and within the
last fifteen years or so the most extreme empiricists
have pinned the pennant of Hume to their lances.

The controversy regarding him has been less about
what he meant than about whether his meaning
should be accepted or rejected: his meaning, it was
assumed, was clear, so that there was nothing more to
do than to test it by one's own philosophical standards
and take sides. This assumption that the exegesis of
Hume was in effect finished needs to be challenged.
The exegesis has become rigidified in the text-books of
the history of philosophy, where it has doubtless served
a useful paedagogical purpose. Locke, we are there
told, started the "way of ideas" by translating Descartes into empiricist terms, could find no empirical
ground for the notion of substance, expounded physical causality as an analogue of mental effort, and left
the proof of an external world in a parlous condition;
Berkeley denied material substance, material causality,
and an external world; and Hume completed the cor-
rosive process by denying spiritual substance also and

[1] *The Philosophical Works of David Hume*, ed. T. H. Green
and T. H. Grose, 4 vols. (London, 1874–75).

all causality, leaving us with nothing but the sequence of momentary personal experiences, rich indeed, but significant of nothing beyond themselves. The scheme is, of course, too simple: distinguished thinkers cannot be aligned in so neat a way. So far as Hume is concerned, it can be questioned in two general respects, each susceptible of much specification: it presupposes that Hume was a philosopher, in either motive or achievement, only in Book I of his *Treatise* (with the *Enquiry concerning Human Understanding* as a watered-down version of this), and it presupposes further a particular interpretation of that Book.

The customary concentration of attention on Book I reduces Hume to an epistemologist. Now he certainly did not think of himself as being most importantly the author of that Book, or of the *Enquiry concerning Human Understanding*. In the short autobiography which he left behind at his death he expresses the judgment that his *Enquiry concerning the Principles of Morals* "is of all my writings, historical, philosophical or literary, incomparably the best." That is, he thought of himself primarily as a moralist. We are at liberty, of course, to rank his epistemological achievement higher than his ethical, but we are unlikely to reach a just understanding of either the man or his work unless we take into account his judgment upon himself, which, it seems to me, is borne out by all his works, and is further confirmed by the more intimate glimpses which we get of him in his letters, and yet further by the probity of his life.

The first change which viewing Hume as a moralist introduces into the traditional presentation of him is that it opens our eyes to aspects of his mentality which the original horror, the later criticism, and the recent laudation of him have all alike obscured. A moralist takes life seriously, and has a deeply-felt concern about his fellow men. That Hume was a moralist in this sense, and not a completely detached thinker, is the cumulative impression that he leaves on me. The cool and easy manner of his writing for the public conceals it; so also does his banter (perhaps modelled on Shaftesbury); and so also does the radicalness of his questioning. But his banter and his pointed probing were directed to the exposure of pretentiousness in religion, religious morality, theology, theological ethics, and philosophy. They were intended to be purgative, not destructive. He would have weaned no man from simple religion and simple morality. On the nature of the first he was somewhat reticent, because of, I believe, a reverent agnosticism; on the nature of the second he was explicit and emphatic, handling all the common virtues with respect, and providing for them what he thought to be irrefragable grounds. His *Principles of Morals* is a sincere defense of justice and benevolence; his *Political Discourses* shows a care for good government; and his *History* is written with feeling, and abounds with moral judgments the sincerity of which cannot fairly be questioned. In all these writings he seems to be campaigning, in his own restrained way, for the betterment of life, by recalling the sophisticated section of society from indulgence in intellectual conceit to the honest and sagacious following of what he calls "human nature." There is a similar point in Book I: the well-known passage in which he speaks of his turning from philosophy to the game of backgammon is, beneath its apparent levity, a parable of his most general purpose.

The character-portrait of Hume deserves to be redrawn. He was a man of sentiment. Why should this be surprising, since his writings are an open championing of sentiment? The tearing out of Book I of the *Treatise* from the remainder of that work, and the neglect of his other writings, have falsified our picture of him. The earliest document that gives us a direct glimpse of his mind, a letter written when he was twenty-three to a physician in London, tells of a "distemper" of mind that had afflicted him since he was eighteen, showing itself in an alternation of spiritlessness and "inflamed imaginations." This turmoil, due apparently to a tension between an adolescent emotionality and an already adult intellectuality, and made more severe by the excitement of his discovery, even so early, of his philosophical programme—this turmoil may well be a clue to those aspects of his inner experience about which he was reticent throughout his later life. Instead of daring to follow the clue with any pretence of evidence, I shall only confess that as I read Hume I find myself every now and then imagining a man of strong feelings who has mastered them by a severe self-discipline that was consciously moral, and I suspect that the discipline was virtually complete before corpulence, with the easy temper that usually accompanies it, came upon him.

What was it that Hume set himself to do? The same letter gives us the answer: every moral philosopher, he writes, "consulted his fancy in erecting schemes of vir-

tue and of happiness, without regarding human nature, upon which every moral conclusion must depend.
This therefore I resolved to make my principal study,
and the source from which I would derive every truth
in Criticism [i.e., the investigation of the standards of
aesthetic judgment] as well as in Morality."[2] He left
Criticism out of the *Treatise*, reserving it for his *Essays, Moral and Political* (1742). Observe that in addition only Morality is mentioned, and the seriousness with which he regarded this is indicated externally
by his anxiety to get the judgment of the grave Dr.
Joseph Butler on the draft of Book III of the *Treatise*,
which is wholly concerned with ethics (Greig, *loc. cit.*,
p. 25). The temporal priority of his ethical interest is
an outstanding biographical fact; the continuing, or at
least spasmodically recurrent, dominance of that interest seems to me to be a cogent inference from the
general study of his writings and letters. That temporal
priority, and many features in Books II and III of the
Treatise, have led Professor N. Kemp Smith, in a
masterly work to which I am deeply indebted,[3] to put
forward the revolutionary judgment that these Books
were thought out, and to a large degree written out,
before the famous Book I. The detailed evidence which
he has marshalled is to me entirely convincing. His
radically new point of view illuminates many of the
questions which almost force themselves on the mind
of anyone who reads the *Treatise* from cover to cover.

[2] *The Letters of David Hume*, ed. J. Y. T. Greig, 2 vols. (Oxford, 1932), I, 16.
[3] N. Kemp Smith, *The Philosophy of David Hume: A Critical
Study of its Origins and Central Doctrines* (London, 1941).

There is an apparently strange lack of relationship between some of the doctrines of Book I and the rest. For example, the self that is denied there is here assumed and sometimes explicitly affirmed. Book I is intelligible as an afterthought; it is puzzling if taken as laying down a groundwork of epistemological doctrine with which Books II and III must be consistent; and some of its own internal inconsistencies become explicable when we return to it after reading II and III for their own sake. As only I is usually read (for II is tedious, and instead of III we commonly read the *Principles of Morals*), those points tend to be overlooked. The *Treatise* as a whole is a labyrinth, not a highway. No scholar has seen as adequately as Kemp Smith has done its labyrinthine character, and I do not think that anyone else has found a way through it.

Yet the *Treatise*, despite its inconsistencies, has a unity of purpose and method. It is partly indicated in the passage quoted above from his letter of 1734—that "every moral conclusion" depends on "human nature"; and more fully in the subtitle of the *Treatise* itself—"An attempt to introduce the experimental method of reasoning into moral subjects," where "moral subjects" means the whole sphere of mental phenomena, considered apart from their material affiliations. Hume, then, confessedly set out to make an empirical study of mind; and an empirical study of mind is psychology. True, Hume did not always hold fast to the psychological field; he turned aside to epistemological and ethical considerations; but unless his predominantly psychological treatment is seen as such, his work will be misunderstood. To take a crucial example from

Book I: he did not deny causality (the assumption that he did makes nonsense of his very arguments about it), though he denied the rationality of the causal principle. What he did do was to devote most of his pages on the subject to a *psychological* account of the *process* of causal *inference*. Another important part of Book I is the working out of a *psychological* theory of belief; and Book II is wholly psychological.

This psychologizing, it might be retorted, is after all only the natural expression of his empiricism, and everybody knows that he was an empiricist. This is true; but his psychologizing has not been given the prominent place in exegesis which it has in Hume's text, and—this being a more serious fault—much of his psychology in Book I has been read as if it were epistemology.

Empiricism is undoubtedly the right name for Hume's general attitude, but we must detect the special form which he gave to it. As a label it does not narrow our thought down to his distinctive doctrines. It does not, for instance, distinguish him sharply enough from Locke and Berkeley. What it really expresses is his deep sense of the precariousness of all theorizing, which Locke had in a much lesser degree, and which Berkeley scarcely had at all (he was a metaphysician). Hume's own key word is "human nature." The dissection of *this* is what he set himself to do. He meant by it the outstandingly stubborn, virtually universal, and therefore presumably generic beliefs, emotions and reactions, and the introspectively evident processes by which they are brought about and connected with one another. Some opinions, some feelings, and some practical adjustments are so changeable as to be assignable to the margins of our nature (though their linkages with one another show generic uniformities), but others remain steadily with us, and must therefore be regarded as constitutive, indeed so basically a part of us that Hume found some of them present in animals.[4]

Now his empiricism consists not merely in the identification and causal explanation of these constitutive features, but in the *acceptance* of them. He saw no point in repudiating what we cannot get rid of. It seemed plain to him that, since even philosophers are men, they cannot argue away their humanity, and only make fools of themselves if they try. Here he takes his stand; here he sets down what we must call his fundamental value-judgments, from which he never moves. In Book III, where Hume is more moral than many of his critics have seen, his position is that in fact we do and must seek happiness; that we cannot help seeking the good of others as well as our own (his answer to Hobbes and Mandeville); and that certain qualities of mind in others compel our approval, and certain other qualities our disapproval with equal uniformity. In Book I, where Hume is much more commonsensical than the customary exegesis has allowed him to be, he declares that we do, shall, and must believe in a world independent of our sense perception, a world of things that persist in the intervals of our perceiving them, and are connected by an inexorable causality;

---

[4] Book I, Part III, Sect. 16, *Of the Reason of Animals*; II, I, 12 *Of the Pride and Humility of Animals*; II, II, 12, *Of the Love and Hatred of Animals*. In morals he offers no such parallel.

and he assumes that causality rules nearly as much in
the mental as in the physical world. These are not mere
personal confessions; they are doctrines in the *Treatise*.
They have been either overlooked or treated as curious or shocking inconsistencies by most of his readers,
who have concentrated their attention on his other
doctrine, that our moral attitudes and our belief in an
external world of causally connected events and things
cannot be *rationally* justified. This is, indeed, as in-
expugnable a part of his teaching as the other statements are, but to take it without these is to miss the
precise meaning of one of his chief contentions, which
at one point he expresses in the well-known sentence,
"Reason is the slave of the passions," and which at
other points he expresses more aptly (i.e., without the
aggressive hyperbole which he often slips into), in the
form that our basic beliefs and moral attitudes are a
causal consequence of our constitution, that causal
reasoning can only serve them, that intellect can in
no way illuminate them, and that nevertheless these
features do not discredit them.

We seize the peculiar form of Hume's empiricism
when we note its twofold expression in his ethics and
his epistemology. (1) In Book III it led him to adopt
an autonomous ethic: our general moral judgments
are sufficient and final, are ultimates that need no
props from metaphysics, whether theological or otherwise. He denied the possibility of a metaphysic; he
affirmed the inevitability and rightness of an ethic (the
content of which he took largely from the examples
and maxims of the Romans). Regarding him bio-
graphically, we could say that he was very probably

recoiling from the current religious orthodoxy that tied morality so strongly to religious belief as to maintain that without the latter the former can neither be justified nor practiced. Exegetically, we could say that he was following Shaftesbury (except that the latter was not antimetaphysical), and following Shaftesbury's two most distinctive ethical tenets, namely, that the moral life stands on its own feet, and must do so if it is to retain its purity, and that its judgments are akin rather to aesthetic taste than to rational insight. Shaftesbury's moral empiricism had a decisive effect on British ethics in the eighteenth century. Hume was strongly influenced by it, partly directly, and partly through Hutcheson, whom he consulted about Book III on the eve of its publication. (2) In Book I Hume's empiricism takes a parallel form. Our spontaneous realism and causalism are invincible, belonging to our nature, and neither spring from intellect nor are justifiable by it. We believe in material and causally connected things on the same ground as that on which we act benevolently and approve benevolence in others. The parallel is strongly stressed by Professor Kemp Smith. His hypothesis that Hume moved from ethics to epistemology, from Book III to Book I, and not *vice versa*, is both intrinsically plausible and helpful in the understanding of passages in both Books which the converse supposition leaves obscure. Whether his hypothesis be accepted or no (I accept it), his detection of what he calls a Hutchesonian or "biological" attitude in Book I seems to me irrefutable.

We may now confine ourselves to Book I. That the "biological" attitude only underlies it, and does not dominate the way in which the various topics are handled, must be admitted. Much more evident is the influence of Locke's *Essay*, of Newton's mechanism, especially his theory of gravitation, and of the scepticism of Montaigne and Bayle. These diverse influences conspire to make the Book piebald. The Book is certainly extremely difficult to understand; it is the most badly constructed and confusing piece that Hume ever wrote. His own dissatisfaction with it was expressed quickly—in the Appendix which he added in Book III, and in private letters written soon after its publication. Its imperfections of structure, and some of its inconsistencies and extravaganzas, were removed in the rewriting of it as *Philosophical Essays* (later called *Enquiry*) *concerning Human Understanding*. Nevertheless, Book I of the *Treatise* is acuter than this *Enquiry*; his intellect there plays more sharply and over a wider range of detail, and the reader is given, perhaps not better doctrines, but certainly a better philosophical education. In any case, there the Book stands as something to be read, and the problem is how to read it. What are its dominant lines of thought?

As we have seen, the aim is not to question either causality or the reality of a corporeal world. These are affirmed, and Hume's arguings frankly assume them. There is little left to do, then, but to psychologize, and this is what for the most part Hume does do. In doing so he felt himself inspired by a novel idea—that just as Newton had shown that the fundamental changes in the physical world can be explained by the principle of "attraction" (gravitation), so the processes of knowing, so far as they consist in inferring presumed fact from actual fact, can be explained by the principle of association. It was *this* theme that excited him, this for which he claimed originality, this by which he hoped to win fame, this on which he spent his heaviest labor—*not* the questioning of causality, substance, and an external world. He was sure that he had found a comprehensive law, and what further kindled his enthusiasm was that the law satisfied his empirical scruples: like Newton with gravitation, he could exhibit association as a fact of experience, without any pretence of formulating for it an occult cause. In what has recently been identified as Hume's own summary of the *Treatise*, he says at the end: "If anything can entitle the author to so glorious a name as that of inventor, it is the use he makes of the principle of the association of ideas, which enters into most of his philosophy."[5] He did not, of course, discover this principle; but while Locke, for instance, had brought it in as an afterthought, in a later edition of the *Essay*, and to explain error, Hume uses it as a major instrument, and to account for truth. His zeal, by the way, soon cooled: there is far less pressing of the principle in the *Enquiry*, and when he came to rewrite Book II, in which it is tiresomely pressed to the extreme, he reduced that Book to a very short essay ("Of the Passions," in *Four Dissertations*, 1757; from 1758 onwards appended to the *Enquiry*).

A further dominant feature is Hume's theory of be-

[5] *An Abstract of a Book lately published, entituled* A Treatise of Human Nature (London, 1740). Identified as Hume's by J. M. Keynes and P. Sraffa. See their edition, under the same title (Cambridge, 1938).

lief, in which also he is very self-consciously original. "This act of the mind," he writes in Book I (Part III, Sect. 7, note), "has never yet been explained by any philosopher," and more strongly in the *Abstract* (p. 17), "Here is a new question unthought of by philosophers." The theory plays both a prominent and a basic rôle in Book I, being quite necessary to the account of causal inference. His usual expression of it is rather lame: belief is a "liveliness" or "vivacity" of impressions and of certain ideas, is a manner in which these present themselves. In other places he refers it not to these but to the act of apprehending them. In the *Abstract* (p. 19) he says that he is "sensible that it is impossible by words to describe this feeling." He is thinking only of belief in matters of fact, in existence, not in the connections of mere ideas or in value-distinctions; and his point is that existence is never a part of the content apprehended, is not itself an idea —denying a hitherto unchallenged assumption, and preparing here (as also in his denying that the causal principle is analytic) a way for Kant. The existent is that to which what we might nowadays call the reality-feeling is attached. The definition, it must be observed, is a psychological one, not metaphysical.

It is with this theory of belief, together with the principle of association (specified in the three laws of resemblance, contiguity and causality), that he approaches the topic of causality. That he uses the law of causal association to explain the idea of causality would be a glaring *petitio principii* if his inquiry were an epistemological one. His inquiry is psychological; and there is plainly no impropriety whatever in the search for the cause of the idea of causality, and also —Hume emphasizes this further problem—for the cause of our *belief* in specific causal connections. I must sketch the bare outline of his argument in order to show how it is determined by his principle of association and his theory of belief.

The problem is the idea of necessary connection— for Hume refuses to reduce causality to mere uniformity, and had he done so he would have reduced the psychological associational law of causality to that of contiguity. On the ground of the theory (taken over from Locke, but greatly sharpened) laid down at the beginning of the *Treatise*, that every "simple" idea is a *copy* of an impression (its being a copy and not merely a derivative is Hume's gloss on Locke), his task is to find the impression that supplies the content of the idea of necessary connection. We do in fact have the idea; therefore there must be a correspondent impression. Like Locke and Berkeley, he cannot find the impression in sensation. Also like Locke he finds it in an impression of reflection, in an ultimate inner experience. But whereas Locke locates it in a sense of power, Hume finds it in a transition of attention. When A and B have been experienced together many times, the experience of either will bring before us the idea of the other. The transition becomes inevitable, except when interfered with by another association. Frequency of contiguity produces a natural, a psychological bond—a habit; and the reflex sense of compulsion is the impressional source and archetype of the idea of necessary connection. That is the solution of the first problem. Hume passes to the second. In causal inference, when we sensorily perceive A (or B) we find ourselves not only having the idea of B (or A), and not only expecting B to happen, but also *believing* B to exist. This is the point at which Hume's theory of belief comes into play. Belief as reality-feeling belongs originally to impressions and to nothing else. It cannot be transferred by any act of will. It can be communicated to ideas only by a natural process. This process is the associational one. When an habitual connection between A and B has been established, an impression of either will, besides rousing the idea of the other, infect the idea with the reality-feeling, with belief. The account, it will be noticed, is mechanistic, somewhat analogous to what the physicists were saying when they spoke of the communication of motion by impact. It is the Newtonian strain in the *Treatise*.

Such, slightly simplified, is Hume's most famous argument. What it amounts to is that causal inference does not consist in the rational inspection of the relations of objects, but is a psychologically determined process; that it has no logical ground, but only a cause; that it is itself an instance, not a detection, of causality —"the necessary connection depends on the inference, instead of the inference's depending on the necessary connection" (Book I, Part iii, Sect. 6). It rests on a twofold process of association, of content with content and of belief with content.

Hume's explanation of our belief in an external material world is similarly psychological. By that world we mean things that persist when we are not sensing them, and that are independent of our sensing. The persistence of things cannot be a datum of sense just because we are not always sensing them. Neither can their independence, for this is not in fact a part of the presented content; and if it were, it would be the product not of bare sensation but of an act of comparison, of distinguishing between the self and a not-self—which is scarcely possible, since at the unreflective level we have only a very vague idea of the self (and at the philosophical level, none). Nothing is given except fleeting and subjective perceptions, and from these a world of enduring and external things cannot be inferred in the logical sense of this term. How then does the belief, which we in fact have and cannot discard, in such a world arise? Hume again resorts to the mechanism of association. A thing in its interrupted appearances to us (Hume writes in realistic terms because of his doctrine that realism is really unavoidable) gives us similar perceptions, which in accordance with the law of resemblance become associated. Now resembling associations are apprehended smoothly, and such smooth apprehension resembles, and is unreflectively felt to resemble, the steady apprehension of a continuing object; and this felt resemblance leads the imagination to fill in the gaps in presentation and to fashion the idea of a really continuing object. The associative force of resemblance thus operates in a twofold way. Further, our *belief* in the continuing object is also naturally, not rationally, produced; for in this connection the ideas are *memories* of perceptions, and memories of impressions are directly infected with the belief (or "liveliness") that belongs primarily to impressions. When therefore the sequent ideas are run together into one idea, this idea receives the memorial belief that was attached to them. Once more Hume is writing in his mechanistic strain, though here and there the "biological" note creeps into his account and confuses it, as when he speaks of the activity of the *mind* and of an original bias in our *nature*.

In short, Hume gives psychologically a subjectivist account of our knowledge of matters of fact, while holding to an objectivist postulation of them. He does not conceal the contradiction between these two positions; on the contrary, he advertises it, and ends Book I with the proclamation that it cannot be resolved. It is in this proclamation that his scepticism consists. In the knowledge of matters of fact reason, in the traditional sense of the term, does not and cannot operate; it is confined to the apprehension of the relations of ideas *qua* ideas, that is, of the logical affiliations of contents not asserted to be existents. Also in moral evaluation reason, again in the traditional sense of the term, has no place. The peculiar character of Hume's scepticism would have stood out more clearly if he had not allowed himself to use the term "reason" on many occasions for the process of associatively determined causal inference, a process which, because it is not logical but natural, he assigns in his more careful moments of writing to the imagination. It is, of course, reason in this shockingly loose sense that he asserts to be the "slave of the passions." Reason in the strict sense "mortifies" them—or, rather, would do in a perfectly pure philosopher, which, he implies, no one can become.

DAVID HUME: HIS PYRRHONISM
AND HIS CRITIQUE OF PYRRHONISM

RICHARD H. POPKIN

> The wise in every age conclude,
> What Pyrrho taught and Hume renewed,
> That dogmatists are fools.[1]

David Hume has always been considered one of the greatest sceptics in the history of philosophy, yet little attention has been given to determining the precise nature of his sceptical point of view. John Laird, in his *Hume's Philosophy of Human Nature*, states that "Hume remained a complete Pyrrhonian regarding all *ultimate* principles."[2] However, Laird did not discuss the nature and extent of Hume's Pyrrhonian scepticism. In this paper I shall attempt such an examination, based upon what I conceive to be the key to Hume's entire sceptical outlook—namely, the recurrent criticisms in all of the Scottish sceptic's major philosophical writings of "that fantastical sect," the Pyrrhonian sceptics. A thorough examination of these

From *The Philosophical Quarterly*, Vol. I (1951). Reprinted by permission of the author and *The Philosophical Quarterly*.

[1] Original version of a poem by Thomas Blacklock, as it appeared in Hume's letter of April 20, 1756 to John Clephane, in *The Letters of David Hume*, ed. J. Y. T. Greig (Oxford, 1932), I, 231.

[2] John Laird, *Hume's Philosophy of Human Nature* (London, 1932), p. 180.

objections will reveal, as this paper will show, that Hume, himself, actually maintained the only "consistent" Pyrrhonian point of view.[3]

In every one of his discussions of the extreme sceptical view of the Pyrrhonians, Hume contended that such a position could not be refuted by reason, and yet, at the same time, could not be believed. The Pyrrhonian point of view is the logical outcome of philosophical analysis, and, yet, there is something in the nature of human beings that prevents one from accepting it. "Philosophy would render us entirely Pyrrhonian, were not nature too strong for it."[4]

Before proceeding to examine the basis for Hume's claim, it is necessary to outline in brief the position that Hume designates by the term "Pyrrhonian." Bayle had defined Pyrrhonism as "l'art de disputer sur toutes choses, sans prendre jamais d'autre parti que de suspendre son jugement."[5] Hume, however, considers it not as an art, but as a series of arguments which lead

---

[3] It is not within the scope of this paper to attempt to uncover the sources of Hume's knowledge of, or objections to, Pyrrhonian philosophy. None of his discussions refer to the classical statement of the position by the Hellenistic sceptic, Sextus Empiricus. Hume was acquainted with the works of Sextus by 1751 since he referred to certain passages of those works in *An Enquiry concerning the Principles of Morals*. The discussions regarding Pyrrhonism may refer to the doctrines advocated by Sextus himself, or may refer to various versions of Pyrrhonism which appear in works like Montaigne's *Apologie pour Raimond Sebond*, Bayle's *Dictionnaire Historique*, *La Logique ou L'Art de Penser*, Crousaz's *Examen du Pyrrhonisme*, or Huet's *La Faiblesse de l'Esprit Humain*. Some suggestions as to sources appear in Laird, *op. cit.*, pp. 180–85.

[4] Hume, *An Abstract of A Treatise of Human Nature*, ed. J. M. Keynes and P. Sraffa (Cambridge, 1938), p. 24.

[5] Bayle, *Dictionnaire Historique et Critique*, 4th ed. (Amsterdam, 1730), p. 732.

to the development of a certain type of attitude towards all intellectual and practical problems. The main
theme of the arguments is that for any problem whatsoever, no rational basis can be given for determining
what the solution may be. If two possible judgments
conflict, there is no rational basis for preferring either
of them. There is no area of intellectual or practical
concern in which one can attain certain and indisputable knowledge. Therefore, dogmatic acceptance of any
proposition or set of propositions is without adequate
reasonable foundation, since "all is uncertain and . . .
our judgment is not in *any* thing possest of *any* measure of truth and falsehood."[6] Owing to this inability
to discover adequate grounds for any opinion, the
Pyrrhonian sceptic proposes that one should, or will,
suspend judgment with regard to all questions. The
proper sceptic will develop an attitude of mind in
which he will have "no opinion or principle concerning
any subject, either of action or speculation."[7]

In this brief sketch of the doctrines of Pyrrhonian
scepticism, as Hume conceived them in his *Treatise,
Enquiries,* and *Dialogues concerning Natural Religion,* it is worth noting two ways in which the theory,
so stated, differs from the standard formulation of it in
Sextus Empiricus. First of all, Hume's version is more
dogmatic than that of Sextus. The latter attempted to

---

[6] Hume, *A Treatise of Human Nature,* ed. L. A. Selby-Bigge
(Oxford, 1888), p. 183. (This work will be referred to hereafter
as *Treatise*).

[7] Hume, *An Enquiry concerning Human Understanding,* in
The Philosophical Works of David Hume, ed. T. H. Green and
T. H. Grose, 4 vols. (London, 1874–75), IV, 122. (This work
will be referred to hereafter as *Enquiry*).

list a series of arguments, pro and con, on many questions, and then suspended judgment on them, instead
of dogmatically holding that all questions are unanswerable.[8] Secondly, Hume's rendering of Pyrrhonism
omits any reference to the basis that the Pyrrhonian
offers for deciding practical questions once the suspensive attitude has been adopted. Sextus maintained that
the sceptic could accept appearances undogmatically,
and live naturally. The former means that one can assent to, or recognize, or have opinions about what appears to be the case, without giving up one's suspensive attitude as to what really is the case. The latter
doctrine states that one can live "naturally," without
having to make any judgments, by obeying one's natural compulsions unconsciously, or by habit, and by accepting, without judging their worth, the customs and
regulations of one's social and cultural environment.[9]

In various parts of Hume's philosophical writings,
he indicated that he believed that a portion of the Pyrrhonian doctrine was the logical outcome of philosophical analysis. An examination of the grounds for
our judgments concerning matters of fact, matters of
value, or even mathematical matters, reveals, according
to Hume, that the basis for any of these judgments is
neither rational nor certain, and that no judgment can
be considered more firmly based than another.

The *intense* view of these manifold contradictions
and imperfections in human reason has so wrought
upon me, and heated my brain, that I am ready to

[8] Cf. Sextus Empiricus, *Outlines of Pyrrhonism*, ed. R. G.
Bury, 3 vols. (London and Cambridge, Mass., 1933–36), *passim*.
(This work will be referred to hereafter as *Outlines*).
[9] Sextus Empiricus, *ibid.*, Sections 13–24.

reject all belief and reasoning, and can look upon no opinion even as more probable or likely than another.[10]

Not only is this the case, but in addition, any attempt to overcome this basic defect in our knowledge only exposes more fundamental and insurmountable difficulties.

> This sceptical doubt, both with respect to reason and the senses, is a malady, which can never be radically cur'd, but must return upon us every moment, however we may chace it away, and sometimes may seem entirely free from it. 'Tis impossible upon any system to defend either our understanding or senses; and we but expose them farther when we endeavour to justify them in that manner.[11]

A close examination of Hume's views will show that he agreed with the Pyrrhonian theory of the inability to find any rational and certain basis for our judgments to the extent that an epistemological analysis of the nature and grounds of human knowledge would reveal that there are no rational or certain grounds for our judgments, and that we have no ultimate criterion for determining which of our conflicting judgments in certain fundamental areas of human knowledge are true, or to be preferred.[12]

[10] *Treatise*, pp. 268–69.
[11] *Ibid.*, p. 218.
[12] It is interesting to note that in one of the most Pyrrhonian passages in Hume's writings, the conclusion to Book I of the *Treatise*, Hume applies this sceptical view to his own theories and asked, "Can I be sure, that in leaving all establish'd opinions I am following truth; and by what criterion shall I distinguish her, even if fortune shou'd at last guide me on her foot-steps? After the most accurate and exact of my reasonings, I can give no reason why I shou'd assent to it; and feel nothing but a *strong*

In the discussion of Pyrrhonism in the *Enquiry concerning Human Understanding*, Hume distinguished
two types of sceptical arguments that the Pyrrhonians
present, a popular type which is trivial and weak, and
a philosophical type which is irrefutable. The former
consists of arguments about the fallaciousness or con-
tradictoriness of sense information, the natural weaknesses of the human understanding, the long and
tedious history of disagreement among men on almost
every conceivable subject, the variability of our judgments depending on internal and external circumstances, etc., or, in brief, the main sort of arguments
propounded in the ten tropes of Pyrrhonism as found
in Sextus. These arguments are weak and trivial, first
of all, because, according to Hume, the difficulties involved in sense information only prove that the senses
alone cannot be completely depended upon, and must
be corrected by other sources of information, such as
memory or reason. This, then, would not show that all
our knowledge is unreliable owing to our faulty senses,
but only that the senses, considered alone, are insufficient to yield a satisfactory basis for judgments.[13] Secondly, these popular arguments are weak and trivial
because they assume that the value of the type of judgments they are directed against depends upon their
certitude. Hume believed that these popular arguments were directed against the sort of judgments
made in everyday common life. Then, these arguments
show that there are grounds for doubting the certitude

propensity to consider objects *strongly* in that view, under which
they appear to me" (*ibid.*, p. 265).
[13] *Enquiry*, p. 124.

of such judgments, but the judgments themselves have a pragmatic rôle in our ordinary endeavors which is unaffected by these doubts. On the common sense level, Hume contended, it is both necessary, at all times, to make judgments without reference to the grounds or evidence on which they were based, and to evaluate the judgments without such reference. The epistemological objections raised by the Pyrrhonist are beside the point.[14]

The philosophical types of argument show that, at bottom, there is no rational or certain basis for either our factual and moral judgments, or the rational (mathematical) judgments that we make. This type of argument shows the most fundamental strength of Pyrrhonism, namely that our rational and factual judgments sometimes conflict, and that there is no basis whatever for choosing one judgment in preference to another. Such a line of reasoning, culminating in so radical a conclusion, Hume contended was irrefutable, and, on the epistemological level of analysis, completely devastating to any and every attempt to discover certain knowledge. The evidence adduced by Hume in support of these Pyrrhonian conclusions is first of all the result of his analysis of those factual judgments which are more than mere reports of immediate appearances. All our evidence for any matter of fact which is not obvious at a given moment is based on the relation of cause and effect or constant

---

[14] "These objections are but weak. For as, in common life, we reason every moment concerning fact and existence, and cannot possibly subsist, without continually employing this species of argument, any popular objections, derived from thence, must be insufficient to destroy that evidence" (*ibid.*, p. 130).

conjunction. There is no rational basis for believing that those objects that have constantly been conjoined in the past, will still be so conjoined in the future. It is only custom, or "a certain instinct of our nature," that makes us believe that they will be so conjoined, and this instinct which may be hard to resist psychologically, may well be fallacious and deceitful.[15] The basis for all factual and probable reasoning is thus irrational, determined by certain natural instinctive forces resulting in certain emotional effects.[16]

In the case of value judgments, similar psychological factors are even more in evidence, showing that these judgments too, are not based on rational evidence. Here Hume maintained that moral, or value distinctions can be known to us neither by the comparison of ideas by reason, nor by an examination of matters of fact.[17] Reason cannot be the source because (*a*) moral ideas influence our passions, whereas rational ones do not, and (*b*) reason compares ideas seeking truth or falsity in terms of their agreement or disagreement, whereas in the case of moral ideas we cannot meaningfully look for truth or falsity, but instead seek

[15] *Enquiry*, pp. 130–31.

[16] "Thus all probable reasoning is nothing but a species of sensation. 'Tis not solely in poetry and music, we must follow our taste and sentiment, but likewise in philosophy. When I am convinc'd of any principle, 'tis only an idea, which strikes more strongly upon me. When I give the preference to one set of arguments above another, I do nothing but decide from my feeling concerning the superiority of their influence. Objects have no discoverable connexion together; nor is it from any other principle but custom operating upon the imagination, that we can draw any inference from the appearance of one to the existence of another" (*Treatise*, p. 103).

[17] For Hume's discussion of this point, see *Treatise*, Book III, Part I.

for what is laudable and blameable. Matters of fact can have nothing to do with moral distinctions since they are not features of any object. Our knowledge of moral distinctions is based entirely upon some sentiments within us due to our moral sense. "Morality, therefore, is more properly felt than judg'd of."[18]

These two arguments concerning matters of fact and moral distinctions constitute the most elementary Pyrrhonian level, showing that in two main areas of inquiry, our opinions are based on non-rational factors. The more radical and perplexing levels of Pyrrhonism are, for Hume, those that introduce a doubt regarding the rationality of our reasonings, and their compatibility with our obvious information derived from the senses and common life.

In the beginning of Book I, Part III of the *Treatise*, Hume had drawn a distinction between knowledge and probability, and had maintained that perfect demonstrative knowledge regarding quantity or number was possible, and could be obtained through chains of reasoning about certain types of relations between

---

[18] *Treatise*, p. 470. The clearest statement of Hume's view is: "Take any action allow'd to be vicious: Willful murder, for instance. Examine it in all lights, and see if you can find that matter of fact, or real existence, which you call *vice*. In which-ever way you take it, you find only certain passions, motives, volitions and thoughts. There is no other matter of fact in the case. The vice entirely escapes you, as long as you consider the object. You never can find it, till you turn your reflexion into your own breast, and find a sentiment of disapprobation, which arises in you, towards this action. Here is a matter of fact, but 'tis the object of feeling, not of reason. It lies in yourself, not in the object. So that when you pronounce any action or character to be vicious, you mean nothing, but that from the constitution of your nature you have a feeling of sentiment of blame from the contemplation of it" (*ibid.*, pp. 468–69).

ideas. Such a contention would seem to be at variance
with the Pyrrhonian view, since, at least in regard to
the science of arithmetic, certain and rational knowledge would appear to be attainable. The sceptical view,
enunciated in both the second book of Sextus's *Outlines of Pyrrhonism* and in Montaigne's *Apology for
Raimond Sebond,* to the effect that no true proof
could ever be given of anything, is apparently denied
by Hume at this point. However, in Book I, Part IV
of the *Treatise* Hume presented some rather novel arguments to show that one must adopt a "scepticism
with regard to reason."

The first of these arguments attempts to show that
we can never have any reason for believing that a given
chain of reasoning is logically correct, even though, if
it were correct, it would constitute a legitimate proof.
Thus, the argument tries to establish that there can
never be adequate rational evidence for a judgment of
the type "I know that P is a legitimate proof." Such an
argument is to be distinguished from the usual Pyrrhonian contention about proofs, to the effect that
one must suspend judgment as to the truth of a judgment of the type "P is a legitimate proof." Hume raised
doubts as to the ability of any human being ever to be
sure that he could recognize a legitimate proof, but he
did not doubt the possibility of there being legitimate
proofs. However, the result of the Pyrrhonian and
Humean argument is the same, to show us that we
must suspend judgment with regard to the claim that
any proposition has been proven.

Hume's argument on this matter is as follows:
Everyone knows from experience that his ability to

carry out a chain of reasoning is not perfect. Therefore, in judging the accuracy of any piece of reasoning,
the reasoner will have to take into account the probability that he has reasoned accurately in this case. This
probability will be less than 1, and thus the judgment,
"I know that P is a legitimate proof" can only be probable, but never completely true. Further, our ability to
judge when we have accurately reasoned is not perfect,
and hence there is a further probability, namely
whether we have judged properly in evaluating our
reasoning. Hume contends that the probability of the
new judgment was the product of the probability that
we reasoned properly and that we judged the accuracy
of our reasoning properly. Since both probabilities are
less than 1, the product is smaller than either of them.
Then, there is a further question as to whether or not
we have properly evaluated our ability to judge our
judgments about the accuracy of our reasoning properly. Since both probabilities are less than 1, the product is smaller than either of them. Then, there is a
further question as to whether or not we have properly
evaluated our ability to judge our judgments about the
accuracy of our reasonings, etc. This process of introducing new probabilities, each less than the preceding
ones, can go on *ad infinitum*, and thus, the probability
that we could ever recognize, without the slightest
shadow of doubt, that a particular piece of reasoning
was correct, approaches zero.[19]

This argument may not lead to Pyrrhonian doubts
about logical rules and inferences, but it does raise
some doubts as to the ability of any human being ever

[19] *Ibid.*, pp. 181–83.

to be positive that he is reasoning logically. If one depended upon complete assurance that one's ability to
reason was perfect before accepting any proof whatsoever, then, Hume claimed, this argument introducing
probability considerations into our judgments about
our reasonings would "utterly subvert all belief and
opinion."

> But as experience will sufficiently convince any one,
> who thinks it worth while to try, that tho' he can find
> no error in the foregoing arguments, yet he still con-
> tinues to believe, think, and reason as usual, he may
> safely conclude, that his reasoning and belief is some
> sensation or peculiar manner of conception, which
> 'tis impossible for mere ideas and reflections to de-
> stroy.[20]

Hume then offered a psychological theory explaining
why these arguments bring about no diminution of
our faith in our reasonings, suggesting that this is due
to the fact that the mind cannot "stretch" itself into
the uncomfortable position from which to make judgments about its judgments.[21] Thus, what preserves our
faith in our reasonings is not rational evidence, but
only some psychological quirks of our constitution,
and hence the Pyrrhonian contention that we have no
rational basis for defending our opinion is once again
illustrated.

In order to undermine further our confidence in our
reasonings, and to show yet more forcefully that the
Pyrrhonian position is irrefutable, Hume presented
the contradictions which arise between "proper" rea-

20 *Treatise*, p. 184.
21 *Ibid.*, pp. 184–86.

sonings on the one hand and sense-information and common-sense beliefs on the other. These contradictions concern the existence of external objects, the status of primary qualities, the nature of the "self," and the conclusions of arithmetic and geometry. The first arises because we all naturally believe that the objects we perceive with our senses are real objects, in that they are distinct from the observer, and exist continuously whether observed or not, and yet, at the same time, our rational enquiries force us to conclude that all our perceptions exist in us, and cannot exist apart from us. Hume maintained, in both the *Treatise* and *Enquiry*, that men were led by a natural instinct to suppose that there is an external universe existing independently and continuously, and that our sense images belong to this universe.[22] "But this universal and primary opinion of all men is soon destroyed by the slightest philosophy."[23] All that we ever perceive are sense images. The Pyrrhonian evidence is overwhelmingly in support of the view that these images are dependent upon us, in that the images can be altered by our state. We do not believe that when we affect the image, e.g. by pressing one eyeball, the object is similarly changed. The images can be no more than a feature of our mental world. Hence, the philosophers have invented their dualistic solution, that the images are different from the objects. But this system is no aid, since all we ever can know are images, and hence it can never offer any rational evidence in

[22] *Ibid.*, pp. 187–88, and *Enquiry*, p. 124.
[23] *Enquiry*, p. 124.

support of the dualistic view.[24] The crux of the problem is that our instinctive realistic beliefs conflict with
our rational views on the subject, and yet no rational
solution can be given to overcome the difficulty. Both
our common-sensical and our rational views are determined by "trivial qualities of the mind," and so we
seem to be led by our reason into an insoluble contradiction with our instinctive beliefs.[25]

The second of these contradictions is due to a conflict between the contentions that secondary qualities
are nothing but impressions in the mind, and that
there is an external material world. Hume first agreed
that the same reasoning (mainly Pyrrhonian arguments about illusion and the concomitant variability
of our state and our perceptions) that led one to deny
the extra-mental existence of secondary qualities compelled one to deny the extra-mental existence of primary qualities. Here he employed some of Berkeley's
arguments to show that there was no epistemological
basis for distinguishing the type of qualities that in-

[24] On this problem see *Treatise*, pp. 210–16, and *Enquiry*,
pp. 124–26.

[25] "This is a topic, therefore, in which the profounder and
more philosophical sceptics will always triumph, when they endeavour to introduce an universal doubt into all subjects of human knowledge and enquiry. Do you follow the instincts and propensities of nature, may they say, in assenting to the veracity of
sense? But these lead you to believe, that the very perception or
sensible image is the external object. Do you disclaim this principle, in order to embrace a more rational opinion, that the perceptions are only representations of something external? You here
depart from your natural propensities and more obvious sentiments; and yet are not able to satisfy your reason, which can
never find any convincing argument from experience to prove, that
the perceptions are connected with any external objects" (*Enquiry*, p. 126).

clude motion and extension from the type that include color and sound. In addition Hume tried to show that our knowledge of primary qualities was actually knowledge of certain arrangements of secondary qualities. The conclusion to be drawn from these points is, then, that all of the qualities of bodies are impressions of the mind, and that there is nothing meaningful that we can call an external material object.[26] Thus, if we believe the theory of secondary qualities,

> we utterly annihilate all these [external] objects, and reduce ourselves to the opinions of the most extravagant scepticism concerning them. If colours, sounds, tastes, and smells be merely perceptions, nothing we can conceive is possest of real, continu'd, and independent existence. . . .[27]

Therefore, once again the natural belief in an external world turns out to be contrary to our rational principles, and the latter seem to be indefensible. The only conclusion Hume could come to from such conflicting views was:

> Thus there is a direct and total opposition betwixt our reason and our senses; or more properly speaking, betwixt those conclusions we form from cause and effect, and those that persuade us of the continu'd and independent existence of body.[28]

Another contradiction is to be found in the analysis

[26] *Treatise*, pp. 225–31, and *Enquiry*, pp. 126–27.

[27] *Treatise*, p. 228. In the *Enquiry*, Hume stated, "Bereave matter of all its intelligible qualities, both primary and secondary, you in a manner annihilate it, and leave only a certain unknown, inexplicable *something*, as the cause of our perceptions; a notion so imperfect, that no sceptic will think it worth while to contend against it" (*Enquiry*, p. 127).

[28] *Treatise*, p. 231.

of personal identity. Hume's discussion of this subject
led him to conclude that we have no impression and,
hence, no idea of a "self," and that all we can mean by
the term is a succession of some particular perceptions.
What makes us believe that these perceptions are
bound together by some connection which gives them
an identity and simplicity is a strong feeling we have
when viewing the perceptions. No real connections are
ever discoverable by human beings. In the *Appendix*
to the *Treatise,* Hume announced that the above conclusions contained a labyrinth of contradictions and
absurdities, which he was unable to render consistent.

The difficulties here do not seem to be due to logical
contradictions, but to violations of common sense beliefs. The whole discussion in this *Appendix* note
points out that Hume's analysis leads to a view that
there is no real unity discoverable amongst our perceptions, and yet a unifying connective principle is
needed to make this square with common sense opinion about the nature of the self. Since Hume was unable to make his theory about the "self" agree with
ordinary views on this matter, all that he could do was
to announce that he was a sceptic on this issue, and
the difficulties on this head were sufficient to make
anybody a complete sceptic.[29]

The final contradictions are the result of rational
mathematical conclusions, some of which are "big with
contradiction and absurdity."[30] Hume felt that the
mathematical demonstrations about the infinite divisi-
bility of extensions and time, though as logically sound

[29] *Treatise, Appendix,* pp. 633–36.
[30] *Enquiry,* p. 129.

as any other mathematical proof, and though based ultimately on the same premises, were paradoxical in that they conflicted with our common sense notions. The conception of the angle of contact between the circumference of a circle and its tangent which is proved to be infinitely smaller than any acute angle is at variance with our ordinary notions, etc.[31] Some of the mathematical proofs lead to such "absurd" results from the point of view of common sense (and, fortunately, Hume lived too early to know about the even stranger theorems of modern set theory with its hierarchy of infinities) that

> Reason here seems to be thrown into a kind of amazement and suspence, which, without the suggestions of any sceptic, gives her a diffidence of herself, and of the ground on which she treads. She sees a full light, which illuminates certain places; but that light borders upon the most profound darkness. And between these she is so dazzled and confounded, that she scarcely can pronounce with certainty and assurance concerning any one object.[32]

All these many arguments show, according to Hume, that the extreme scepticism of the Pyrrhonians cannot be refuted, and that it is the logical result of an epistemological analysis of the bases of our beliefs in factual, moral, and demonstrative matters. In all these beliefs we find that our views are determined by non-rational factors, and in general that it would be impossible to offer any satisfactory rational evidence for our opinions. In addition to this, our opinions derived

[31] *Ibid.*, pp. 127–29.
[32] *Ibid.*, p. 129.

from reason conflict with our senses, or common-sense beliefs. We have no criterion whatsoever for preferring one belief to another.

In the conclusion to Book I of the *Treatise*, Hume revealed despairingly that this epistemological Pyrrhonism was all that philosophy could lead us to. All that we could ever know by memory, senses, or understanding, is founded on the irrational psychological quirks of the imagination. Even the acceptance of Humean philosophy could only be advocated on the grounds that some people have a strong propensity to consider the world in this way.[33] But even worse, these natural psychological factors which determine our opinions, compel us to have conflicting views on the same subjects, like the status of the external world, etc. Here two different principles by which we irrationally come to have opinions force us to have different opinions. If all our opinions are founded on these psychological principles, how can we ever choose one set as preferable to another? What can we do about the unfortunate fact that reason is in conflict with common sense?

> Shall we, then, establish it for a general maxim, that no refin'd or elaborate reasoning is ever to be receiv'd? Consider well the consequences of such a principle. By this means you cut off entirely all science and philosophy: You proceed upon one singular quality of the imagination, and by a parity of reason must embrace all of them: And you expresly contradict yourself; since this maxim must be built on the preceding reasoning, which will be allow'd to be sufficiently refin'd and metaphysical. What party, then, shall we

33 *Treatise*, p. 265. See note 12 for quotation to this effect.

choose among these difficulties? If we embrace this principle, and condemn all refin'd reasoning, we run into the most manifest absurdities. If we reject it in favour of these reasonings, we subvert entirely the human understanding. We have, therefore, no choice left but betwixt a false reason and none at all.[34]

Thus, according to Hume,

if reason be considered in an abstract view, it furnishes invincible arguments against itself, and that we could never retain any conviction or assurance, on any subject. . . .[35]

The epistemological analysis of human knowledge leads to a complete Pyrrhonian scepticism. Yet Hume held, as we have seen, that this analysis fails when applied to common sense beliefs, and fails to undermine our convictions in them, since they are not really rational beliefs. The Scottish sceptic went much further in his judgment of the merits of this extreme sceptical view, holding that no one could ever believe it, regardless of the fact that it was philosophically unanswerable. In common life, the Pyrrhonian doubts are ignored.[36] On the pihlosophical level, this scepticism is just not believed. "Whoever has taken the pains to refute the cavils of this *total* scepticism, has really disputed without an antagonist."[37]

Let us now turn to this other side of Hume's views

---

[34] *Treatise*, p. 268.

[35] Hume, *Dialogues concerning Natural Religion*, ed. Norman Kemp Smith, 2nd ed. (London, 1947), p. 135. (This work will be referred to hereafter as *Dialogues*).

[36] *Treatise*, p. 268.

[37] *Treatise*, p. 183. In fact, Hume claimed, "it is certain that no man ever met with any such absurd creature" as the complete sceptic (*Enquiry*, p. 122).

about Pyrrhonism. On the one hand, Pyrrhonism cannot be refuted, and yet nobody ever did or can believe
the view. The explanation of this rather paradoxical
observation that sceptical arguments *"admit of no answer and produce no conviction"*[38] is that " 'tis happy,
therefore, that nature breaks the force of all sceptical
arguments in time, and keeps them from having any
considerable influence on the understanding."[39]

The Pyrrhonist, according to Hume, maintains that
the suspensive attitude ought to result from and does
result from showing that in no area whatsoever have
we the slightest rational basis for holding to an opinion. Hume agreed that this does happen with regard to
speculative reasoning. Here, the sceptic's discovery
that we have no rational basis for our views undermines our belief in them, and leaves us suspending
judgment.[40]

The sceptic has the strange opinion, also common
to the Stoic, that what a man can do sometimes, and
in some conditions, he can do at all times and in all
conditions.[41] However, this is definitely not the case.
The same sort of natural factors by which our biologi-

[38] *Enquiry*, p. 127 n. Hume made this point in showing why
he considered Berkeley's arguments those of a sceptic. All that
Berkeley's reasonings accomplish "is to cause that momentary
amazement and irresolution and confusion, which is the result of
scepticism."

[39] *Treatise*, p. 187.

[40] "But it is evident, when our arguments . . . run wide of
common life, that the most refined scepticism comes to be upon
a footing with them, and is able to oppose and counterbalance
them. The one has no more weight than the other. The mind
must remain in suspense between them; and it is that very suspense or balance which is the triumph of scepticism" (*Dialogues*,
pp. 135–36).

[41] *Ibid.*, p. 133.

cal existence is shaped, determine our psychological existence as well, and require us to hold to opinions sometimes regardless of evidence.

> Shou'd it here be ask'd me, whether I sincerely assent to this argument, which I seem to take such pains to inculcate, and whether I be really one of those sceptics, who hold that all is uncertain, and that our judgment is not in *any* thing possest of *any* measures of truth and falsehood; I shou'd reply, that this question is entirely superfluous, and that neither I, nor any other person was ever sincerely and constantly of that opinion. Nature, by an absolute and uncontroulable necessity has determin'd us to judge as well as to breathe and feel; nor can we any more forbear viewing certain objects in a stronger and fuller light, upon account of their customary connexion with a present impression, then we can hinder ourselves from thinking as long as we are awake, or seeing the surrounding bodies, when we turn our eyes towards them in broad sunshine.[42]

Therefore, the sceptical view that we ought not and do not hold any opinions is false. We must hold opinions since nature forces us to. It is not really a question of what we should do, but rather a question of what we have to do.

We are required to judge about (i) factual, (ii) moral, and (iii) rational matters, regardless of the legitimate evidence that we have at our disposal. (i) As Hume explained at great length, our belief in judgment about matters of fact is not due to rational evidence, but is the result of a custom or habit, which produces a strong feeling in us regarding certain ideas

[42] *Treatise*, p. 183.

usually conjoined with an impression now present to the senses or memory. The judgments that we believe concerning such matters impose themselves upon us because of our mental constitution. Thus, it is nature and not logical reasoning that leads us to make all causal inferences. It is this type of inference which "peoples the world" and allows us to talk of matters not immediately present to sense or memory.

(ii) With regard to moral judgments, Hume's entire thesis is to the effect that they are the result of a moral sense which when operating normally leads us to have certain feelings with regard to various objects and events. We evaluate naturally and not by reflective analysis. An opinion that something is good, or meritorious, is the result of a pleasant feeling, and an opinion that it is evil or deplorable the result of an unpleasant feeling. We are so constituted that at every moment in our experience we have certain feelings accompanying what we perceive. Thus, in this area, too, nature compels us to have opinions, though the sceptic shows that we have no basis for them. Now there is a very famous statement of Hume's which may appear to be in contradiction to what I am asserting here and throughout the paper, namely, "Reason is, and ought only to be the slave of the passions, and can never pretend to any other office than to serve and obey them."[43] What I term Hume's complete Pyrrhonism is, in part, that reason *is* the slave of the passions, that all our allegedly rational conclusions are based upon various psychological and biological factors. The additional point that reason *ought* to be the

[43] *Treatise*, p. 415.

slave of the passions seems to imply that there is more to Hume's view, namely that he held to a positive theory of moral irrationalism stating that there is something right about the fact that we function irrationally. If Hume held such a view, then, for him, philosophy does not end in Pyrrhonism, but in a dogmatic theory, from which it follows that what I have been developing is not the real Humean point of view. However, I believe that this passage is open to another kind of interpretation when it is examined in its actual setting in Book II of the *Treatise*. Here it appears in answer to the rationalist view that reason and the passions are in conflict, and that virtuous action consists in following reason, or that rational men are obliged to regulate their actions according to reason. In its context I think that the passage in question can be interpreted as an exuberant or over-enthusiastic denial to Hume's opponents, instead of its being considered as conflicting with Hume's general Pyrrhonian scepticism. As evidence that this is a possible and plausible interpretation, it should be noted first that the reasons that Hume offered to refute his opponents are exclusively of the sort which show that reason is the slave of the passions, or that reason alone is not a motivating force in our actions, and hence cannot conflict with the passions. None of the evidence adduced by Hume relates to the point that reason ought to be the slave of the passions. Furthermore, after the passage in question, which Hume admitted "may appear somewhat extraordinary," several additional considerations were offered to defend his view. And here, too, none of the points made relates to whether or not reason ought

to be the slave of the passions, but only further confirm the points previously made. That crucial matter of
whether it is right that reason is so dominated is just
not discussed in these considerations.[44] As a last point
in defense of the plausibility of my interpretations,
there is a passage[45] where Hume made "an observation, which may, perhaps, be found of some importance," namely that a proposition involving *ought* does
not follow from one involving *is*. Thus, presumably,
Hume realized that evidence proving reason to be the
slave of the passions does not establish that reason
ought to be the slave of the passions. Thus, I think
that the context of the passage in question and the
observation on inferring a normative proposition from
a factual one suggest that Hume's meaning was not
that he advocated a positive theory of moral irrationalism, but rather that he denied a positive theory of
moral rationalism. His strong way of stating the denial
makes it look as if he meant more. But all that he
offered as evidence was a series of psychological considerations to show that reason does not direct our actions, and that reason is the slave of the passions.
Hence, it does not seem to be unreasonable that that
was all that he meant to say. And if this was all that he

[44] It is also interesting that in Norman Kemp Smith's excellent study, *The Philosophy of David Hume* (London, 1941), in
the sub-chapter entitled *In Morals, as in Belief, Reason acts in
the Service of Feeling and Instinct*, pp. 143–47, the explanation
of the passage in question, of which Kemp Smith considers the
obligatory feature to be basic, contains no statements explaining
why reason ought to be the slave. The entire explanation of
Hume's meaning, and the reasoning behind it, relates only to
why reason cannot conflict with the passions, and why reason *is*
the slave of the passions.
[45] *Treatise*, pp. 469–70.

meant to say, then the passage does not deny that Hume was a complete Pyrrhonist on philosophical matters, but rather serves as one more indication of the point.

(iii) The sceptical arguments indicating that we can never acquire certain demonstrative knowledge likewise conflict with what nature compels us to believe. Hume felt that his argument that we are never able to be sure that any demonstrative reasoning is correct was unanswerable, and yet, it does not prevent people from being sure on this head. Our assurance is, however, not rationally grounded, but is due to natural factors. The mind is unable to carry doubt of its ability to judge its judgments *ad infinitum* because this puts the mind in an uneasy posture, "the spirits being diverted from their natural course."[46] And this very inability is what saves us from the force of the sceptical argument. We reason by nature, and, by a very fortunate quirk of the mind, we are unaffected by doubts cast on our reasoning abilities.

Nature not only compels all men, including the sceptic, to reason and believe concerning factual, moral, and demonstrative matters, though there is no rational defense of doing so, but nature also compels us to believe in the existence of certain types of metaphysical objects, though there is no proof that they exist, and though a belief in their existence leads to paradoxes. Hume seemed to be of the opinion that nature led us to believe in the existence of body, mind, and God, Descartes's three substances, though by no argu-

[46] *Ibid.*, p. 185.

ments of philosophical reasoning could these beliefs
be defended.

The problem of the existence of bodies is prefaced
by the remark that

> he [the sceptic] must assent to the principle concern-
> ing the existence of body, tho' he cannot pretend by
> any argument of philosophy to maintain its veracity.
> Nature has not left this to his choice, and has doubt-
> less esteem'd it an affair of too great importance to be
> trusted to our uncertain reasonings and speculations.
> We may well ask, *What causes induce us to believe
> in the existence of body?* but 'tis in vain to ask,
> *Whether there be body or not?* That is a point, which
> we must take for granted in all our reasonings.[47]

In the *Enquiry* Hume said that the belief in the existence of an external world was due to following "the
instincts and propensities of nature."[48] But, as has
been pointed out above, Hume contended that this
belief was not only indefensible, but at variance with
our best reasonings on the subject. Nature, by an odd
type of propensity, leads us to believe that the objects
which we perceive exist continuously, though not always perceived. We naturally tend to consider our interrupted preceptions as continuous, and even though
this may be in conflict with our reasonings. Even after
Hume pointed out that our natural belief in the existence of body was in complete conflict with our reasonings, that there was no way he could discover to
reconcile the conflict, and that this led to the most
profound sceptical doubts, he still insisted that "whatever may be the reader's opinion at this present mo-

[47] *Treatise*, p. 187.
[48] *Enquiry*, p. 126.

ment [after reading Hume], an hour hence he will be persuaded there is both an external and internal world."[49] The natural propensity to believe in the existence of bodies was too strong to be overcome by even the most insurmountable metaphysical difficulties.

The case with regard to the natural belief in the existence of mind, or self, is harder to make out, but I believe it is the only interpretation which can account for Hume's apparently strange reversal on the question of personal identity in the *Appendix* to the *Treatise*. The discussion of personal identity is not intended, as often supposed, just to show that we have no impression of a continuing "self." Almost all of Hume's analysis on this point is concerned with the development of an answer to the question,

> What then gives us so great a propension to ascribe an identity to these successive perceptions, and to suppose ourselves possest of an invariable and uninterrupted existence thro' the whole course of our lives?[50]

The belief in personal identity is a natural one, in that everyone holds to it without or prior to any reflection on the subject.[51] But it is also a belief without any basis in Hume's epistemological analysis. The clear indication of this fact makes it look as if Hume denied

[49] *Treatise*, p. 218.
[50] *Ibid.*, p. 253.
[51] Cf. Charles W. Hendel, *Studies in the Philosophy of David Hume* (Princeton, 1925), pp. 242–43. Hume, in the *Treatise*, pp. 317 and 320, in asserting the common man's view claimed that we are always conscious of ourselves. On these passages, see John Laird, *op. cit.*, pp. 161–62.

that anyone ever actually had a belief that the "self"
existed. However, Hume showed, on his psychological
principles, how such a "fictitious" belief occurs, which
amounts to showing the natural causes of such a belief. In his discussion in the *Appendix*, Hume said that
his account of personal identity was contradictory. He
stated that he was unable to reconcile two of his principles that he employed in this account: that all our
distinct perceptions are distinct existences, and that
the mind never perceives any real connection among
distinct existences. Now, as Kemp Smith pointed out,
these two principles do not conflict, but the second
happens to be a corollary of the first. No logical difficulty whatever in Hume's doctrine is pointed out in
the *Appendix*.[52] So that any contradiction that Hume
found is of a different variety entirely. One interpretation, which renders intelligible Hume's assertion
that his doctrine is contradictory, is that his analysis
seems to lead to a denial of the natural belief in personal identity.[53] His analysis shows that knowledge of
a "self" is impossible, yet, by his own admission, there
is a natural propensity to unite our fleeting impressions and believe in a "self." In the *Appendix*, Hume
said that the difficulty might be solved if we could find
something for our perceptions to inhere in, or find
some real connection between our perceptions.[54] In
other words, the problem would be ended if we could
justify the natural belief. If this interpretation is cor-

[52] Norman Kemp Smith, *op. cit.*, p. 558, and *Treatise*, pp.
633–36.
[53] This interpretation is also offered by Kemp Smith, *loc. cit.*
[54] *Treatise*, p. 636.

rect, then the belief in the existence of mind is like the belief in the existence of body. We have natural propensities to believe in both, and in both cases what we naturally believe is indefensible within Hume's epistemology.

Although Hume was certainly a consistent anti-religionist, he did contend that the belief in the existence of a deity was natural. A statement like this must be carefully qualified to avoid any suggestion that Hume believed in the Deity of the Judeo-Christian tradition, or in any sort of personal God. What he himself believed in is quite difficult to determine, especially since, as Kemp Smith pointed out,[55] Hume became less and less theistically inclined as time went on, and more and more antagonistic to all religious views. Also, Hume made several remarks in his writings, which taken out of their context would indicate a much stronger religious attitude on his part than his works, and especially the *Dialogues*, could possibly support.

In *The Natural History of Religion*, Hume attempted to present some of the causal factors which induce men to believe in a deity. Here he differentiates between two types of beliefs, the superstitious ones which the common man is led to adopt by natural causes, and the more "rational" ones that thinking men are made to accept by other natural factors. The common man in ancient days was polytheistically inclined because of all the amazing and apparently irregular occurrences in the world. The common man would be completely baffled by the world he meets,

[55] *Dialogues*, introduction by Kemp Smith, pp. 37–44.

resulting from causes that he cannot know, "were it
not for a propensity in human nature."[56] This propensity is the universal tendency to anthropomorphize
nature, and conceive of natural forces and events as
endowed with human capacities. Popular religion develops from this anthropomorphic polytheism to a
more theistic view, not by reasoning, but by a gradual
exaggeration of one of the deities whom human beings
think they most depend upon, until this conception
becomes that of a completed unified and infinite deity
who created the world.[57] This conception which grows
naturally just happens to coincide "by chance, with the
principles of reason and true philosophy."[58] Hume felt
that popular religion, besides being in conflict with
our rational notions, led to the excesses of "enthusiasm" and superstition.

True religion, or more properly, the religion of the
learned, arises from different natural principles. It
arises from a recognition of the order in the universe.

> The whole frame of nature bespeaks an intelligent au-
> thor; and no rational enquirer can, after serious re-
> flection, suspend his belief a moment with regard to
> the primary principles of genuine Theism and Re-
> ligion.[59]

Although Hume was, perhaps, the most severe and
devastating critic of the argument from design who

[56] Hume, *The Natural History of Religion*, in *The Philosophical Works of David Hume, op. cit.*, IV, 316–17. (This work will
be referred to as *Natural History* hereafter.)
[57] *Ibid.*, pp. 328–35.
[58] *Ibid.*, p. 330.
[59] *Ibid.*, p. 309. This same view is expressed several times in
the *Natural History*. Cf. pp. 313, 315, 325, 328–29 and 361.

ever wrote on theological questions, he yet maintained
that the order obvious in the world compelled any rational man to admit that one could infer from the order to the existence of some guiding intelligence,
which, for want of a better term, may be called God.[60]
Order naturally leads a rational man to believe in an
intelligent source of the order.

Thus, according to Hume there is a "universal propensity to believe in invisible, intelligent power."[61]
This may be due to an original instinct or a general
feature of human nature. The vulgar believe because
of their fears, and their anthropomorphizing tend-
encies; the intelligent because of the order in the
world. (Of course, it must be recalled that Hume regarded the vulgar religion and the usual dogmatic the-
ologies as utter absurdities and perversions, insisting
that no positive attributes of God or moral commands
of God could ever be discovered, and hence, one
should accept only theological views that are forced
upon us, and not any superstitions or absurdities
added to them. Nature does not allow us to be athe-

[60] Philo in the last of the *Dialogues* maintained that one could
not suspend judgment on the existence of such a guiding cause.
"That the works of nature bear a great analogy to the productions
of art is evident; and according to the rules of good reasoning,
we ought to infer, if we argue at all concerning them, that their
causes have a proportional analogy" (*Dialogues*, pp. 216–17).
Later on Philo stated the one proposition left to natural theology,
*"that the cause or causes of order in the universe probably bear
some remote analogy to human intelligence"* (*ibid.*, p. 227). Or,
lastly, there is the stronger statement in the *Natural History*, "A
purpose, an intention, a design is evident in everything; and when
our comprehension is so far enlarged as to contemplate the first
rise of this visible system, we must adopt, with the strongest conviction, the idea of some intelligent cause or author" (p. 361).
[61] *Ibid.*, p. 362.

ists, but does not force us to assent to the vagaries of popular superstition or refined theology.)[62]

Not only does nature require us to make judgments on all these matters, though we lack adequate evidence for these judgments, but, also, some of us are required to philosophize. The sceptic may realize that no speculative questions can ever be settled, but this does not mean that he can avoid reasoning and even holding opinions about them. The pleasures and satisfactions of philosophizing, regardless of the merits of the enterprise, are often sufficient to entice even the sceptic, and make him enter into so futile a task. We philosophize when we feel like it.[63] This may be just the confession of Hume's reasons for philosophizing, but it indicates at least one way in which nature leads us on into speculative activities.

Hume apparently believed that nature did all these

[62] *Dialogues*, p. 218. Cf. the story of Hume's meeting with Baron d'Holbach, which is reprinted in Kemp Smith's introduction to the *Dialogues*, pp. 37–38. See also *ibid.*, pp. 226–28, and *Natural History*, p. 363.

[63] *Dialogues*, p. 134. "At the time, therefore, that I am tir'd with amusement and company, and have indulg'd a *reverie* in my chamber, or in a solitary walk by a riverside, I feel my mind all collected within itself, and am naturally *inclin'd* to carry my view into all those subjects, about which I have met with so many disputes in the course of my reading and conversation. I cannot forbear having a curiousity to be acquainted with the principles of moral good and evil, the nature and foundation of government, and the cause of those several passions and inclinations, which actuate and govern me. . . . . . . I feel an ambition to arise in me of contributing to the instruction of mankind, and of acquiring a name by my inventions and discoveries. These sentiments spring up naturally in my present disposition; and shou'd I endeavour to banish them, by attaching myself to any other business or diversion, I *feel* I shou'd be a loser in point of pleasure; and this is the origin of my philosophy" (*Treatise*, pp. 270–71).

amazing things to us in order to protect us, and allow us to live in this world. Our reasoning faculties are so weak and fallacious, as all the philosophers from Montaigne and Descartes to Locke and Bayle had pointed out, that had we been forced to depend upon them to determine what we must believe in order to survive in this world, we would have perished long ago. These beliefs which we are compelled to accept are "of too great importance to be trusted to our uncertain reasonings and speculations."[64] It is so essential to human existence that we make judgments and inferences that nature has made these instinctive, just as the use of our limbs is.[65] And this leads to the last, and perhaps, principal reason why Pyrrhonism is incredible: it is incompatible, according to Hume, with the actions necessary to support human life.

> . . . he [the Pyrrhonist] must acknowledge, if he will acknowledge any thing, that all human life must perish, were his principles universally and steadily to prevail. All discourse, all action would immediately cease; and men remain in a total lethargy, till the necessities of nature, unsatisfied, put an end to their miserable existence.[66]

[64] *Ibid.*, p. 187.

[65] *Enquiry*, pp. 46–47. Here Hume employed the concept of the pre-established harmony between the succession of our ideas and the order of nature. There is no rational connection between what we think and what goes on in the world, but there is a correspondence established by nature through custom and instinct. This notion seems to be similar to Malebranche's view of the pre-established harmony after the Fall of Man; cf. Nicholas Malebranche, *Dialogues on Metaphysics and on Religion*, tr. Morris Ginsberg (London, 1923), Dialogue IV, esp. pp. 132–33.

[66] *Enquiry*, p. 131. "The great subverter of *Pyrrhonism* or the excessive principles of scepticism, is action, and employment, and the occupations of common life" (*ibid.*, p. 130).

The natural safeguards which enable us to live are at variance with the proposed suspensive attitude of the Pyrrhonians, and hence, nature being stronger than Pyrrhonism, the necessary actions which we must perform to live destroy all possibility of being Pyrrhonian.

Hume maintained that, in order to exist in this world, to act as human beings do, one must hold to some opinions. Our actions are not based upon a rational philosophy, but on irrational natural instincts and mechanisms which allow us to persevere. This is true of all men, including the Pyrrhonian sceptics.[67] What we believe, in order to act, is not a matter of rational choice, and did we not believe these matters we would perish. The Pyrrhonian sceptic would, if he were sincere, have no basis for doing one thing rather than another, for drinking water rather than vinegar, or for employing doors rather than windows as means of exiting.[68] But the conduct of the Pyrrhonian shows that in practical matters he has "the firmest reliance on all the received maxims of science, morals, prudence, and behaviour."[69] Though he may suspend judgment on the validity of any such maxims, in practice he accepts them all the time. No matter how much the extreme sceptic undermines the reasons for what we do, he will never prevent us from doing it. "Nature will always maintain her rights, and prevail

[67] "To whatever length any one may push his speculative principles of scepticism, he must act, I own, and live, and converse like other men; and for this conduct he is not obliged to give any other reason than the absolute necessity he lies under of so doing" (*Dialogues*, p. 134).

[68] *Ibid.*, p. 132. This is the old objection of Epictetus.

[69] *Ibid.*, p. 137.

in the end over any abstract reasoning whatsoever."[70]

Thus, Pyrrhonian scepticism, if believed and acted upon, could only have the unfortunate result of destroying the believer. As long as the doctrine leads to a suspense of all action it can have no other result and no adherent. If the sceptic is really sincere, Hume maintained, he will soon cease bothering anyone. This doctrine is unique in that it is the only one with no alleged useful or beneficial end. If believed, the believer does nothing. Other doctrines propose to tell people what the world is like, or how to live better; this one tells us nothing, and leaves the believer to perish.[71]

[70] *Enquiry*, p. 36. Pyrrhonism may be believed in the sceptic's school or closet, but in the everyday world our natural instincts drive it away. "These principles [Pyrrhonism] may flourish and triumph in the schools; where it is, indeed, difficult, if not impossible, to refute them. But as soon as they leave the shade, and by the presence of real objects, which actuate our passions and sentiments, are put in opposition to the more powerful principles of our nature, they vanish like smoke, and leave the most determined sceptic in the same condition as other mortals" (*ibid.*, p. 130). "And though a PYRRHONIAN may throw himself or others into a momentary amazement and confusion by his profound reasonings; the first and most trivial event in life will put to flight all his doubts and scruples, and leave him the same, in every point of action and speculation, with the philosophers of every other sect, or with those who never concerned themselves in any philosophical researches. When he awakes from his dream, he will be the first to join in the laugh against himself, and to confess, that all his objections are mere amusement, and can have no other tendency than to show the whimsical condition of mankind, who must act and reason and believe; though they are not able, by their most diligent enquiry, to satisfy themselves concerning the foundation of these operations, or to remove the objections, which may be raised against them" (*ibid.*, pp. 131–32). See also, *Dialogues*, pp. 132–33, and *Treatise*, Conclusion to Book I, and p. 455.
[71] *Ibid.*, p. 131.

What philosophical merits does this "naturalistic" criticism of Pyrrhonism have? The criticism is not intended to, nor does it, show that the Pyrrhonian theory which Hume accepted has any logical difficulties.[72] The main force of the criticism is psychological and practical, and amounts to an explanation of what we do, if it is actually the case that Pyrrhonism is unanswerable. The reasons why people believe or do not believe a given doctrine are not necessarily comments on its truth or falsity. If people do not believe Pyrrhonism, as Hume portrayed it, because of certain natural attitudes that they have, this is no philosophical reflection on Pyrrhonism. However, pointing out the incredibility of a doctrine, and the unfortunate consequences of believing it, has often sufficed, historically, for leading people to give up a doctrine. E.g., consider Hume's criticism of popular religion, or Voltaire's of optimism. Neither of these proves the doctrines at issue to be incorrect logically, but are sufficient to raise great doubts as to their merits.

Hume really showed how one lives in a Pyrrhonian universe. None of our naturally acquired beliefs are offered as truths, as knowledge, with which to refute the Pyrrhonist. They are all irrational, but as Hume

[72] Hume did not believe the usual logical refutation of Pyrrhonism, namely, that if the sceptical arguments were strong, they showed that something could be known, and if weak, not in need of refutation. Hume maintained that the sceptical reasonings were always as strong as those to which they were opposed, in that any dogmatic conclusion allowed for a sceptical answer. An unanswerable question can be asked on the basis of whatever dogmatic maxims are used. If the dogmatic maxims are disavowed because of the sceptical arguments, then both the sceptical and dogmatic conclusions are invalidated, and not just the former. See *Treatise*, pp. 186–87.

pointed out, necessary in our existence. We judge because we have to, and we act because we have to. Neither our judgments nor our actions prove that we possess any rational basis for what we do.

What I wish to show, as the philosophical significance of Hume's criticisms of Pyrrhonism, is that it is the only "consistent" version of the original sceptical theory, more consistent than even the formulation in Sextus Empiricus. Other Pyrrhonians have been either too sceptical or too dogmatic to hold to the position consistently. Hume, as I shall try to prove, found the proper mixture of dogmatism and scepticism, of belief and suspense, for a Pyrrhonist.

Hume, for the various reasons presented above, accepted the Pyrrhonian analysis of human knowledge, so long as that analysis was restricted to the theoretical foundations of human knowledge. He contended, however, that the acceptance of such an analysis could not be accompanied by the development of a suspensive attitude towards any and every question because our natural constitution would not permit it. This contention is merely a legitimate extension of the Pyrrhonian principle of living according to nature. The classical Pyrrhonians, as was mentioned earlier, had never held the view as it appears in Hume's remarks, in that the original holders of this view had not advocated total suspense of opinion and action. Sextus had said:

> Adhering, then, to appearances we live in accordance with the normal rules of life, undogmatically, seeing that we cannot remain wholly inactive. And it would seem that this regulation of life is fourfold, and that

one part of it lies in the guidance of Nature, another in the constraint of the passions, another in the tradition of laws and customs, another in the instruction of the arts. Nature's guidance is that by which we are naturally capable of sensation and thought; constraint of the passions is that whereby hunger drives us to food and thirst to drink; tradition of customs and laws, that whereby we regard piety in the conduct of life as good, but impiety as evil; instruction of the arts, that whereby we are not inactive in such arts as we adopt. But we make all these statements undogmatically.[73]

In this statement there are two important points which Hume never recognized as part of the Pyrrhonian thesis, and therefore attacked the Pyrrhonians for omitting, first that we cannot remain wholly inactive, and second, that sensation and thought are natural occurrences and are to be accepted as such. Hume really offered a radical form of the old doctrine by showing what the ancient Pyrrhonians never realised —that almost everything we believe is due to nature's guidance and that our activity commits us to accepting far more than they expected. If we live according to nature, we then suspend judgment only when it is natural to do so, and, as Hume contended, it is not natural to do so solely because we lack rational evidence for coming to a decision. E.g., in discussing the question, "Does motion exist?", Sextus maintained that it was evident to our senses that it does, while our reasoning showed that this was impossible, and therefore we should "suspend our judgment—in view of the contradiction between appearances and arguments—

[73] Sextus Empiricus, *Outlines*, I, Sect. 23–24.

regarding the question as to the existence or non-existence of motion."[74] Hume pointed out that in asking people to suspend judgment on such a question, the Pyrrhonian may be asking them to do something very unnatural. If the Pyrrhonian view consists in showing that there is no basis for any opinion, and that the way in which one does live if this is the case is by the guidance of nature, then the consistent Pyrrhonist, like Hume, will believe in whatever he is naturally compelled to, and will suspend judgment on that which he is compelled to. Nature leads us to this suspensive attitude when the dogmatist's arguments go too far away from the affairs of common life. On the other hand, nature does not lead us to a suspensive attitude on many unfounded beliefs about the common affairs of mankind.[75] It is really only on the basis of a psychological investigation that one can determine when, in actual life, we do suspend judgment. This cannot be discovered merely by investigating the grounds for our opinions. The ancient Pyrrhonians, even if they were not guilty of the failure to see the need for some sort of human activity, were guilty of too much dogmatism, in thinking that one should and could suspend judgment on all questions. They were guilty of the same sort of dogmatic rationalism that

[74] *Ibid.*, III, Sect. 81.

[75] Sextus admitted this with regard to certain types of non-rational inferences. E.g., the sceptic assents to the fact that smoke signifies fire, though the existence of the fire is not deducible from the occurrence of the smoke, since this is the way we operate. Cf. *ibid.*, II, Sect. 102. On the other hand, Sextus insisted that "the Pyrrhonian philosopher assents to nothing that is non-evident" (*ibid.*, I, Sect. 13). This, as Hume showed, is unnatural, and just stubbornness.

they were trying so hard to overthrow, in that they thought a conclusion was to be accepted because it followed logically. The proper Pyrrhonian view separates the problems of rational evidence for beliefs, and the psychology of beliefs. One believes for various psychological causes, which often have nothing to do with the evidence at hand. One is sceptical for various psychological causes, also. Hence, the Pyrrhonist ought to hold, as Hume did, that one believes when one must, one doubts when one must, though, on the epistemological level, no opinion of doubt or belief can be justified. And this is following nature's guidance.[76]

Not only were the Pyrrhonians too dogmatic in their scepticism, in insisting on their suspensive attitude on all matters, they are too sceptical in trying to be undogmatic at all times. Sextus insisted that the sceptic never makes any positive assertions, but only asserts what appears to be the case at any time, undogmatically.[77] But is this natural? Hume contended that we are dogmatic at times owing to the various psychological and biological factors operating upon us.

> Nor is it only proper we shou'd in general indulge our inclination in the most elaborate philosophical researches, notwithstanding our sceptical principles, but also that we shou'd yield to that propensity, which inclines us to be positive and certain in *particular points*, according to the light, in which we survey

[76] This distinction between epistemological scepticism and psychological ability to doubt is different from the classical distinction between theory and practice, since, according to Hume, the Pyrrhonian analysis applies to both theoretical and practical matters, and psychological factors determine our ability to doubt on matters on either level.

[77] Cf. *ibid.*, I, Sect. 4 and 13–15.

them in any *particular instant*. 'Tis easier to forbear all examination and enquiry, than to check ourselves in so natural a propensity, and guard against that assurance, which arises from an exact and full survey of an object. On such an occasion we are apt not only to forget our scepticism, but even our modesty too; and make use of such terms as these, *'tis evident*, *'tis certain*, *'tis undeniable*; which a due deference to the public ought, perhaps, to prevent. I may have fallen into this fault after the example of others; but I here enter a *caveat* against any objections, which may be offer'd on that head; and declare that such expressions were extorted from me by the present view of the object, and imply no dogmatical spirit, nor conceited idea of my own judgment, which are sentiments that I am sensible can become no body, and a sceptic still less than any other.[78]

Thus, the sceptic, in stating what seems to him, will be as dogmatic as he feels at that moment, or as sceptical as he feels. This is the natural way. The ancient Pyrrhonian who wanted to be undogmatic at all times, was confusing his desire to be undogmatic on the epistemological level with his natural propensity to state his opinions of the moment in a dogmatic way. The proper Pyrrhonist has no rational basis for his opinions, but still has strong opinions owing to his psychological and biological constitution.

The ancient Pyrrhonians always claimed that their

[78] *Treatise*, pp. 273–74. It is interesting that the reviewer of the *Treatise* in the *Bibliothèque Raisonnée des Ouvrages des Savans de l'Europe*, Vol. 24 (1740), who considered the work entirely Pyrrhonian, remarked satirically about this passage, "And, in truth, one would have to be madly Pyrrhonian to refuse to believe him" (p. 355). See also E. C. Mossner, "The Continental Reception of Hume's *Treatise*, 1739–41," *Mind*, LVI (1947), 34–38.

attitude, if accepted, would have therapeutic results. The sceptic would attain a state called "quietude" by ceasing to dogmatize about anything. "The man who determines nothing as to what is naturally good or bad neither shuns nor pursues anything eagerly; and, in consequence, he is unperturbed."[79] However, if Hume is correct, the orthodox Pyrrhonist will not attain peace of mind, and instead will go mad. Only the Humean Pyrrhonist has any hope for quietude. The former will be continually fighting nature in his unnatural effort to retain a suspensive attitude and to be undogmatic at all times. His passions, propensities, etc., will every moment be leading him to judge and to judge dogmatically, while the Pyrrhonian will, on principle, be trying desperately to resist. Both the Humean and the orthodox Pyrrhonist may be at ease as to the intellectual merits of any dogmatic view, but only the former is able to have a peaceful attitude towards the view, since how he feels about it will be natural, and there will be no attempt to combat his inclinations.

To conclude, then, Hume was trying to show the psychological impossibility of accepting a certain version of Pyrrhonism, and in doing so offered the only "consistent" formulation of that extreme sceptical view. One does not and cannot suspend judgment merely because of lack of rational basis for any conclusion. Epistemological Pyrrhonism, though the only possible conclusion of philosophical analysis, according to Hume, cannot cause us to adopt a practical Pyrrhonian attitude. This attack can be pushed, beyond the truncated version of Pyrrhonism that Hume

[79] Sextus, *Outlines*, I, Sect. 28. See also I, Sect. 10, 12, 25–30.

attacked, against the original version as well, when the ancient sceptics tried to insist on too dogmatic an attitude on suspending judgment, and too sceptical an attitude towards being dogmatic. Both of these points are in fact determined by nature and not by theory. Hence, if one is really Pyrrhonian, as Hume was, one will be as dogmatic and as opinionated as one is naturally inclined to be.[80]

Hume's full view of himself as the "consistent" Pyrrhonist comes out in the picture that he painted of what the true sceptic is like, both in the character of Philo in the *Dialogues*, and in various remarks in all his philosophical writings. The true Pyrrhonist is both a dogmatist and a sceptic. In being entirely the product of nature he welds his schizophrenic personality and philosophy together. He believes whatever nature leads him to believe, no more and no less. He is compelled to believe, and in accepting the compulsion he is exhibiting his scepticism. He is led to philosophize by certain natural inclinations, and through them to come to certain conclusions, and in so doing he is again exhibiting his scepticism. "I may, nay I must yield to the current of nature, in submitting to my senses and understanding; and in this blind submission I shew most perfectly my sceptical disposition and

[80] There is, of course, a point at which even Hume's formulation of "consistent" Pyrrhonism breaks down. Hume requires a theoretical framework in order to distinguish between epistemological Pyrrhonism and one's psychological abilities. Such a framework will constitute a systematic position not open to Pyrrhonian attacks if the distinction between epistemology and psychology which is made within it is any more than a strong natural belief of David Hume.

principles."[81] Even the more "mitigated scepticism" which Hume proposed, as an alternative to extreme scepticism, at the end of the *Enquiry*, comes to no more than this. This sceptic, once thoroughly convinced of the force of the Pyrrhonian doubts, and seeing that it is only the strong power of natural instinct that allows him to go on, will philosophize because he gains pleasure from it, and because he has a propensity to reason.[82]

Such a sceptical philosopher will restrict his reasonings within the compass of our faculties, and will only be organizing the principles of common life. Philosophy, as a natural pursuit rather than the haughty speculations of the dogmatists, whether dogmatic dogmatists or dogmatic sceptics, is not a search for sufficient reasons, but only an extension and clarification of ordinary, natural reasonings.[83]

Such a sceptic will be modest, diffident, and careless. He will come to some degree of doubt, and will always see the lack of rational basis for any conclusion. He will, sometimes, realize that he reasons in the careless manner of speculating owing to an inclination of the moment, of accepting a conclusion *pro tem.* because of the way it strikes him, etc.

[81] *Treatise*, p. 269. "In all the incidents of life we ought still to preserve our scepticism. If we believe, that fire warms, or water refreshes, 'tis only because it costs us too much pains to think otherwise. Nay, if we are philosophers, it ought only to be upon sceptical principles, and from an inclination, which we feel to the employing ourselves after that manner. Where reason is lively, and mixes itself with some propensity, it ought to be assented to. Where it does not, it never can have any title to operate upon us" (*ibid.*, p. 270).

[82] *Enquiry*, p. 133.

[83] *Ibid.*, p. 133, and *Dialogues*, p. 134.

The conduct of a man, who studies philosophy in this careless manner, is more truly sceptical than that of one, who feeling in himself an inclination to it, is yet so over-whelm'd with doubts and scruples, as totally to reject it. A true sceptic will be diffident of his philosophical doubts, as well as of his philosophical conviction; and will never refuse any innocent satisfaction, which offers itself, upon account of either of them.[84]

The final portrait of the sceptic, according to Hume, comes out in the very odd footnote in the last of the *Dialogues:*

It seems evident, that the dispute between the sceptics and dogmatists is entirely verbal, or at least regards only the degrees of doubt and assurance, which we ought to indulge with regard to all reasoning: And such disputes are commonly at the bottom, verbal, and admit not of any precise determination. No philosophical dogmatist denies, that there are difficulties both with regard to the senses and to all science: and that these difficulties are in a regular, logical method, absolutely insolveable. No sceptic denies, that we lie under an absolute necessity, notwithstanding these difficulties, of thinking, and believing, and reasoning with regard to all kind of subjects, and even of frequently assenting with confidence and security. The only difference, then, between these sects, if they merit that name, is, that the sceptic, from habit, caprice, or inclination, insists most on the difficulties; the dogmatist, for like reasons, on the necessity.[85]

Who ever heard of such a dogmatist, or such a sceptic? Certainly no Cartesian, Spinozist, or Leibnizian would accept the fact that there are absolutely insoluble diffi-

---

[84] *Treatise*, p. 273. See also, *Enquiry*, p. 132.
[85] *Dialogues*, p. 219 n.

culties in our reasonings. Certainly, no sceptic of ancient times ever granted that there is an absolute necessity for believing on all sorts of subjects. The only such dogmatist and sceptic was Hume himself, the complete Pyrrhonist. He alone believed that both the difficulties and the necessity exist. The picture of the two, the dogmatist and sceptic, is a picture of the perfect Pyrrhonist in his two moods, his split personality. In one mood, the difficulties overcome him, in another, the necessities do. Only by being both can one be a philosopher, and live according to nature.[86]

[86] Perhaps it was Hume's view that any "honest" philosopher would be this sort of schizophrenic Pyrrhonist. A note seems due here with regard to a disagreement between John Laird and Norman Kemp Smith as to whether Hume was a Pyrrhonist or a naturalist. I submit that they are the same. Hume, the naturalist who subverts all reason to emotion, was just Hume the Pyrrhonist in his dogmatic mood. Hume the reasoner was Hume the Pyrrhonist in his sceptical mood.

HUME'S THEORY OF MENTAL ACTIVITY

ROBERT PAUL WOLFF

Ever since Norman Kemp Smith's brilliant paper on "The Naturalism of Hume" fifty-five years ago,[1] students of philosophy have acknowledged the fact that David Hume's *Treatise of Human Nature* is very much more than an encyclopedia of skepticism. Hume, it is now realized, was engaged in Book I of the *Treatise* in a serious attempt to answer some of the central problems of philosophy. However, there is rather less clarity about just what his answers were. No doubt the obscurity of Hume's positive theory is due in part to his smooth and jesting style, free of the ponderous terminology which in other works alerts the reader to the least touch of a theory. But I think the real reason for Hume's failure to get across his very novel suggestions is the fact that they carry him beyond the limits of his own system, so that he is forced to express his best ideas in language totally unsuited to them. To put the point in a sentence, Hume began the *Treatise* with the assumption that empirical knowledge could be explained by reference to the contents of the mind

From *The Philosophical Review*, Vol. LXIX (1960). Reprinted by permission of the author and *The Philosophical Review*.
[1] N. Kemp Smith, "The Naturalism of Hume," *Mind*, XIV (1905), 149–73; 335–47.

alone, and then made the profound discovery that it was the activity of the mind, rather than the nature of its contents, which accounted for all the puzzling features of empirical knowledge. This insight, which was so brilliantly exploited by Kant, and has become today a focus of attention through the studies of disposition terms and language habits, was used by Hume to clarify the nature of causal inference and to explain the origin of our concepts of material objects.

In this paper I shall try to extricate Hume's theory of mental activity from the associationism and copy theory of ideas in which it is embedded. Hume nowhere sets out whole the theory which I attribute to him, but every part of my interpretation, with the exception of several terminological clarifications, is amply supported by passages in the *Treatise*. I have tried to exhibit the *Treatise* as more than a dated work of purely historical interest. If my interpretation is correct, Hume can still make a useful contribution to current epistemological and metaphysical debates.

I

The best way to get hold of Hume's new theory is to discover the precise point at which the framework of his system distorts his exposition and forces him to cramp his thoughts into ill-suited categories. That point, in my opinion, is reached when Hume attempts to explain the necessity of causal inference by appeal to "impressions of reflection." It is worth our while to explore a bit Hume's discussion of this category of impressions, for through it we will see what he was trying to say and why he had such difficulty saying it.

There are, Hume tells us, two sorts of impressions. The first are impressions of sensation, which "without any introduction make their appearance in the soul" (p. 275).[2] These are dependent upon "natural and physical causes," the examination of which, Hume says, would lead him "into the sciences of anatomy and natural philosophy" (p. 276). He therefore turns to the second category: impressions of reflection. It sometimes happens that an idea, which in its turn is derived from some precedent impression, will "return upon the soul" (p. 8) to produce new impressions, of pride, humility, ambition, vanity, hope, fear, desire, aversion, or any of the countless "passions and other emotions resembling them" (p. 275; also pp. 276–77). The category of impressions of reflection finds its most natural employment in Books II and III of the *Treatise*, where Hume discusses the passions and moral sentiments. Kemp Smith has based on this fact his claim that Books II and III were earlier in composition than Book I.[3] According to Kemp Smith, who seems to me quite convincing, the analyses of causation, space and time, and material objects are intended by Hume as extensions of a theory first advanced in connection with problems of ethics. The beliefs arising from the "impression" of causal necessity are viewed as analogous to the moral sentiments produced in the soul by

[2] All parenthetical references are to Hume, *A Treatise of Human Nature*, ed. L. A. Selby-Bigge (Oxford, 1888).

[3] Cf. N. Kemp Smith, *The Philosophy of David Hume* (London, 1941), pp. 12–20, 44–46.

the mechanism of sympathy. *"Belief,"* says Hume, *"is more properly an act of the sensitive, than of the cogitative part of our natures"* (p. 183, italics Hume's).

There are two important similarities between moral sentiment and passions on the one hand and empirical beliefs on the other, which seem to me to have led Hume to group them together as "impressions of reflection." First of all, Hume believed that neither passions nor beliefs are "rational" in the strict sense of "justifiably derivable from relations of ideas" (cf. p. 70). Passions, of course, are not the products of reasoning, nor, thought Hume, are the sentiments of approbation and disapprobation. Now the whole point of his attack on the rationalists was to show that empirical beliefs are also not justifiable by an appeal to relations of ideas. They spring from "nonrational" sources in the soul. It is for this reason that Hume wrote, "Belief is more properly an act of the sensitive, than of the cogitative part of our natures." Second, and in my opinion even more important, Hume believed that moral sentiments, passions, and empirical beliefs are all responses of the mind to the presented world rather than given contents of experience. Just as love, hatred, approval, and disapproval are second-level reactions of the mind to experience, so also the beliefs in causal necessity and physical objects result from the mind's "reflection" upon its sensations. What I suggest is that these similarities of beliefs to passions and moral sentiments led Hume to identify them and to use in Book I the tool—impressions of reflection—which had worked so well in Books II and III. For notice that impressions of reflection are (1) nonrational in origin, and (2) contributed by the mind to experience rather than derived directly from perception. These are just the ways in which passions, moral sentiments, and beliefs are similar, on Hume's view.

But if there are similarities, still there are striking differences. Perhaps the most troubling difference is that the so-called "impressions of reflection" cited by Hume to explain the origins of empirical beliefs are remarkably elusive and hard to find. Hume feels no need to prove the existence of love or anger or desire. But when it comes to the "impression of necessary connexion" he does not simply say, "Look and see." Rather, he eliminates alternatives, argues by *reductio ad absurdum*, and generally does just what we would expect of a philosopher attempting to pin down an unknown quantity. The reason for this odd behavior is not difficult to discover. Hume began the *Treatise*, as I have suggested, by assuming that all empirical concepts could be explained in terms of some combination of the contents of perception. He very quickly came to see that knowledge and belief result from what the mind *does* with its contents rather than simply from the nature of those contents. Hence, most of Book I is devoted to a discussion of the activities of the mind. Having no category in which to put mental activities, however, Hume tried to squeeze them into the slot labeled "impressions of reflection." Now in order to remove some of the confusion thus caused, we must attempt a systematic restatement and interpretation of Hume's discussion of mental activity. After a general statement, we can look to the text for confirming evidence.

II

Hume begins his analysis of the mind's operations
with an appeal to associations of ideas. Modeling his
discussion on the Newtonian theory of gravitation, he
attempts to explain the phenomena of cognition without referring to secret causes and without framing hypotheses concerning ultimate qualities (p. xxi). The
central thesis is that there is a "uniting principle"
among ideas which can be regarded as a "gentle force,"
influencing the imagination in its arrangements and
rearrangements of perceptions (pp. 10–11). It is at
this point unclear whether some special condition of
the mind is necessary for the working of the force.
Hume's emphasis is all on the nature of the ideas
themselves. The imagination, if subjected repeatedly
to the gentle force of association, develops certain
habits or *customs*. It comes to anticipate the conjunction of perceptions which past experience has exhib-
ited. Much as Pavlov's dog would begin to salivate at
the sound of a bell, so the mind generates the idea of
an "effect" if presented with the "cause." Indeed, says
Hume, the habit of thinking an idea when presented
with an impression is all there is to causal inference.
The gentle force, so unassuming in its first appearance,
is the adhesive for all experience.

This explanation, based on an analogy between
gravitation and association, is not satisfactory as it
stands. According to Newton, two bodies attract one
another without (so far as we know) the intervention

of any third thing. This is at least intelligible, for bodies can literally move about, toward or away from each other. But an impression clearly is not a body which approaches or recedes from other impressions. When Hume says that the cause and effect are "associated," he means that the mind tends to think of one when presented with the other. Thus the metaphor of a "gentle force" is misleading. The impressions affect the mind, not one another. The question remains, by what means does the observed contiguity and resemblance become translated into a habit of association? Then, too, the theory of association fails to explain the striking similarity in the habits of different minds, or of one mind at different times. Despite a bewildering variety in perceptual experience, the mind, according to Hume, seems always to come up with the same few types of association: causes, objects, the self. These are only a few of the inadequacies of the simple associationism of the early pages of the *Treatise*. Hume soon moves past this theory to a more complicated analysis of cognition, basing his account on a theory of mental propensities.[4]

A "propensity" can be described as the disposition to develop a disposition, or as a "second-level" disposition. When we attempt to explain the behavior of Pavlov's dog, for example, it is not enough to state that Pavlov rang the bell every time the food was offered. That is, of course, a necessary part of the explanation, but we must add that the dog was *capable*

---

[4] What follows is a reconstruction of Hume's view. In the third and fourth sections of this paper I have assembled the evidence for its defense.

of being conditioned. If it were not, no amount of bell-ringing could produce the conditioned reflex of salivation. Let us use the term "disposition" to describe the fact that an entity is prone to act or react in certain ways under certain conditions. Let us use the term "propensity" to describe the fact that an entity is prone to *develop certain dispositions* under certain conditions.[5] Then we can say that the dog's salivation upon the ringing of the bell is a manifestation of a disposition (in this case a conditioned reflex) and the disposition in turn is a manifestation of the dog's propensity (to form dispositions of this sort).

There are several simple facts about stimuli, dispositions, and propensities which it will prove helpful to keep in mind when considering Hume's theory. First, the stimuli are, of course, sensory in nature. They are the instigators or "proximate causes" of the conditioning process, as well as the triggers of the disposition already formed. Second, the sensory stimuli are the individuating conditions of the dispositions being formed. The nature of the stimulus determines the precise character, or content, of the disposition. For example, by choosing a different stimulus, we can make the dog salivate at the blowing of a whistle or a clap of the hands rather than at the ringing of a bell. Third, dispositions are distinguished from propensities by their logical type. As mentioned above, propensities are second-level dispositions, or dispositions to form dispositions. Therefore, dispositions depend upon the

[5] This is not the usage followed by Hume. He does not observe strict distinctions among "habit," "custom," "propensity," and "disposition."

conditioning stimuli and follow after them, while propensities precede both stimuli and dispositions. Propensities are thus necessary conditions for the development of dispositions.

With these few points outlined, I can now state the theory of mental activity which I claim to find in Book I of the *Treatise*. The proof of my claim, of course, will come in the detailed examination of Hume's account of our concepts of causal inference and material objects. Put briefly, the theory runs like this: The human mind has a small number of innate propensities, or "dispositions to form dispositions." When the mind is presented with perceptions conjoined in certain ways, its propensities are activated and it develops dispositions. These dispositions determine the mind to reproduce in imagination certain impressions when it experiences certain others.[6] The mind, in another of Hume's phrases, forms a "habit of association." The factors in cognition which Hume labeled impressions of reflection—such as the impression of necessary connection—are really dispositions, and the ideas of necessary connection, substance, and so forth, are not copies of impressions but ideas of mental dispositions. The innate propensities constitute the basic "machinery" of the mind. They are the necessary and universal conditions of all our ideas of causes and objects. In Hume's words:

> In order to justify myself, I must distinguish in the imagination betwixt the principles which are permanent, irresistible, and universal; such as the customary

[6] The impressions, of course, are reproduced in a less vivid form, as ideas (p. 93).

transition from causes to effects, and from effects to causes: And the principles, which are changeable, weak, and irregular; such as those I have just now taken notice of. The former are the foundation of all our thoughts and actions, so that upon their removal human nature must immediately perish and go to ruin (p. 225).

Now let us examine the arguments of the *Treatise* in more detail.

III

I shall begin with Hume's discussion of causal inference, which occupies Part III of Book I. After completing his famous and devastating attacks on the rationalists, Hume translates the problem of causation into two questions: (1) What is the nature of the idea of necessary connection? and (2) "Why [do] we conclude that such particular causes must *necessarily* have such particular effects; and what is the nature of that *inference* we draw from the one to the other, and of the belief we repose in it?" (p. 78).[7] Hume chooses to answer the second question first, leaving the "idea of necessary connexion" for later.

When we examine specific causal reasoning, we find four components: an impression, an inference, an idea, and a belief. All causal reasoning begins with an *im-*

---

[7] Hume also asks "For what reason we pronounce it *necessary* that every thing whose existence has a beginning shou'd also have a cause?" (p. 78). However, he nowhere accounts for our belief in this "causal maxim," and this may be why he omits all mention of it from the *Enquiry concerning Human Understanding.* Cf. Kemp Smith, *The Philosophy of David Hume*, pp. 405–13.

pression of sensation which is present before the mind and acts as the anchor of the entire process. The second component is the *inference* by which the mind passes from the present impression to an *idea*. This idea, related to the impression, is the third component of the reasoning process. Fourth, there is the *belief* which we then repose in the idea.

The impression needs no explanation. To account for the inference to the idea, Hume introduces the factor of "constant conjunction." Upon examining causally related objects, and reflecting back over past experience, we discover that whenever we label one object cause of another, we can recall pairs of contiguous and successive objects which resemble the present impression and idea. As the objects appear again and again in similar relations to one another, they become "associated" in the imagination. By a natural mental process, the habit is inculcated of conceiving of the one when the other is perceived. When the impression of the cause, let us say, is present to the mind, then the disposition created by past conjunction determines the mind to reproduce the idea of the effect. The essence of the causal inference lies in this transition. There remains only the belief, which I discuss below.

Hume returns in Section 14 of Part III to the first question, What is the nature of the idea of necessary connection? His analysis of particular causal inferences has produced three conclusions which, he believes, permit him now to answer the question. The conclusions are

that the simple view of any two objects or actions,

> however related, can never give us any idea of power,
> or of a connexion betwixt them: *that* this idea arises
> from the repetition of their union: *that* the repeti-
> tion neither discovers nor causes any thing in the ob-
> jects, but has an influence only on the mind, by that
> customary transition it produces (p. 166).

But every idea, says Hume, is a copy of some impression. As the idea of necessary connection is not derived
from any quality or relation of objects, it cannot be a
copy of an impression of sensation. The only available
impression of reflection is the "feeling" attached to the
disposition of the mind to pass from an object to the
idea associated with it (p. 165). Therefore the idea
of necessary connection must be the idea of this mental transition. This analysis of causal inference depends
on three points, each of which requires some comment. The points are: (1) the nature of the "transition" from impression to related idea; (2) the nature
of the "impression of necessary connexion" on which
we base our idea of causal influence; and (3) the nature
of the mechanism of belief, whereby we assent to the
inference and take the associated idea as objectively
representative. Let us consider them in turn.

The "transition" of which Hume speaks is not to be
understood as a passing of the mind from one present
perception to another *present* perception. What happens is that the mind, perceiving the first, "forms an
idea of its usual attendant" (p. 93). In other words,
the mind reproduces in imagination a copy of the impression which has lately been associated with the
present impression. This process of recall is the manifestation of a mental disposition or "habit" which is

inculcated by experience. The mind is confronted with a succession of resembling impressions, and thereupon develops a disposition to conceive the one when it perceives the other. As I have already noted, the proneness of the mind to develop such a disposition is itself a disposition; it is what I called a "propensity." Hume now sets to one side the aspects of causal reasoning which are independent of the mind's inferences. The contiguity and succession of objects is indeed separate from our thought, as is the constant association of like objects (p. 168). These relations are "independent of, and antecedent to the operations of the understanding" (p. 168). But the necessity of their connection is a property of our inference upon them and derives from the mind's "habit." In the terminology which I have adopted, the associated impressions act as stimuli to activate an innate propensity; the result is a mental disposition to imagine a related idea when presented with an impression.

The second element of Hume's analysis is the "impression of necessary connexion" from which the idea of causal influence is copied. We are here presented with a common problem of textual interpretation. What Hume says is not the same as what Hume says he says. As I have suggested, the natural development of his argument leads him in one direction, but the prior strictures of his system require a different and conflicting move. Hume talks as if the impression of necessary connection, like an impression of love or envy, were a directly observable mental content arising from the workings of the imagination. But the description which he actually gives of this impression is peculiar, to say the least. The "internal impression," he claims, is the "propensity, which custom produces, to pass from an object to the idea of its usual attendant" (p. 165). Again, the "customary transition is the same with the power and necessity" (p. 166). Hume is not saying here that the impression arises from the transition or is conjoined with the transition or is dependent upon the transition; he is saying that the impression *is* the transition. Now this is plainly an error in classification. "Customary transitions" and "propensities" are mental operations or powers, not contents of consciousness. If the idea of necessary connection is a copy of the transition from an impression to its usual attendant, then it is a copy of a mental activity. It is in fact the idea of the mind's disposition to reproduce related perceptions in imagination. This is just the muddle which I referred to above, when discussing impressions of reflection. In these passages we can observe Hume shifting toward explanation in terms of mental activities, while still tied to the language of mental contents. Later on we shall see him move even further in this direction when he deals with the problem of external objects.

Finally, let us consider the problem of *belief*. Hume holds that to believe in the existence of an object is not to conjoin an idea of existence to the idea of the object (p. 94). He casts about, therefore, for some quality common to all the ideas and impressions in which we repose belief, and he hits upon "the *manner* of our conceiving them." The belief in an idea is nothing but an increased force and vivacity by which our conception is heightened and enlivened (p. 96). This theory, as Hume himself recognized, is open to serious objections. One of these is the fact that there are many common beliefs which cannot be explained as "enlivened ideas." When we form an inference upon the evidence of historical traces, and reason from a present impression of manuscripts to the past existence of a historical personage, the resultant belief cannot be attributed to the force of the impressions of the text before us (pp. 145–46). We could not, for example, strengthen the belief by illuminating the page more brightly or recasting the print more sharply.[8] Hume appears to take account of this objection in several passages, the first of which contains a turn of phrase suggesting a possible revision:

> For suppose I form at present an idea, of which I have forgot the correspondent impression, I am able to conclude from this idea, that such an impression did once exist; and as this conclusion is attended with belief, it may be ask'd, from whence are the qualities of force and vivacity deriv'd, which constitute this belief? And to this I answer very readily, *from the present idea.* For as this idea is not here considered as the representation of any absent object, but as a real perception in the mind, of which we are intimately conscious, it must be able to bestow on whatever is related to it the same quality, call it *firmness, or solidity, or force, or vivacity,* with which the mind reflects upon it, and is assur'd of its present existence (pp. 105–6).

The key phrase is the last clause but one of the final

[8] It is the existence of the beliefs, not their truth, which is at stake here. The trouble with Hume's theory is that it fails to explain why we do *not* believe vivid and affecting fiction, and yet *do* believe dull history books.

sentence. The present idea, serving as the "impression" from which the inference proceeds, must possess that firmness or solidity or force or vivacity *with which the mind reflects upon it*. The force is not a quality of the perception, but rather a quality of the way in which the mind conceives it. Hence any idea or impression, however weak, may serve as the starting point for a causal inference, if only the mind reflects upon it with the solidity of belief. Now in the passage I have quoted, Hume uses this locution only to explain our inference from a present idea to the past impression *of which it is a copy*. But in the Appendix he extends the same description to all belief. There he states that the "feeling" of belief is a *"firmer conception, or a faster hold, that we take of the object"* (p. 627; cf. p. 626). Belief is not a hold that the object takes on us, but that we take on the object. Here again we see a shift in emphasis from the characteristics of perception to some activity of the mind.

IV

Hume's theory of mental activity reaches its fullest development in his treatment of our belief in material objects. The argument is carried on in several different passages in Book I of the *Treatise*, and a great deal of restatement and interpretation is needed to present it in coherent form. The first passage is a discussion of substance which comes as part of an examination of relations, modes, substances, and abstract ideas in Part I. It is little more than a page in length, and the laconic manner in which it proceeds suggests that Hume did not consider his views especially original. Nevertheless, his remarks are exceptionally suggestive, albeit brief.

What is our idea of substance? asks Hume (p. 15).[9] Does it derive from an impression of sensation or of reflection (p. 16)? Surely neither, he answers, for no one impression is the origin of the idea of a substance. Hence it must be an idea of "a collection of particular qualities" (p. 16). To the qualities, or their ideas in our mind, is attached a name, by which we may recall all or some of them when necessary. As we learn more about those qualities which bear an intimate relation to the given collection, our idea of it expands, and the number of ideas which its name recalls becomes larger. Thus, a first idea of gold may include the qualities yellow, hard, and heavy. When the quality of solubility in *aqua regia* is learned, this is added to the collection, and henceforth the word "gold" is capable of calling it to mind.

Now Hume adds a highly significant sentence, which unfortunately is left without comment: "The principle of union [of the qualities] being regarded as the chief part of the complex idea, gives entrance to whatever quality afterwards occurs, and is equally comprehended by it, as are the others, which first presented themselves" (p. 16). Ideas of substance are distinguished by this fact from ideas of modes. Modes are also collections of qualities, to be sure. But the qualities are either not closely connected by the relations of contiguity

_____

[9] He means, what is our idea of *a* substance; that is to say, what is our idea of gold or wood or a man?

and causation—Hume offers the example of a dance
—or else are united together, but in such a way that
"the uniting principle is not regarded as the foundation of the complex idea" (p. 17). To introduce a *new*
quality, therefore, destroys the particular unity to
which the name is attached, and occasions a new name.
Thus an arrangement of colors may be beautiful, but
the beauty is not a substance. For if it were, one could
attach other related qualities to the collection without
destroying the idea of the beauty. What in fact happens, of course, is that any addition or subtraction
produces a *new* idea—of an equal beauty, perhaps, but
different from the old idea (p. 17). On the other hand,
one can subtract from or add to the qualities of a
substance without thereby destroying its unity. A man
is still the same substance whether he gains weight,
cuts his hair, gets a tan, or even loses several limbs.
So, too, for other substances. They remain the "same
thing" through a variety of changes. Indeed, on Hume's
view it would make no sense to speak of learning
about a *thing*, unless our concept of it were in some
way more than an idea of the qualities we conceive
it to possess. For otherwise an added quality would be
part of a *new* thing, not a new quality of the old thing.

Three questions are raised by Hume's preliminary
analysis of the idea of substance. First, what is the
"principle of union" by which the imagination unites
the qualities of a substance? Second, how does the
imagination form the principle of union? And third,
what does Hume mean by his statement that the principle of union is the "chief part" of the idea of a substance?

The principle of union is described by Hume as being the manner in which the various qualities "are united by the imagination, and have a particular name assigned to them, by which we are able to recall, either to ourselves or others, that collection" (p. 16). This description is so remarkably similar to the account of "abstract ideas" given in the very next section of the *Treatise* that I shall draw on that account for an expansion of Hume's brief analysis of substance. Why he did not himself unite the two is a mystery, for he would thereby have strengthened considerably his entire theory of our concepts of objects.

In the light of the section "Of Abstract Ideas" we can construct the following interpretation of Hume's view of the unity of a substance. The "principle of union" is a habit or custom of the mind to which is attached a word. The habit determines the mind to reproduce in imagination one or more of a set of ideas, when the word for that set has been uttered or thought or otherwise invoked. Once the mind has formed the habit, it can reinvoke it at will, and by "one of the most extraordinary circumstances" of the mind's powers (p. 21), a false assertion about the membership of the set will often provoke the mind to reproduce just that member which will effectively belie the ascription. Thus, if the mind ascribes the quality of dryness to water, it will immediately recall the idea of wetness without running through the qualities of coldness, lucidity, and so forth. It will, furthermore, recognize the idea of wetness as having been called forth by the habit associated with the word "water." Hume does not pretend to know how or why this delicate capacity is possessed by the mind. He says that "To explain the ultimate causes of our mental actions is impossible. 'Tis sufficient, if we can give any satisfactory account of them from experience and analogy" (p. 22).

Returning to Hume's example, we see that the mind has formed the habit of calling up yellowness, weight, malleability, and fusibility when it conceives the word "gold." These several ideas are united solely by the mind's habit, though they are *associated* by the relations of contiguity and causation (p. 16). We are brought then to the second of our three questions: how does the imagination *form* the habit which unites the qualities? The full answer to this question is only developed by Hume in Part iv of Book I, which I shall examine presently. In this earlier section, however, he indicates the line which his argument will take. The difference between the qualities of a substance and those of a mode, he tells us,

> consist[s] in this, that the particular qualities, which form a substance, are commonly refer'd to an unknown *something*, in which they are supposed to inhere; or granting this fiction should not take place, are at least supposed to be *closely and inseparably connected by the relations of contiguity and causation* (p. 16; italics mine).

As in the case of causal inference, the mind forms a habit of reproducing perceptions as the result of certain perceived relations of objects.[10]

---

10 The analysis is complicated by the fact that causal belief, itself the result of a habit of the imagination, plays here the role of stimulus. Equally, causal belief involves belief in the existence of objects which are causally related. Hume never succeeded in

Finally, in what sense is the habit or principle of union the chief part of the idea of a substance? A possible answer is that Hume means to call the principle of union a *necessary condition* of the idea of the substance. The idea, to be sure, must contain some quality-ideas, for otherwise it would consist of a principle of union with nothing to unify. The mind would have a habit of reproduction which did not dispose it to reproduce anything at all. But among the several qualities which we impute to a substance, no single one is essential to our conception. One man's idea of gold may include the qualities yellowness, heaviness, malleability; another's conception might omit the color yellow and yet include solubility in acid, and so on. The principle of union, on the other hand, *is* a necessary element in the idea of any substance. It is for this reason that it is the "chief part" of the idea. If it is omitted, the mind is left with an unstructured assortment of ideas which are not bound up in any manner warranting the assignment of a special name.

The major discussion of the belief in material objects occurs in the long section, "Of scepticism with regard to the senses," which forms the core of Part IV. Hume defines his subject as "the *causes* which induce us to believe in the existence of body . . . ," for, as he says a few lines earlier:

> We may well ask *What causes induce us to believe in the existence of body?* but 'tis in vain to ask *Whether there be body or not?* That is a point, which

___

sorting out the complicated relationships between causal and substantial beliefs.

we must take for granted in all our reasonings (p. 187).

Specifically, it is our belief in the *continued* and *independent* existence of bodies which needs explanation. As this belief does not arise from the impressions alone, it must arise "from a concurrence of some of their qualities with the qualities of the imagination" (p. 194). Hume discovers two kinds of regularity in our impressions: constancy and coherence. Constancy is the simpler, for it depends solely upon the repetition of resembling impressions, while coherence depends upon a second-order regularity, namely, constancy of the principle of alteration. Nevertheless, Hume discusses coherence first.

It frequently happens that an impression which has in the past been regularly associated with another will make an appearance in perception alone, thereby "contradicting" past experience. For example, the sound of a squeaking door, if not accompanied by a sight of the door, runs against the past experience in which the two have been conjoined. In order to preserve the coherence of my experience, I assume a door (or, better, the visual aspect of a door) to exist, even though I do not perceive it. This would seem to involve a new propensity of the mind (p. 198).

But, Hume announces, the propensity to preserve and extend coherence is very different from the customs and habits which explained causal belief (p. 197). Mere habit can explain a belief only in what is actually inculcated by experience. If we condition a parrot to say "Two plus two is four," knowing that it has the capacity to learn simple phrases, we ought not to be surprised if it speaks the words back. But if, one day, the bird is heard to say "Two plus three is five," then we shall either discover who has been secretly coaching it or be very surprised indeed. Now our believing in the continued existence of objects is like the parrot saying "Two plus three is five," for although experience teaches us to expect coherence in the impressions we perceive, it does not, and obviously could never, teach us to expect perceptions to continue to exist when we do *not* perceive them. The mind here actually imparts to its perceptions a *greater* regularity than they naturally possess.

This is the first suggestion of the manner in which the causal connections of perceptions lead to our conceptions of objects. Taking Hume's example, the mind is accustomed to perceiving the movement of the door together with the squeak, *which is its effect*. When presented only with the squeak, the mind makes a causal inference in the manner described above, concluding that the door exists though it is unperceived. This in turn supports the causal belief, for the isolated squeak can then be interpreted as a positive, rather than a negative, instance of the causal relation. Were the mind limited merely to its causal beliefs, the force of the connection would be weakened. By creating the "fiction" of a continued and independently existing object, the mind is enabled to preserve and increase the order of its perceptions. In a manner of speaking, the mind's propensity reinforces the causal inference, protecting it from the excessive disconnectedness of experience. The two propensities together subdue a chaos which would overwhelm the "causal" propensity and greatly diminish its effectiveness.

The second characteristic common to "objective" impressions is the constancy with which they reappear in experience. We must explain the effect of this constancy upon the mind, says Hume, for coherence and the propensity it invokes are "too weak to support alone so vast an edifice, as is that of the continu'd existence of all external bodies" (p. 198–99). Hume summarizes his explanation before presenting it in detail:

> When we have been accustom'd to observe a constancy in certain impressions, . . . we are not apt to regard these interrupted impressions as different (which they really are) but on the contrary consider them as individually the same, upon account of their resemblance. But as this interruption of their existence is contrary to their perfect identity . . . we . . . are involv'd in a kind of contradiction. In order to free ourselves from [it we suppose] that these interrupted perceptions are connected by a real existence, of which we are insensible (p. 199).

As Hume intends to explain why we impute a continued and independent existence to objects, he must first make clear what we mean when we speak of various impressions as being the impressions of *an object*. Although the perceptions are distinguishable (and hence discrete) we treat them as one, supposing the object to be identical with itself at different times. But one impression gives the idea of *unity*; several impressions give the idea of *number* or multiplicity.

Betwixt unity and number there can be no medium.

> . . . After one object is suppos'd to exist, we must either suppose another also to exist; in which case we have the idea of number: Or we must suppose it not to exist; in which case the first remains at unity (p. 200).

The escape from the dilemma lies in the relation of time to our awareness of mental contents. Time is the idea of the manner in which successive impressions appear to the mind. Now imagine a series of exactly similar impressions, among which the mind distinguishes no mark of difference. If attention is paid to the passage of time (by noticing the alteration of other impressions, for example) then we distinguish among the members of the series and conceive the idea of number.[11] If only their invariable and uninterrupted similarity is attended to, then we conceive the idea of unity. The idea of identity is a mixture, or confusion, of the ideas of number and unity. As Hume puts it:

> By this means we make a difference, betwixt . . . object and . . . itself, without going to the length of number, and . . . without restraining ourselves to a strict and absolute unity (p. 201).

But experience all too rarely provides the mind with conditions for the conception of identity. Even resembling impressions are interrupted in their appearance. Hume now explains why the mind extends its identity-judgments to these faulty series.

The resemblance of impressions induces in the

---

[11] Though Hume does not say so, the distinction is presumably a "distinction of reason" (pp. 24–25). Successive resembling impressions are unlike in being dissimilar to a third impression, say one which is *contemporaneous* with the first, but *precedent* to the second.

mind a habit of recollecting them together. The habit
or disposition by which the mind recalls an uninterrupted series is, to be sure, different from the habit
by which it recalls a discontinuous series. But the two
dispositions are *alike* (p. 203), and just as the mind is
prone to associate like impressions, so it is prone to
confuse similar dispositions. "Whatever ideas place
the mind in the same disposition or in similar ones,"
Hume says, "are very apt to be confounded" (p. 203).

No sooner has the mind confused its several dispositions and denominated the discontinuous impressions
"identical" than it is thrown into the baldest contradiction. The successive impressions are obviously *not*
continuous and uninterrupted. Hence they ought not
to be called identical (p. 205). Confronted with this
conflict, the mind chooses the bolder alternative, and
rather than declare the impressions different, "unite[s]
these broken appearances by the fiction of a continu'd
existence" (p. 205). Apparently this means that the
mind, in recollecting the discontinuous series, "fills in"
the lacunae by reproducing other resembling perceptions in positions where none were experienced. Hume
says:

> Our memory presents us with a vast number of
> instances of perceptions perfectly resembling each
> other, that return at different distances of time, and
> after considerable interruptions. This resemblance
> gives us a propension to consider these interrupted
> perceptions as the same; and also a propension to
> connect them by a continu'd existence, in order to
> justify this identity, and avoid the contradiction, in
> which the interrupted appearance of these percep-
> tions seems necessarily to involve us (pp. 208–9).

In the terminology which I have employed, the mind approaches experience with the propensities which, in the case of each object-belief, operate to develop two dispositions. The dispositions together produce the idea of a continued and unified object.

V

Now let us pull together the results of the analysis of Book I, and see whether the interpretation outlined in Section II of this paper has been substantiated. It was there suggested that Hume had developed a theory of mental activity in which the key elements are certain innate propensities, and the dispositions which result when those propensities are "activated" by sensation. I think it is now clear that the various "principles" invoked by Hume do have the characteristics of dispositions and propensities. Consider first the role of sensation in the formation of empirical belief. The mind is presented with a variety of impressions which rapidly come and go in regular patterns. Stimulated by these perceptual regularities, certain mental propensities are activated, and the mind becomes disposed to reproduce its perceptions in imagination according to some established rule. Thereafter, this disposition can be "touched off" by the appearance of a suitable impression, which acts as stimulus to the mind. The similarity to the conditioning of Pavlov's dog is evident: first the bell and salivation together (first the cause and effect together), then the bell alone (the cause alone), and by virtue of the conditioned reflex (the mental disposition) the salivation (idea of the effect) occurs (is produced).

Furthermore, the impressions serve as the individuating factors of a disposition. For example, the disposition to recollect together the properties of gold may be based on a general propensity to develop such "substance-dispositions," but that the mind should associate hardness and malleability with *yellow* rather than with *green* is a result of the particularities of sensory experience. Were the patterns of perception different, the mind would associate together different qualities. It is easy to imagine a well-ordered, comprehensible world in which fire is cold, rocks are soft, gold is brittle, and water tastes like honey. But in such a world, there would be causes and effects and there *would* be continuous independent objects,[12] for our conception of causes and objects depends on the propensities of the mind itself. Without them, Hume tells us, "human nature [would] immediately perish and go to ruin" (p. 225). Thus the impressions of sensation are the stimuli which activate propensities and individuate dispositions. The "permanent, irresistible, and universal" principles, or propensities, lie ready for experience. The dispositions, on the other hand, wait upon experience, for their individual nature is determined by the qualities of the impressions.

Finally, these propensities and dispositions are all *mental* principles. Hume at times conceals this important fact by his associationistic language. In some passages he seems to suggest that perceptions are attracted

[12] More properly, there would be causal *beliefs*, and object *beliefs*.

to one another by a "gentle force" of association (pp. 10–11), without the interference of the mind. When he actually comes to describe the "transitions" and "principles of union," however, he makes it clear that the transition is a transition *of the mind* from one perception to another; that the principle of union is a principle by which the imagination recalls a set of perceptions; and in general that the propensities which precede experience and the dispositions which result are mental pronenesses to reproduce perceptions in imagination.

We are now in a position to make a list of the propensities which Hume describes in Book I of the *Treatise*. Hume never groups them together in this fashion, but if he had, the result might well have been labeled a "Table of Categories," for the propensities actually play a role quite similar to that of the categories in the *Critique of Pure Reason*. The list is as follows.

1. The propensity to develop, under the stimulus of repeated conjunction of resembling pairs of objects, a disposition to reproduce the idea of the one when presented with the impression of the other.[13]

2. The propensity to develop, under the stimulus of a set of impressions which (by the first propensity) are conceived as causally interrelated, a disposition to reproduce the impressions together, and by confusing the related set with a series of resembling impressions, to conceive the reproduced perceptions as identical.

3. The propensity to develop, under the stimulus of

[13] The clumsiness of these definitions is occasioned by the attempt to include in them all three of the elements of mental activity: propensity, stimulus, and disposition.

a causal inference from a present object to an absent object, a disposition to conceive that absent object as existent, and hence to reinforce both the causal inference and the belief in continued existence of objects.

4. The propensity to develop, under the stimulus of a discontinuous series of resembling impressions, a disposition to reproduce the series as if it were continuous, filling in the lacunae with suitable ideas, and thus permitting the ascription of *identity* and *continuity* to the series.

5. The propensity to develop, under the stimulus of a present perception, a disposition to conceive an associated perception with a greater firmness of belief, the more firmly the present perception is conceived and the closer the association between them.

The first propensity is responsible for our causal inferences. The second, dealing with the "principle of union," the third, which depends on "coherence," and the fourth, whose stimulus is "constancy," are jointly responsible for our conception of unified, independent, continuous objects. The fifth propensity is the source of the *belief* in causal influence and an external world. Taken together, these five propensities comprise the principles which Hume calls "permanent, irresistible, and universal" (p. 225). The first four propensities determine *which* perceptions the mind reproduces, and the fifth determines the *manner* in which they are reproduced.

HUME'S TWO DEFINITIONS OF "CAUSE"

J. A. ROBINSON

The text of Book I of the *Treatise of Human Nature*
makes curiously difficult reading. As J. A. Passmore has
remarked of Hume's writings in general (*Hume's Intentions* [Cambridge, 1952], p. 1), we meet there
with admirable simplicity and clarity in each individual
sentence, and yet find an overall intricacy of logical
architecture and involved argument which often baf-
fles and exasperates the student just as much in its own
way as does the writing of Hegel or Kant. This judgment is especially applicable to that segment of Book I
of the *Treatise* which dominates the rest, namely the
long and complex discussion of the notion of a "cause"
in Part III. In this sequence we encounter *par excel-
lence* the characteristic contrast between local lucidity
and global obscurity which renders Hume's meaning
so often elusive.

I think that the chief reason for this difficulty is to
be found in the fact that Hume is very nearly always
—and particularly so in the "cause" sequence—doing
two quite disparate things at one and the same time.
On the one hand, Hume is propounding what amounts

From *The Philosophical Quarterly*, Vol. XII (1962). Reprinted by permission of the author and *The Philosophical Quarterly*.

to an empirical law of psychology, the merits of which might today seem dubious but which was a source of great pride to him and which he thought would serve to explain a wide variety of mental, emotional and behavioral phenomena in man and even in the higher animals. On the other hand, Hume is simultaneously pursuing the philosophical task of analyzing and clarifying certain concepts, notably the concept of "cause." The two themes, empirical psychology and philosophical analysis, are so closely intertwined and indeed interdependent, that one sometimes suspects that Hume himself was not always able to keep them distinct in his own mind. Certainly this duality of motive and intention leads to interestingly mistaken interpretations of Hume's treatment of causation, as for example in the case of Professor Norman Kemp Smith, as we shall argue in detail in the sequel.

Perhaps the most strikingly bizarre symptom of Hume's twofold treatment of the causal relation is to be found in the fact that it culminates in *two* different definitions of the term "cause." This would not be so noteworthy a circumstance if the two definitions were equivalent to each other, either intensionally or extensionally, but even a casual inspection of them reveals that they are not equivalent in either sense. They differ, not only in meaning, but also in that the class of cases to which each applies evidently contains members which are not in the class of cases determined by the other. Let us verify this lack of equivalence. The first definition is stated as follows:

(1) We may define a *cause* to be 'An object precedent and contiguous to another, and where all the ob-

jects resembling the former are placed in like relations of precedency and contiguity to those objects that resemble the latter.'[1]

and the second definition is stated as follows:

(2) 'A *cause* is an object precedent and contiguous to another, and so united with it that the idea of the one determines the mind to form the idea of the other, and the impression of the one to form a more lively idea of the other.'[1]

It will be noted that (1) determines a class of ordered pairs (x,y) of particular occurrences, each pair having the completely objective property of being *an instance of a general uniformity*. We may write "C(x,y)" as an abbreviation for the statement that the ordered pair of particular events (x,y) satisfies the conditions laid down in (1). If in any particular case we have a pair (x,y) for which C(x,y), we may note that (*a*) the fact that C(x,y) in no way depends upon anyone's having *observed* either x or y to have occurred: (*b*) even if x, or y, or both *are* observed by someone to occur, it would not be necessary *for him to be aware that* he had witnessed an instance of a general uniformity, in order that C(x,y); (*c*) the fact that C(x,y) depends on very much more than the circumstances immediately surrounding the particular occurrences x and y.

On the other hand, (2) determines a class of ordered pairs (x,y) of particular occurrences by means of a property which is defined quite essentially in terms of certain *mental* phenomena. If we write "D(x,y)"

[1] Hume, *A Treatise of Human Nature*, ed. L. A. Selby-Bigge (Oxford, 1888), p. 170.

as an abbreviation for the statement that the conditions of (2) are satisfied for the ordered pair of particular occurrences (x,y), we may note that (*d*) there
is a definite implication, from the fact that D(x,y),
that some human observer *has* observed either x, or y,
or both to occur, or has previously observed other particular occurrences of the same kind to occur, and in
either case that he now has the disposition to pass
from the idea of an occurrence like x to an idea of an
occurrence like y, and to pass from an observation of
an occurrence like x to an expectation of an occurrence
like y; (*e*) it is possible to determine from the circumstances immediately surrounding the occurrences x and
y whether or not D(x,y).

We conclude from these remarks that (1) and (2)
certainly differ in *meaning*, and that even if the class
C of ordered pairs determined by (1) has precisely the
same members as the class D of ordered pairs determined by (2), this could not be *deduced* from (1)
and (2). Nevertheless, it is logically possible that C
and D may just happen, as a matter of contingent fact,
to contain precisely the same members; it therefore
remains for us to argue that they do not.

Indeed, no one will disagree (in particular Hume,
who admits that there can be and are "secret" and
"conceal'd" causes) that C must contain a vast multi-
tude of pairs (x,y) of occurrences which are never observed, of which no one even suspects that C(x,y);
let alone that no one has the disposition to pass from
an idea of x to an idea of y. Conversely, it is clear
that there are in fact cases where a pair (x,y) is to be
found in D without being a member of C; it is a famil-

iar predicament, in which we have all found ourselves at some time, to expect the occurrence of an event y after having observed an occurrence x, and yet to be disappointed when y does not in fact take place.

It is inescapable, then, that (1) and (2) are equivalent neither in their meanings nor by virtue of having the same extension. This being so, it seems strange that Hume should put forward (1) and (2) as *definitions* of the *same* term. He does the same thing again in the severely pruned version of his treatment of causation in the *Enquiry concerning Human Understanding*, stating there an essentially unchanged formulation of (1), followed by a somewhat trimmed-down reformulation of (2):

> (2′) [A *cause* is] an object followed by another, and whose appearance always conveys the thought to that other.[2]

What, then, are we to make of this extraordinary ambivalence? Many are no doubt tempted to write off the matter as being due to Hume's carelessness and informality, and to come away with the conclusion that Hume's account of causation amounts to saying little more than that, like beauty, causation is in the eye of the beholder.[3] I believe, however, that the puzzle can be resolved in a satisfactory way by taking the

[2] Hume, *Enquiry concerning Human Understanding*, ed. L. A. Selby-Bigge, 2nd ed. (Oxford, 1902), p. 77.

[3] The only commentator I have found who gives a correct account of these two definitions is A. H. Basson, in his recent book on Hume in the Pelican philosophy series, where he briefly states the view maintained in the present paper (*David Hume* [London, 1958], pp. 75–78). I had in fact reached this view independently, but in any case it is worth stating at greater length and in contrast to the more traditional views.

difference between (1) and (2) seriously and probing further beneath the surface to find some reason for their bald juxtaposition. An important clue is to be found in the words with which Hume introduces the two definitions in the *Treatise:*

> There may two definitions be given of this relation, which are only different by their presenting a different view of the same object, and making us consider it either as a *philosophical* or as a *natural* relation; either as a comparison of ideas, or as an association betwixt them (p. 170).

Definition (1) is then the definition of the cause-effect relation "as" a philosophical relation, while (2) is its definition "as" a natural relation. Although Selby-Bigge confessed in his Introduction to Hume's *Enquiries* that this distinction between philosophical and natural relations was for him "very hard to follow" and "indeed most bewildering," it is in fact utterly fundamental for a clear understanding of what Hume's philosophy is all about. I suspect that it is the failure to get this distinction clear which is responsible for most of the misunderstanding and confusions which exist concerning Hume's treatment of causation. The importance of the distinction lies in its being the foundation of Hume's psychological theory of the Association of Ideas. The reason the distinction is so often muddled is that Hume has frequently been taken as espousing an Idealist or Phenomenalist ontology and as therefore not to be entitled to use language and concepts dealing with physical objects and events and relations between physical objects and events. In fact Hume uses such language constantly, and indeed cannot avoid doing so in stating his theory about the Association of Ideas. Let us now discuss this theory, and show how the concept of a "natural" relation is the basic working concept of the theory.

Starting from the observable fact that, as Hobbes puts it at the beginning of the *Leviathan*, "when a man thinketh on anything whatsoever, his next thought thereafter is not altogether as casual as it seems to be; not every thought to every thought succeeds indifferently," Hume sets out to discover a general *explanatory theory* of this psychological phenomenon. He wants to be able to say *why* the "bond" or "tie" of association exists between a pair of ideas, when it is found to exist between them, and he wants also to be able to *predict* the pairs of ideas between which associative links will occur, on the basis of the observations and experiences of the person involved. A theory analogous to Newtonian mechanics would take the form of isolating an *intrinsic* property, analogous to *mass*, of the entities between which the interaction is found to occur, i.e. the mental entities, *thoughts*, *ideas* and *impressions*, and of stating a law connecting this intrinsic property, via perhaps a relational property analogous to *distance*, with the interaction to be explained. Despite the fact often-noted that Hume was consciously aware of the illustrious example of Newtonian mechanics as an immensely successful explanatory theory applied to the physical world, he did not choose to pursue the analogy in the details just now envisaged. Newtonian mechanics was for him simply the paradigm of *explanation*, whereby from a few hypotheses (of whatever form) of great generality, together with, in particular applications, ancillary information serving as "initial values" and "boundary conditions" characterizing the case at hand, the desired information descriptive of the phenomenon to be explained or predicted could be deduced. A theory having this general logical structure was what Hume was after, and, to judge by the theory he adopts, he must have reasoned somewhat as follows.

It seems like a good move, given that, for example, the idea of A is associated with the idea of B, to turn one's attention from the *ideas* towards the entities A and B, and to ask whether or not there may be some *relation* between A and B (which would usually be a pair of physical objects or physical occurrences, hence Hume's need to use a language enabling him to talk about such things), possessing some property which would account for the existence of an association between the *idea* of A and the *idea* of B. If this were to be found to be the case, then perhaps a theory might be constructible along the lines of relating the subject's previous history of experience and observation of A's and B's to the *setting up* or *inducing* in the subject's mind of dispositions to pass from the idea of A to the idea of B, and from the observation of A to the idea of B.

It was in as simple a way as this, it seems to me, that the notion of a "natural" relation suggested itself to Hume. *Naturalness* is then simply the property of any relation R between a thing or event A and a thing or event B (*not* between the *idea* of A and the *idea* of B) whereby the observation of A and B standing to each other in the relation R is enough to induce an association between the idea of A and the idea of B. There may not *be* any relations R having this property of naturalness, since it is a purely contingent feature of a relation R that it should be natural, and it may happen to be the case that *no* relation between things or events possesses this property. If so, then no theory involving the property of being natural would be possible, and Hume would have had to try another tack. However, Hume tells us that his investigations revealed that there are in fact *three* relations between things or events which apparently, in the world we happen to live in, possess the property of being natural. These are (*a*) resemblance, or similarity, (*b*) close spatial or temporal proximity; and (*c*) *the cause-effect relation.*

Now it is one thing to *analyze* or *define* a relation R, and quite another thing to *state* that a given relation R possesses a contingent empirical property. Indeed, the latter would presuppose that the relation was already well-specified or defined, in order that it could be talked about meaningfully. So that to say a relation is *natural* is not to define it or philosophically analyze it, but rather is to presuppose that this has already been done. In particular, to say *of the cause-effect relation* that *it* is a natural relation *is not to define it, nor to contribute in any way to its philosophical analysis, but to presuppose that this has already been done.* To say that the cause-effect relation is a natural relation is to state an empirical psychological theory involving it, namely that observation of ordered pairs of particular occurrences standing to each other in the cause-effect relationship is sufficient to induce an *as-*

sociation between the idea of events like x and the
idea of events like y.

Hume therefore has two tasks to carry out in the
portion of Book I of the *Treatise* which is devoted to
causation: (A) he must analyze the cause-effect relationship between events and give a clear definition of
it, and (B) he must expound his claim that the cause-
effect relation, *so defined,* is a natural relation, and
pursue the factual consequences of this claim. (A) is a
philosophical task, a logical preliminary to (B), which
is a task of empirical science.

This, then, is what is involved in a relation's being
natural. On the other hand, to say that a relation R
is "philosophical" is to make a factually empty statement; *all* relations are philosophical. The term is introduced by Hume simply in order to emphasize what
a difference there is between the logical notion of a
relation, as such, and the man-in-the-street's notion of
"some sort of a connection" between things which
leads one of them to recall the other in our thoughts,
from which he borrowed his own more technical concept of "natural" relations. It must not be thought
that here we have a classification of all relations into
two kinds, philosophical on the one hand and natural
on the other. Thus the cause-effect relation, being a
relation, is *ipso facto* a philosophical relation, and
therefore to define it "as" a philosophical relation is,
simply, to define it.

Definition (1), therefore, is Hume's *definition* of
the cause-effect relation, embodying his analysis of it
as nothing more than an instance of a general uniformity of concomitance between two classes of par-

ticular occurrences, and as quite independent of any associations of ideas which may or may not exist in human minds. "As to what may be said, that the operations of nature are independent of our thoughts and reasoning, I allow it," he writes, "and accordingly have observed, that objects bear to each other the relations of contiguity and succession; that like objects may be observed, in several instances, to have like relations; and that all this is independent of, and antecedent to, the operations of the understanding" (*Treatise*, p. 169).

Definition (2), on the other hand, is now seen not to be a definition at all, but simply a restatement of the proposition that the (already defined) cause-effect relation is a *natural* relation, in a somewhat elliptical formulation. It is clearly an error on Hume's part to have offered it *as a definition*, and admittedly an extremely misleading error, leading to misinterpretations and confusions as to what he was trying to say about causation. But diagnosis and correction of the error leave intact both his analysis of the cause-effect relation and his psychological theory concerning it, and in pointing out this error we are in no way modifying either his philosophical or his psychological claims.

Something can be said, however, in exoneration of Hume for having put forward the formulation (2) alongside (1). One of the applications he makes of his psychological theory, that causation is a natural relation, is to try to *explain* how it is that his philosophical analysis (1) of the cause-effect relation appears to many people to have omitted an element which they would wish to include in it. This element is that of the *necessity* or *inevitability* of the occurrence of y, given the occurrence of x, and given that x causes y. In Hume's view it is a philosophical error to include this element in the analysis of the causal relation, and he believes that many people commit it precisely because the cause-effect relation *is* a natural relation. The explanation consists of observing that, since the cause-effect relation is a natural relation, it is responsible for the inducement of dispositions to pass from the ideas of events which are causes to the ideas of events which are their effects; when these dispositions are actuated, the transition from the *idea* of x to the *idea* of y is "projected" by the subject onto *the transition from x to y.* Hence the prevailing belief that the element of inevitability belongs to the cause-effect relation itself is *explicable* on the view that the causal relation is natural, but *mistaken* on the view that the cause-effect relation is to be analyzed as in definition (1). Realizing, therefore, that definition (1), omitting the element of inevitability or necessity, will shock those who believe, mistakenly, that it should be included therein, Hume offers in (2) a "compromise" characterization of the cause-effect relation which, as it were, encapsulates the explanation given above.

It is therefore ironic that Norman Kemp Smith's interpretation of Hume's views on the cause-effect relation includes the attribution to Hume, as part of Hume's philosophical claim, of the very belief which Hume thought to be erroneous, namely that the analysis (1) of the cause-effect relation omits the essential element of necessitation or inevitability. Kemp Smith writes:

But Hume is no supporter of what is usually meant by the "uniformity" view of causation. As he is careful to insist, causation is more than sequence, *and more also than invariable sequence.* We distinguish between mere sequence and causal sequence; and what differentiates the two is that the idea of necessitation (determination or agency) enters into the latter as a quite essential element.[4]

Again later in his book, Kemp Smith repeats this claim:

What, now, makes the causal problem for Hume so difficult of solution is that from the start he refuses to accept as adequate any mere regularity view. He is, of course, ready to admit that contiguity and succession are all that can ever in any single instance be *observed;* it is precisely upon this that he is himself insistent. . . . But this does not lead him to conclude that there is no such thing as causal agency, and that what has been mistaken for it is merely constancy or uniformity of sequence. On the contrary, he is convinced that it is a form of *connexion,* and further that it is a connexion which is necessary, and that it is this *necessity* which is its essential differentia (p. 369).

After each of these two passages, Kemp Smith quotes the same remark of Hume's, on which this interpretation leans heavily:

Shall we then rest contented with these two relations of contiguity and succession, as affording a complete idea of causation? By no means. An object may be contiguous and prior to another, without being considered as its cause. There is a *necessary connexion*

[4] N. Kemp Smith, *The Philosophy of David Hume* (London, 1941), pp. 91–92 (italics not in original).

to be taken into consideration; and that relation is of
much greater importance, than any of the other two
above-mention'd (*Treatise*, p. 77).

This remark occurs at a point in Hume's minute
analysis where he has exhaustively examined what
there is about a particular occurrence x, a particular
occurrence y, and the relation R between them, which
is necessary in order that x should *cause* y to occur.
He has, at this point, isolated the fact that the relation
R must be that of spatiotemporal contiguity, which
we may take to mean that (*a*) y occurs immediately
after x occurs, and (*b*) y occurs in the immediate geo-
graphical neighborhood of x. It will be noted that (*a*)
and (*b*) are both the sort of facts about x and y which
can be ascertained without reference to *other* times,
other places, and *other* particular occurrences x′, x″,
. . . , and y′, y″, . . . which are like x and y respectively. The facts (*a*) and (*b*) depend only on the *immediate context* of the particular occurrences x and y
themselves.

Now Hume remarks, in the very passage which
Kemp Smith quotes and which we have reproduced
above, that (*a*) and (*b*) are, though they jointly constitute a *necessary* condition (in the logical sense) for
x to be the cause of y, by no means a *sufficient* condition for x to be the cause of y. *But this point applies
solely to the conditions (a) and (b).* It does NOT
apply to the third condition that (*c*) ALL particular
occurrences which are like x are such that a particular
occurrence like y occurs immediately afterwards in the
immediate vicinity. This condition (*c*) is what is referred to by the expressions *"constant* conjunction,"

"uniformity," "regularity." At the point in the analysis at which Hume makes the comment upon which Kemp Smith's interpretation leans, condition (*c*) *has not yet been introduced*, nor is it introduced for the first time in the analysis until ten pages later on (in the Selby-Bigge edition). Yet Kemp Smith cites the comment twice (p. 92 and p. 369) to support the view that in it Hume is "carefully insisting" that "causation is more than sequence, and *more also than invariable sequence*." More than sequence, yes; for conditions (*a*) and (*b*) are, although necessary, not sufficient: more than *invariable* sequence, no; for Hume has not yet mentioned this factor. Indeed, when he finally introduces condition (*c*) into the analysis, it is precisely with the purpose of providing, in the joint condition comprising (*a*), (*b*) AND (*c*), a condition both necessary AND sufficient for x to be the cause of y. His comment at *this* point is worth close study:

> Thus in advancing we have insensibly discovered a *new* relation betwixt cause and effect, when we least expected it, and were entirely employed upon another subject. This relation is their CONSTANT CONJUNCTION. *Contiguity and succession are not sufficient to make us pronounce any two objects to be cause and effect, unless we perceive that these two relations are preserved in several instances.* We may now see the advantage of quitting the direct survey of this relation, in order to discover the nature of that NECESSARY CONNECTION which makes so essential a part of it (*Treatise*, p. 87; italics not in original; capitals represent italics which are in the original).

The "new" relation, now introduced over and above

contiguity and succession, or (*a*) and (*b*), is heralded here as the sought-for missing condition which was needed to provide, with (*a*) and (*b*), a *sufficient* condition for x to cause y, and therefore to provide the analysis of the extra element of necessitation which was lacking when (*a*) and (*b*) alone had been adduced earlier.

If the class X of particular occurrences x, x′, x″, . . . , and the class Y of particular occurrences y, y′, y″, . . . , may be termed the *event* X and the *event* Y, we may say that the events X and Y are "universally juxtaposed" just in case that *every* occurrence of X, no matter where or when, observed or unobserved, is immediately followed by an occurrence of Y in its immediate spatial vicinity. Let us say that the occurrence x and the occurrence y are *juxtaposed* just in case y follows immediately after x in x's immediate vicinity. With this concept, we may state Hume's analysis of the causal relation more succinctly and perspicuously by saying that an occurrence x *causes* an occurrence y, if and only if x is an occurrence of an event X, and y is an occurrence of an event Y, x and y are juxtaposed, *and X and Y are universally juxtaposed.*

This is the precise content of Hume's definition (1). It belies any attempt, such as Kemp Smith's, to show that "Hume was no supporter of what is usually meant by the 'uniformity' view of causation." Hume most certainly was. But he was also a psychologist and could not refrain from attempting to explain why, once he had given the uniformity analysis of causation, it should be that a great number of people should find this view unpalatable, "correct" (in whatever sense a philosophical analysis can properly be said to be correct) though the uniformity view be.

> 'Tis a common observation, that the mind has a great propensity to spread itself on external objects, and to conjoin with them any internal impressions, which they occasion, and which always make their appearance at the same time that these objects discover themselves to the senses (*Treatise*, p. 167).

In particular, this psychological phenomenon of "projection" is what is at the bottom of people's mistaken supplementation of the uniformity view of causation with an additional illicit ingredient:

> But if we go further, and ascribe a power or necessary connection to these objects, this is what we can never observe in them, *but must draw the idea of it from what we feel internally in contemplating them* (*Treatise*, p. 169; italics not in original).

And what *do* we "feel internally in contemplating them"? Nothing but that the occurrence of which in the mind is explained by Hume's theory of the association of ideas, namely the involuntary transition of the mind from the idea or impression of the cause x to the idea of the effect y, which mental phenomenon is a (factual) consequence of the causal relation's being a *natural* relation.

This entire psychological transaction is implied in Hume's "definition" (2); hence there is some sympathy for those who take it that Hume intended it as an additional requirement for x to be the cause of y that there should be a projected association between the idea of occurrences like x and the idea of occurrences like y. If we may introduce a further concept and say that the event X and the event Y are "associationally juxtaposed" just in case the idea of an occurrence of X entrains in the mind the idea of an occurrence of Y, Hume would then be taken to be analyzing "x causes y" as "x is an occurrence of an event X, y is an occurrence of an event Y, x and y are juxtaposed, X and Y are universally juxtaposed, *and X and Y are associationally juxtaposed*." As I understand him, this is the analysis which Kemp Smith's approach leads him to suppose represented Hume's real view of causation. Earlier commentators have taken the same line. "Any link of causality, or causal connexion, between the phenomena is not in the objects, but in us, who subsequently—by dint of habit and association—read into the objects what is not really there," writes W. Knight,[5] paraphrasing what he takes to be Hume's analysis. H. A. Aikins[6] says that "Hume professed to have no idea of causation but that of two objects frequently perceived in close succession and the idea of one of them suggesting that of the other," while in W. B. Elkin[7] we read that "with Hume, as with Kant, the idea of cause and effect is subjective, and is not valid when applied to suprasensible things; to this extent both agree. According to Hume, however, the idea is empirically derived, by means of the imagination, from repetition, custom, or instinct."

The error behind these interpretations seems to be traceable to the one source, that of construing Hume's

[5] W. Knight, *Hume* (Edinburgh and London, 1886), p. 152.
[6] *The Philosophy of Hume*, ed. H. A. Aikins (New York, 1893), p. 41.
[7] W. B. Elkin, *Hume* (New York, 1904), p. 167.

psychological explanation of a philosophical mistake in the analysis of the causal relation as being itself, somehow, part of Hume's own *philosophical analysis* of the causal relation, and as therefore being contained, for Hume, in the very concept of a cause. Perhaps Hume would have said to these of his commentators, as he wrote in a letter to Dr. John Stewart concerning a somewhat different, though related, misunderstanding of his views:

> Where a Man of Sense mistakes my meaning, I own I am angry: But it is only at myself: For having expresst my meaning so ill as to have given occasion to the mistake.[8]

[8] *The Letters of David Hume*, ed. J. Y. T. Greig, 2 vols. (Oxford, 1932), I, 185.

HUME'S TWO DEFINITIONS OF "CAUSE"

THOMAS J. RICHARDS

In a recent article in *The Philosophical Quarterly* (reprinted in this volume, pp. 129–47 above) Mr. J. A. Robinson argues that the two definitions of "cause" contained in Hume's *Treatise* are not *two* definitions, but a definition followed by an empirical psychological statement about that which has just been defined. This, his major thesis, I cannot accept, even though his minor theses—(*a*) an explication of what Hume meant by "philosophical relation" and "natural relation," and (*b*) that *contra* Kemp Smith, Hume *was* a supporter of the "uniformity" view of causation—are certainly sound. Consequently I wish (I) to explain why Robinson's major thesis is not a true account of Hume's two definitions of "cause," (II) to show that Robinson's conclusion does not follow from his own argument, and (III) to propose an account of Hume's two definitions of "cause" which is a truer account of Hume's intention.

From *The Philosophical Quarterly*, Vol. XV (1965). Reprinted by permission of the author and *The Philosophical Quarterly*.

I

In the passage in which Hume gives his two definitions of "cause" he says:

> There may two definitions be given of this relation, which are only different by their presenting a different view of the same object, and making us consider it either as a *philosophical* or as a *natural* relation; either as a comparison of two ideas, or as an association betwixt them (*Treatise*, pp. 169–70).[1]

A cause as a philosophical relation is defined as:

> An object precedent and contiguous to another, and where all objects resembling the former are placed in like relations of precedency and contiguity to those objects that resemble the latter (p. 170).

A cause as a natural relation is defined as:

> . . . an object precedent and contiguous to another, and so united with it that the idea of the one determines the mind to form the idea of the other, and the impression of the one to form a more lively idea of the other (*ibid.*).

Calling these definitions "(1)" and "(2)" respectively, Robinson argues that (1) and (2) cannot be understood to be defining the same set of objects, for the class of objects of which (1) is true is neither necessarily nor in fact the same as the class of objects of which (2) is true. In particular, it is both logically possible for there to be, and in fact there is, a set of ob-

[1] References are made to the Selby-Bigge edition of the *Treatise*.

jects of which (1) is true but not (2). And since Hume recognized that there *is* such a set of objects, Robinson concludes that Hume cannot be meaning, in all consistency, that (1) and (2) pick out the same set of objects.

Hume in the paragraphs leading up to the two definitions does deal with just such objects, and we read an objector to Hume saying: "As if causes did not operate entirely independent of the mind, and would not continue their operation, even though there were no mind existent to contemplate them, or reason concerning them" (p. 167). Hume says of this: "As to what may be said, that the operations of nature are independent of our thought and reasoning, I allow it; . . . this is independent of, and antecedent to, the operations of the understanding" (p. 168). Robinson himself mentions Hume's talk of "secret" and "concealed" causes—causes which Hume is in no wise concerned to deny. But for Robinson to admit that Hume took cognizance of such causes, and to use this as evidence against the view that the two definitions are defining the same set of objects, is inconsistent with Robinson's own positive thesis that (2) is an empirical comment on the objects defined by (1). For if (2) *were* an empirical comment on the objects defined by (1), then by Robinson's own argument, Hume must have realized that it was a *false* empirical comment, since (2) (under this interpretation of (2)) is not true of all objects defined by (1). If alternatively Hume *didn't* realize he was making a false statement in making (2), then the conclusion of Robinson's position is that Hume was inconsistent in precisely the same way as he was held to be inconsistent on the two-definition view, namely that Hume asserted both that (2) was true of all objects satisfying (1), and that there are some objects which satisfy (1) but not (2).

There can be adduced several other instances which make Robinson's view that (2) is an empirical comment on the objects satisfying (1) seem implausible. Hume says:

> There may two definitions be given of this relation, which are only different by their presenting a DIF-FERENT VIEW of the SAME OBJECT [i.e. same relation, *not* same individuals related], and making us consider it either as a *philosophical* or as a *natural* relation; either as a comparison of two ideas, or as an association betwixt them (pp. 169–70; capitals mine).

Robinson tries to make light of the stressed and repeated "either-or" of this passage, but it is hard to believe that Hume could have said what has just been quoted if he really did hold the view that (2) is an empirical comment on the objects satisfying (1), as Robinson considers he did. Hume wasn't *that* bad on his logic or English.

And Hume reiterates that (1) and (2) are both definitions when he says: "If we define a cause to be [(1)] we may easily conceive that there is no absolute or metaphysical necessity. . . . If we define a cause to be [(2)] we shall make still less difficulty of assenting to this opinion" (p. 172). This passage makes still more difficulty of assenting to *Robinson's* opinion.

II

What is it that Robinson considers (2) is saying about (1), and what is the evidence he gives for this view?

Robinson rightly states that to understand the two definitions we must understand what philosophical and natural relations are. Hume encapsulates the nature of the two in his introduction to the two definitions of "cause" (pp. 169–70) where he says that a philosophical relation is a comparison of ideas and a natural relation is an association between ideas.

The definition of "natural relation" occurs in Book I, Part I, Section 4. Here Hume observes that the union of simple ideas into complex ones must be guided by some universal principles. Of this principle of association he says "we are only to regard it as a gentle force, which commonly prevails, and is the cause why, among other things, languages so nearly correspond to each other; Nature, in a manner, pointing out to every one those simple ideas, which are most proper to be united into a complex one" (pp. 10–11). Hume considers that there are three such qualities or principles which give rise to association of ideas. These are resemblance, contiguity (in time or place) and cause and effect. He says of them: "I believe it will not be very necessary to prove that these qualities produce an association among ideas, and, upon the appearance of one idea, naturally introduce another" (p. 11). He then gives examples in general terms of the association that occurs between our ideas in the first two of these relations.

So Hume defines a natural relation as a relation such that when one term of the relation is given to us in perception or otherwise, our mind by virtue of the way we are constituted, runs on to, or associates that term with, the other term of the relation.

In Book I, Part 1, Section 5, Hume says that "relation" is used in two "considerably different" ways. The first is in the sense just described, namely as the association of ideas. The second is "that particular circumstance, in which, even upon the arbitrary union of two ideas in the fancy, we may think proper to compare them" (p. 13). This is what Hume means by "philosophical relation," and he calls it thus because he considers that the natural or associative meaning of "relation" is the one in common use, whereas the latter use is a philosophical (scientific) one. In support of this he says:

> Thus, distance will be allowed by philosophers to be a true relation, because we acquire an idea of it by the comparing of objects: but in a common way we say, *that nothing can be more distant than such or such things from each other, nothing can have less relation;* as if distance and relation were incompatible (p. 14).

Hume lists seven different types of philosophical relation, two of which are named "resemblance" and "cause and effect," and a third, "space and time," has a sub-class named "contiguity." These three names are also the names of the three natural relations. The question is, what is the relation between philosophical and natural relations of the same name?

Robinson's view is that Hume is saying that all relations are philosophical by definition, but that some
of these produce an association of ideas, i.e. are natural
relations. He says:

> *Naturalness* is then simply the property of any rela-
> tion R between a thing or event A and a thing or
> event B (*not* between the *idea* of A and the *idea*
> of B) whereby the observation of A and B standing
> to each other in the relation R is enough to induce
> an association between the idea of A and the idea of
> B (pp. 136–37).

Of philosophical relations he says:

> . . . to say that a relation R is "philosophical" is to
> make a factually empty statement; *all* relations are
> philosophical. . . . It must not be thought that here
> we have a classification of all relations into two kinds,
> philosophical on the one hand and natural on the
> other. Thus the cause-effect relation, being a relation,
> is *ipso facto* a philosophical relation, and therefore to
> define it "as" a philosophical relation is, simply, to
> define it (p. 138).

From these statements Robinson moves without
further argument to his conclusions about the definitions. Of (2) he says: "Definition (2), on the other
hand, is now seen not to be a definition at all, but
simply a restatement of the proposition that the (already defined [in (1)]) cause-effect relation is a *natural* relation, in a somewhat elliptical formulation"
(p. 139).

It is hard to imagine how it follows from Robinson's
exposition of the two types of relations that (2) is
seen not to be a definition. For a start the considera-

tions adduced in I tell against that. Robinson has forgotten that there are three types of natural relation and that hence there must be statable differences between the three. Consequently there can be given a definition of "cause" as a natural relation: a definition that sorts out natural causal relations from other natural relations.

Further, it must not be thought that Hume anywhere argues that all causal relations are natural. It follows from Robinson's definition of "naturalness" quoted above that if causality is a natural relation, all causal relations are natural. Hume says, however, in connection with the relation of resemblance: "But though resemblance be necessary to all philosophical relation, it does not follow that it always produces a connection or association of ideas" (p. 14). And again, he says of the principles of association among ideas:

> These principles I allow to be neither the *infallible* nor the *sole* causes of a union among ideas. They are not the infallible causes. For one may fix his attention during some time on any one object without looking further. . . . But though I allow this weakness in these three relations . . . ; yet I assert, that the only *general* principles which associate ideas, are resemblance, contiguity, and causation (pp. 92–93).

Hume then does assert that *generally* philosophical causal relations are natural. Or, more precisely, since being observed is a necessary condition for being a natural relation, that *generally* philosophical causal relations can be natural. Now Hume could go on to say (as Robinson holds he does) that the relation between philosophical and natural *causal* relations is more

strict, in that *all* philosophical causal relations are
natural. However, Hume has another job which he
must do, which is to define what it is for a relation
to be a natural causal relation. I have already argued in
I that in the two-definitions passage Hume is not doing the former. Nor is it consistent with the evidence
quoted in I that he is reiterating his weaker version
of the former, that *generally* philosophical causal relations are natural.

In the present section I have presented Hume's exposition of philosophical and natural relations, together with Robinson's summary of that exposition,
in such a way as to make it patent that Robinson's
views on (2) do not follow either from what Hume
says on relations, or what Robinson says about Hume
on relations.

It remains to argue that Hume is, in the two-
definitions passage, doing what he says he is doing,
namely defining the philosophical relation "cause" and
defining the natural relation "cause." To this I now
turn.

III

When an assertion that A causes B is made, there
are two questions which we can ask (among others)
about this assertion. The first is "What is being asserted?" and the second is "What states of affairs must
obtain for the asserter properly to believe that A causes
B?" The two questions are not identical, for if that
which is being asserted is being asserted as an induc-

tion, then we allow the assertion to be made on grounds which are not identical with or do not entail that which is being asserted. Furthermore, with inductive assertions we can often lay down the states of affairs which must obtain for the induction to be a good one.

The answer to the first question above is the definition of "cause" as a philosophical relation, while the answer to the second provides us with the definition of "cause" as a natural relation, in a way which will become clear.

Before defending this thesis it is instructive to note the consequences of this thesis for the other two natural relations, resemblance and contiguity, and to compare these consequences with the consequences of Robinson's view. Of resemblance, Hume says: "When a quality becomes very general, and is common to a great many individuals, it leads not the mind directly to any one of them; but, by presenting at once too great a choice, does thereby prevent the imagination from fixing on any single object" (p. 14). To the man in the street, there is no resemblance between a stone and an umbrella: the idea of the one does not lead to the idea of the other. But a philosopher will point out that they admit of comparison by being both extended, material, shaped, colored. Such properties are *too general*, however, to give rise to an association of ideas.

Hume is not wanting to say, when he claims that resemblance is a natural relation, that wherever two objects have the philosophical relation of resemblance, the ideas of the two objects are associated. He wants to say that wherever the ideas of two objects are associated *by virtue of* some quality or other which they in fact share, we have a case of the natural relation of resemblance between the two objects.

Similarly, when Hume claims that contiguity is a natural relation, he is not saying that whenever two objects are next to one another (have the philosophical relation of contiguity) the ideas of the two objects are associated. Rather, he is saying that whenever two objects are next to each other *in such a way that* the ideas of the two are associated, we have a case of the natural relation of contiguity.

To say these things is not to make the empirical point which Robinson claims is being made. Hume may well be interested in the empirical question of *what it is* about *some* instances of *some* types of relation that leads us to associate the ideas of the two objects thus (philosophically) related. But whatever it is, saying that A and B are related naturally is the same as saying that their ideas are associated.

In the case of causation, Hume having concluded his destructive analysis of necessary connection, lists in (1) the following propositions as expressing the individually necessary and jointly sufficient conditions for it to be true that A causes B:

     (i) .that A and B are contiguous
    (ii) that A is temporally precedent to B
   (iii) that any object like A is precedent and contiguous to some object like B.

Whether we realize it or not, Hume is saying, the conjunction of these three propositions is precisely what we are asserting when we assert that A causes B.

Now the condition stated in proposition (iii) can never be known to be satisfied, yet we do claim to observe and to identify causal relations. So when we assert that what we are observing is a causal relation, we thereby assert that one member of the relation, A, is precedent and contiguous to the other, B; and we also indicate that we believe that any object like A is prior and contiguous to some object like B. That is, we expect any A to be prior and contiguous to some B. Or, in Humean psychology, A is so united with B that the idea of one determines the mind to form an idea of the other, and the impression of one to form a more lively idea of the other.

What must be the case, then, for it to be true that A causes B is (i), (ii) and (iii) (Definition (1)). And what must be the case for a person X properly to assert that A causes B is (i), (ii) and that the ideas of A and B should be associated in his mind, i.e. that X should believe that (iii) (Definition (2)). Object-pairs which obey (i), (ii) and (iii) have the relation "philosophical cause" existing between them. Object-pairs obeying (i), (ii) and so related as to give rise to the belief that (iii) is true of them, have the relation "natural cause" existing between them.

This matter can be put in another way. To say that a relation is natural is to say that the two related objects A and B are related in such a way as to bring about an association of ideas. As *a particular case*, to say that a relation is a natural *cause-effect* relation, as distinct from some other natural relation, is to say that A is prior and contiguous to B, and prior and contiguous to B in such a way as to lead to association of the ideas of A and B. That is why Hume in (2) says ". . . and so united with it that . . ." This phrase is impossible to understand on Robinson's account. Now just what this "way" is, Hume does not investigate, because such an investigation would be an empirical psychological side-issue. (2) does then allude to an empirical psychological matter, but (2) itself is strictly a definition.

Yet another way of putting the difference is this. Hume holds that we want to say that causation consists of priority, contiguity, and necessary connection. But Hume analyses necessary connection into constant conjunction between the objects, together with an association of the ideas of the objects, insofar as the idea of one object conjures up the idea of the other, or the presence of one leads us to expect the presence of the other. Consequently the empirical (philosophical) relation between objects causally connected is priority, contiguity, and constant conjunction. But the conditions under which we assert that A causes B are priority, contiguity, and expectation of continued priority and contiguity. Hume is simply pointing out that since induction is unjustifiable, what we mean by causation is different from the grounds upon which we assert causation.

It will now be realized that (2) is a definition. It tells us what we mean by a natural cause. It is not an empirical assertion as Robinson makes it out to be, which is either false or inconsistent with the rest of what Hume says, for the criteria for A causing B given in (1) correct false assertions made according to (2). When we discover some A not prior and contiguous to some B, we no longer posit a necessary connection, i.e. no longer expect every A (past, present and future) to be prior and contiguous to some B.[2]

[2] I am indebted to Mr. D. A. Lloyd-Thomas of Victoria University of Wellington, and to Mr. A. E. Ralls of St. Andrews University, for the valuable criticism and help which they gave me in the preparation of this paper.

HUME'S TWO DEFINITIONS OF "CAUSE" RECONSIDERED

J. A. ROBINSON

Hume's two definitions of "cause" are as follows:

(1) [A *cause* is] an object precedent and contiguous to another, and where all objects resembling the former are placed in like relations of precedency and contiguity to those objects that resemble the latter.

(2) [A *cause* is] an object precedent and contiguous to another, and so united with it that the idea of the one determines the mind to form the idea of the other, and the impression of the one to form a more lively idea of the other.

Mr. T. J. Richards (pp. 148–61 above) objects to my account (pp. 129–47 above) of (1) and (2), and offers a different one, which seems to me to be wrong.

Underlying my account was the following reasoning: since it is not possible consistently to give two *non-equivalent* definitions of the *same* notion, and since (1) and (2) are not equivalent, either Hume is guilty of an inconsistency or else one of these two characterizations must be construed in some other way than *as defining the very same notion which the other defines.*

Richards does not, as far as one can tell, object to this reasoning. Indeed he gives every indication, short

of saying so, that he bases his own account on this
same foundation. His criticism of my position rather
concerns the particular way in which I proposed to
rescue Hume from inconsistency: I proposed to construe (1) as the "uniformity view" definition of the
causal relation and (2) as the statement that the
causal relation as defined in (1) is a natural relation.
My proposal for (1) is accepted by Richards; in fact he
himself makes the same proposal for (1). However, he
claims that I was wrong in saying that (2) is really
just the statement:

(3) *the causal relation is a natural relation.*

His reasons for denying that (2) expresses (3) are
that (3) is false, and that Hume realized that (3) is
false because he realized that there can be, and are,
cases where no association exists between the idea of
A and the idea of B even though A causes B in the
sense of (1).

Now (3) *may* be false (as I was at pains to point
out) since it is a very sweeping empirical theory. But
Hume certainly did not think that it was—for it is in
fact one of the central propositions of his psychological theory—nor does his concession that there are "secret and conceal'd causes" oblige him to consider (3)
false, *because* (3) *is entirely compatible with there being such "secret and conceal'd causes."*

It is this last point on which Richards seems to me
to have gone astray. It appears that he holds it to be a
necessary condition, for a relation between A and B
to be natural, that an association between the idea of
A and the the idea of B should actually exist in the

mind (". . . saying that A and B are related naturally is the same as saying that their ideas are associated" [p. 158]); whereas Hume's notion of naturalness is *dispositional* in character: A's relation to B is *natural* if observation of A and B standing to each other in the relation in question would produce an association between the idea of A and the idea of B. This allows A and B to be naturally related without ever having been observed, in the same sort of way that a lump of sugar is soluble in water without necessarily having been immersed in any. Richards however says that ". . . being observed is a necessary condition for being a natural relation" (p. 155).

My arguments that (1) and (2) are not equivalent are really arguments which show that (2) cannot consistently mean:

(4) A causes B $\leftrightarrow$ (A is precedent and contiguous to B *and* the idea of A is associated with the idea of B)

if (1) already means:

(5) A causes B $\leftrightarrow$ (A is precedent and contiguous to B *and* every object like A is precedent and contiguous to an object like B)

and (5) is taken to be true by definition. For if (5) is true by definition then (4) is easily seen to be (empirically) false.

Accordingly my proposal was that (2) should *not* be taken to mean (4), but instead should be taken to mean (3). However, Richards apparently takes (3) to mean (4); whereupon he argues that since (5) and (4) are shown to be incompatible by my own arguments, so are (5) and (3) and I am hoist with my own petard. But of course (3) does not mean (4), and that is one of the main reasons why I proposed (3) as an interpretation of (2).

In fact the meaning of (3) has to be rendered somewhat as follows:

(6) A causes B → (A and B are observed → the idea of A is associated with the idea of B)

Richards' own proposal consists of construing (2) as a definition, but as a definition of a *different* notion from that defined in (1). This stratagem certainly makes sense of the fact that Hume does state that (1) and (2) are both definitions; but it surely does not make sense of Hume's further claim, that (1) and (2) are both definitions *of the same notion* ("different views of the same object"). However, any attempt to sort out Hume's intentions in this matter is going to fail to make sense of *part* at least of what Hume said about (1) and (2), and I cannot argue that Richards' proposal is any more inadequate than mine in this respect. His proposal does construe (1) and (2) as *definitions*, though not of the "same object"; my proposal construes (1) and (2) as being "views of the same object," though only one of them as being a definition of that object. Our proposals are thus roughly of equal merit as far as making sense of Hume's whole claim is concerned. But Richards' proposal will not do, for other reasons.

He suggests, in effect, retaining the right-hand side of (4) and modifying the left-hand side so that a term different from "cause" is being introduced definitionally via the biconditional. The term he suggests is "*natural* cause." Thus (4) becomes:

(7) A *is a natural cause of* B ↔ (A is precedent
and contiguous to B and the idea of A is associated
with the idea of B).

The proposal then is to construe (2) as meaning (7).
So far, this amounts to no more than introducing an
abbreviation for the complex of circumstances formulated on the right-hand side of (4); an innocent
enough move.

Richards' error consists in taking "A *is a natural
cause of B*," as defined in (7), to mean, in turn, "*it
may properly be asserted that A causes B*." This
amounts to saying that the right-hand side of (4) sets
forth the grounds on which *it is inductively sound to
assert* the right-hand side of (5). The error here is to
mistake (psychological) *is* for (logical) *ought*. The
right-hand side of (4) sets forth the circumstances under which *it will in fact be believed that A causes B*,
but it is not in the least normative, and Hume would, I
should think, have been most annoyed to have been
interpreted here as smuggling in an *ought* disguised
as an *is*.

Hume's psychological undertaking was to try to explain human thought processes, considered as natural
phenomena. He had to try to show, amongst other
things, what *belief* is, and to give some account of how
beliefs and expectations actually arise in the mind as a
result of interactions between the outside world and
the mind. He did not refrain from investigating matters because the investigations would be "empirical
psychological side-issues" as Richards suggests, on p.
160, that he did. Hume was consciously *doing* empirical psychology a great deal of the time. (Systematic

evasion of empirical questions is an affectation philosophers have acquired in the twentieth century, and it is a very silly one.) Hume's theory of natural relations was an attempt to link *thought processes*, in which ideas and impressions interact through the "force" of association, with *external physical processes*, in which physical events and objects interact in space and time through physical forces. The link comes about through *observation* of the *naturally* related events and objects in the physical world; observation of *them* brings about in the mind the relationship of *association* between their *ideas*, which then accounts for the actual details of the thought processes as they unfold and for the contents of complex ideas.

Now this is a pretty poor theory—vague, unclear, qualitative, full of gaps, impossible to test. But it *is* Hume's theory. It is not a theory about what we ought, rationally, to have in our heads; it is a theory about what we do, in fact, have in our heads, and how it gets there. It is foreign to Hume's whole enterprise to try to read into it any normative aspects.

Richards' proposal, then, will not work, as he frames it. It would have been a far stronger proposal, I think, had he omitted the normative component, and claimed only that (7) lays down the circumstances under which *it will in fact be believed that* A *causes* B; (1) and (2) would, under this modified Richards' proposal, read very nicely as definitions, respectively, of A *causes* B and A *is believed to cause* B. This interpretation would even seem to make *some* sense out of saying that the two non-equivalent definitions are merely "different views of the same object." However, it is still possible, for some A and B, that one of the two assertions A *causes* B and A *is believed to cause* B should be false and the other true.

What (2) appears to be a definition of, on the face of it, is something like: A *is believed to cause* B, *and* A *and* B *are so related that this belief is psychologically unavoidable* (". . . and [A is] so united with [B] that . . ."). How *can* A and B be so related that the belief that A causes B is psychologically unavoidable? If we are not tacitly referring to a single observer, but are including all possible observers at any time and any place, then surely the only way for this to be possible is *for* A *to cause* B in the sense of (1). For if A does *not* cause B, then there is at least one object like A which is not precedent and contiguous to an object like B, and the belief that A causes B *would* then be psychologically avoidable for any person who observed such an object and noted that it was unaccompanied by any object like B.

If we add this further content to the revised Richards' proposal for (2) we get an interpretation of (2) which construes it as defining, in effect: A *is correctly believed to cause* B. This version has the great virtue of entailing A *causes* B, that is, essentially, of subsuming (1) and making it unnecessary. I hasten to stress that the *correctness* of the belief lies in its *truth*, not its "warranted assertability" or anything of that kind.

This last is, I think, the best that can be done by way of a "two definitions" reading of Hume's (1) and (2). I have not been able to find a better "different views of *same object*" reading of (1) and (2) than the one I originally gave and which easily withstands Richards' objections to it.

HUME'S DEFENSE OF
CAUSAL INFERENCE

JOHN W. LENZ

Hume's epistemological writings contain a widely acclaimed examination of causal inference. Yet its precise conclusions are not easily ascertained and, in my opinion, have still to be set forth. Norman Kemp Smith has, beyond all doubt, refuted the Reid-Beattie-Green view of Hume as an extreme sceptic who was advising his readers to stop making causal inferences.[1] Kemp Smith's main thesis that Hume defended these beliefs by showing their natural character is essentially correct.[2] Nonetheless, I am not entirely satisfied with Kemp Smith's naturalistic interpretation. My objections are first, that it has not made clear the precise sense in which Hume *defended* causal beliefs,[3] and second, that it has not clearly delineated the *natural*

From the *Journal of the History of Ideas*, Vol. XIX (1958). Reprinted by permission of the author and *The Journal of the History of Ideas*.

[1] N. Kemp Smith, *The Philosophy of David Hume* (London, 1941), pp. 79 ff.

[2] *Ibid.*, p. 45.

[3] Words like "justification," "defense," and "vindication" are extremely equivocal. I believe that much of the dispute concerning "the problem of induction" has been over what should count as a justification of induction.

character which provides the grounds for their defense.[4]

I shall argue (1) that it is within the context of a deterministic theory of belief that Hume raises the problem of justifying causal inference, (2) that, nonetheless, Hume sharply distinguished between causally explaining a belief and justifying a belief, (3) that for Hume justifying a belief meant showing that it is true, or more specifically, showing that it is caused in such a way that it must be true, (4) that in this sense Hume never did, on his own admission, succeed in justifying causal inferences, and (5) that if Hume thought he had defended these beliefs it was only in the sense that, by showing their natural character, i.e., their unavoidability, he destroyed the point of saying that men ought not hold them.

(1) *Hume's deterministic theory of belief.* In formulating his science of human nature Hume sought to explain mental phenomena, just as Newton had earlier explained physical phenomena, by means of causal laws.[5] Such explanation was possible, Hume thought, because the actions of the mind are as fully determined as the motions of material bodies; in the realm neither of mind nor of matter is there any place for the so-called liberty of indifference or chance. Of course, the necessity with which mental events occur is strictly of the kind implied by Hume's own theory

---

[4] Hume himself pointed out the ambiguity of the word "nature": "our answer to this question [is moral sentiment natural?] depends upon the definition of the word, Nature, than which there is none more ambiguous or equivocal" (A *Treatise of Human Nature*, ed. L. A. Selby-Bigge [Oxford, 1888], p. 474).

[5] *Ibid.*, p. xxi.

of causality. What makes one infer a necessary connection between physical events is their constant conjunction. Since such constant conjunctions are found
in the mental sphere, we must infer that if necessity
is attributed to the physical world, a like necessity prevails in the mind:

> there is no known circumstance, that enters into the
> connexion and production of the actions of matter,
> that is not to be found in all the operations of the
> mind; and consequently we cannot, without a mani-
> fest absurdity, attribute necessity to the one, and re-
> fuse it to the other.[6]

Among the best examples of Hume's deterministic
account of mental phenomena is his discussion of the
passions. There Hume concluded that the various passions are completely determined by the natures and
circumstances of men.[7] What is important for our discussion here is that Hume did not exempt men's beliefs from such causal determination. Not only passions
but their intellectual counterparts, beliefs, however
sophisticated or complex, follow of necessity from the
constitutions and conditions of men.[8]

It follows, therefore, that the difference between

[6] *Ibid.*, p. 404.
[7] *Ibid.*, p. 401.
[8] As John H. Randall, Jr. also notes. Cf. "David Hume: Radical Empiricist and Pragmatist," in *Freedom and Experience*, ed.
Sidney Hook and Milton R. Konvitz (Ithaca and New York,
1947), p. 303. I disagree with Professor Randall, however, when
he goes on to say that the causes of all beliefs are of the same
kind, namely, impressions. Hume points out, for example, that
many beliefs are caused by "education." Cf. *Treatise*, pp. 116–17.
Even causal inferences are not caused simply by impressions, the
force of the imagination playing a prominent rôle.

fiction and *belief* lies in some sentiment or feeling which is annexed to the latter, not to the former, and which depends not on the will, nor can be commanded at pleasure. It *must* [my italics—J.W.L.] be excited by nature like all other sentiments and must rise from the particular situation in which the mind is placed at any particular juncture.[9]

Causal inference well illustrates Hume's deterministic theory of belief. Hume is famous, of course, for having pointed out that neither reason, in the sense of *a priori* intuition or demonstration, nor experience by itself is the source of causal beliefs. But he should be equally famous for having pointed out that the imagination, following definite laws, *must*, under certain circumstances, give rise to such inferences. Given the constant conjunction of objects found in experience, the imagination leads one to infer a necessary connection between such objects. And given the impression of one of these objects, the imagination causes one to conceive vividly the other, or in effect, to believe in the existence of such an object.

This belief [causal inference] is the necessary result of placing the mind in such circumstances. It is an operation of the soul, when we are so situated, as unavoidable as to feel the passion of love, when we receive benefits; or hatred, when we meet with injuries.[10]

We have here isolated one sense in which Hume often spoke of beliefs as "natural." It is the sense of

[9] Hume, *An Enquiry concerning Human Understanding*, ed. L. A. Selby-Bigge, 2nd ed. (Oxford, 1902), p. 48. Note also that Sect. 8 and 9 of Book I, Part 1 of the *Treatise* are concerned exclusively with the causes of various beliefs.

[10] *Ibid.*, p. 46.

"natural," undoubtedly, which Hume used in naming his new science of "human *nature*." Mental events such as beliefs and sentiments are natural in being causally determined. In Book III of the *Treatise*,[11] where Hume distinguished various senses of the term "natural," he points out this use.

> If *nature* be oppos'd to miracles, [that is, to what violates the laws of causality] not only the distinction between vice and virtue is natural, but also every event, which has happen'd in the world.

(2) *Explanation and justification.* There is no doubt that one of Hume's main purposes in writing the *Treatise* was to explain causally the many varieties of belief men hold, especially common-sense beliefs such as causal inference. I believe, moreover, that Hume thought his own explanation of causal beliefs important. Unlike the explanations presupposed by other philosophers, his, he felt, did not overlook the fact that unreflective adults, children, and even animals do make causal inferences.

However, two interpretations of Hume's thought must be avoided. One is that Hume limited himself simply to explaining causal inferences, that he did not attempt, let alone think he had succeeded in defending them. The other is that Hume thought he had, in causally explaining such beliefs, thereby justified them.

The first interpretation would amount to saying that Hume saw himself only as a descriptive psychologist, not as a critic of men's beliefs.[12] The evidence

---

[11] *Treatise*, p. 474.
[12] As J. A. Passmore at times maintains; cf. *Hume's Intentions* (Cambridge, 1952), pp. 12, 41.

against it, however, is overwhelming. It ignores such statements as the famous conclusion of the *Enquiry concerning Human Understanding,* where Hume condemns all but mathematical and experiential reasoning to the flames. In condemning some beliefs and exempting others Hume is not doing descriptive psychology.

The second interpretation would in effect say that Hume equated calling a belief justified with saying a belief can be causally explained.[13] One could, on this interpretation, raise a serious objection against Hume. No doubt "justification" is an ambiguous word; no doubt justifications have taken on many different forms throughout the history of philosophy. Yet anyone who identifies "causally explicable" with "justified" is mis-using language in the interests of a rationalistic metaphysics. That a belief can be causally explained does not mean it is justified. This is evident from our often saying that we can explain why someone holds an unjustified belief.

There is, however, decisive evidence that Hume did not hold this mistaken view either. Had Hume held it he would have had to say that all beliefs are justified, for, as we have seen, on his view all beliefs are causally determined and hence causally explicable. It is readily apparent, however, that Hume held that many beliefs are unjustified, e.g., the superstitions of the ordinary man and the paradoxical beliefs of ancient and mod-

[13] No writer on Hume has, so far as I know, adopted this interpretation. However, the closely related view that Hume confused psychology and logic is, I think, widely held. Cf. for example, John H. Randall, Jr., *op. cit.,* p. 310.

ern philosophers. Hume explicitly pointed out that even fantastic beliefs can be explained causally.

> I am persuaded, there might be several useful discoveries made from a criticism of the fictions of the antient philosophy, concerning *substances, and substantial forms, and accidents, and occult qualities*; which, however unreasonable and capricious, have a very intimate connexion with the principles of human nature.[14]

Hence, when Hume calls causal inferences natural in the sense of being causally determined (and hence causally explicable) he is not saying thereby that they are justified. As a matter of fact, this natural character cannot even be a justifying property of beliefs for it is a property that all beliefs have indiscriminately.

Let me, however, guard myself against being misunderstood. In the first place, I do not want to deny that for Hume any correct justification of beliefs must be consistent with their actual causal origins. That is, while I do think Hume distinguished the question of justifying beliefs from the question of explaining such beliefs, I do not deny that Hume held that the answers to these two questions must be *consistent* with one another.

In the second place, while I have denied that Hume equated "justifying a belief" with "showing that a belief is caused," I have not denied that, for Hume, knowing the cause of a belief is *relevant* to ascertaining whether a belief is justified. I have not, that is, ruled out the possibility that for Hume having a *specific* cause might be a *justifying property* of beliefs.

[14] *Treatise*, p. 219.

In the third place, I do not want to deny that Hume's actual defense of causal inferences is based on their "necessary" character. But, as I shall show in the last section of this paper, this character involves more than causal necessity.

(3) A *justification considered.* Having seen what Hume does not mean by calling a belief justified, let us ask what he does mean. The answer, I think, is plain: to call a belief justified is to say that it is true. This is evident from such passages as the following:

> What then can we look for from this confusion of groundless and extraordinary opinions but error and falsehood? And how can we justify to ourselves any belief we repose in them?[15]

This is also evident from a consideration of the two kinds of cognition Hume regarded as justified: propositions of mathematics and "immediate awareness"; both are true. Propositions of mathematics, which only state relations between concepts, are true in the sense of being internally consistent.[16] Immediate awareness is true in the sense of presenting correctly the appearances of things.[17]

Hume's way of *showing* that certain kinds of cognition are true, and, thus, his way of justifying them can also be seen from his treatment of mathematical propositions and immediate awareness. Hume shows that their respective causes, reason and sensation, can produce only true cognitive claims. Mathematical propositions must be true in the sense of being inter-

[15] *Treatise*, p. 218.
[16] *Ibid.*, pp. 69–70.
[17] *Ibid.*, p. 190.

nally consistent because, says Hume, the mind cannot even conceive their contradictory.[18] Immediate awareness must be correct because its causes are the appearances of which one is aware.[19] In general Hume's method of justifying a belief is to show that it is caused in such a way that it must be true. This is why, for Hume, knowing the actual causes of beliefs is *relevant* to justifying them, why any proposed justification of a belief cannot be inconsistent with the correct account of its genesis.[20]

It is by this method that Hume wanted to justify causal inference. Hume wanted to show that causal inferences are true, that they are caused in such a way that they must be true. Moreover, Hume did, though only temporarily, suggest that these beliefs *were* so justified.

Hume, of course, sharply criticized saying that causal inferences are conclusions of reason and then arguing that, because reason can give rise only to true propositions, these beliefs are true. He agrees, as we have seen, that reason is a faculty which does give rise to true cognitive claims, but he argues that our causal beliefs are not caused by reason. That is, Hume pointed out that this proposed justification is simply inconsistent with the actual causes of these beliefs.

Hume's tentative justification of causal inferences recognizes the imagination as their cause. The imagi-

[18] *Enquiry concerning Human Understanding*, p. 26.
[19] *Treatise*, p. 190.
[20] It is in this way that Hume would challenge Randall's contention that the origins of a belief are irrelevant to its validity. Cf. John H. Randall, Jr., *op. cit.*, pp. 302–5.

nation, Hume claims, causes true beliefs; the imagination has not only weight but also authority.

> If the mind be not engaged by argument to make this step [causal inference], it must be induced by some other principle of equal weight and authority.[21]

Hume claims that the imagination has authority because a benevolent Nature has implanted it within man to give him those true beliefs which are so indispensable for living.[22] Not reason but the imagination is Nature's prime instrument for leading men to truth.[23] Hume further suggests that nature has wisely chosen the imagination as its instrument, for the imagination can give rise to true beliefs without the reflection of which most men, all children, and all animals are incapable:

> as this operation of the mind, by which we infer like effects from like causes, and *vice versa*, is so essential to the subsistence of all human creatures, it is not probable that it could be trusted to the fallacious deductions of our reason, which is slow in its operations, appears not, in any degree, during the first years of infancy, and at best is, in every age and period of human life, extremely liable to error and mistake. It is more conformable to the ordinary wisdom of nature to secure so necessary an act of the mind by some

[21] *Enquiry concerning Human Understanding*, p. 41.

[22] Randall has rightly stressed this pragmatic element in Hume's thought. I disagree with Randall, however, when he says that Hume's final justification of causal and perceptual beliefs was a pragmatic one. A belief, on Hume's view, is pragmatically valuable only if true, and, as I shall show, Hume did not, in the end, think he had shown that they are true. Cf. John H. Randall, Jr., *op. cit.*, pp. 305–11.

[23] Kemp Smith has emphasized this point. Cf. Kemp Smith, *op. cit.*, pp. 543–46, 562–66.

instinct or mechanical tendency which may be infallible in its operations, may discover itself at the first appearance of life and thought, and may be independent of all the laboured deductions of the understanding. As nature has taught us the use of our limbs without giving us the knowledge of the muscles and nerves by which they are actuated, so has she implanted in us an instinct which carries forward the thought in a correspondent course to that which she has established among external objects. . . .[24]

Upon closer examination of Hume's view we see that, strictly speaking, it is not their being caused by the imagination which justifies causal inferences. It is rather their being caused by what is "permanent, irresistible, and universal" in all men's imaginations which justifies them. Only that core of the human imagination common to all men has, presumably, been implanted by Nature; other traits of the imagination which vary from man to man have been formed by other influences, such as education.

But here it may be objected, that the imagination, according to my own confession, being the ultimate judge of all systems of philosophy, I am unjust in blaming the antient philosophers for makeing use of that faculty, and allowing themselves to be entirely guided by it in their reasonings. In order to justify myself, I must distinguish in the imagination betwixt principles which are permanent, irresistable, and uni-

[24] *Enquiry concerning Human Understanding*, p. 55. The unreflective character of many causal inferences also leads Hume to call them "natural," for another meaning of this word is: occurring "without the intervention of thought or reflexion." *Treatise*, p. 484. This natural character is, however, irrelevant to their vindication, for many causal inferences occur with the aid of reflection. *Treatise*, p. 35.

versal; such as the customary transition from causes
to effects, and from effects to causes: And the principles, which are changeable, weak, and irregular. . . .
The former are the foundations of all our thoughts
and actions, so that upon their removal human nature
must immediately perish and go to ruin. The latter
are neither unavoidable to mankind, nor necessary, or
so much as useful in the conduct of life; but on the
contrary are observ'd only to take place in weak
minds, and being opposite to the other principles of
custom and reasoning, may easily be subverted by a
due contrast and opposition. For this reason the former are received by philosophy, and the latter rejected. One who concludes somebody to be near him,
when he hears an articulate voice in the dark, reasons
justly and naturally; tho' that conclusion be deriv'd
from nothing but custom, which infixes and inlivens
the idea of a human creature, on account of his usual
conjunction with the present impression. But one,
who is tormented he knows not why, with the apprehension of spectres in the dark, may, perhaps, be said
to reason, and to reason naturally too: But then it
must be in the same sense, that a malady is said to be
natural; as arising from natural causes, tho' it be contrary to health, the most agreeable and natural situation of man.[25]

In this passage the natural character which justifies
causal inferences is specified. It is not the property of
being caused, but rather the property of being caused
by what in the imaginations of humans is "permanent,
irresistible, and universal."[26]

[25] *Treatise*, pp. 225–26.
[26] Hume also points out this second sense of natural at *Treatise*, p. 484: "Tho' the rules of justice be *artificial*, they are not
arbitrary. Nor is the expression improper to call them *Laws of
Nature*; if by natural we understand what is common to any spe-

In the end, however, Hume rejected this proposed justification of causal beliefs. His rejection was based primarily upon two considerations, both of which cast doubt upon regarding the imagination as a faculty which produces true beliefs.

In the first place, Hume pointed to an inner inconsistency within men's common imagination. The two chief forms which natural belief takes, causal inference and belief in an "external" world, are flatly contradictory. The causal axiom says we can infer the existence of only those objects which we have previously experienced, whereas our perceptual beliefs concern external bodies which, on Hume's view, we can never experience.

> No wonder a principle [the imagination] so inconstant and fallacious shou'd lead us into errors, when implicitly follow'd (as it must be) in all its variations. 'Tis this principle, which makes us reason from causes and effects; and 'tis the same principle, which convinces us of the continu'd existence of external objects, when absent from the senses. But tho' these two operations be equally natural and necessary in the human mind, yet in some circumstances they are directly contrary, nor is it possible for us to reason justly and regularly from causes and effects, and at the same time believe the continu'd existence of matter. How then shall we adjust those principles together? Which of them shall we prefer? Or in case we prefer neither of them, but successively assent to both, as is usual among philosophers, with what confidence can we afterwards usurp that glorious title, when we thus knowingly embrace a manifest contradiction? [27]

---

cies or even if we confine it to mean what is *inseparable* [my italics—J.W.L.] from the species."

[27] *Ibid.*, pp. 265–66.

In the second place, Hume found that at least one of the ordinary beliefs resulting from men's common imagination is clearly fallacious. The ordinary man, and the philosopher in his ordinary moments, identify the very impressions experienced with the external objects themselves. But, Hume claims, reflection on the relativity of sensations will show this to be a mistake.[28] Since it is the human imagination which leads us to have this erroneous belief, Hume insists that doubt is cast upon regarding this faculty as trustworthy in the case of causal inference as well.

> [The sceptic] seems to have ample matter of triumph, while he justly insists that all our evidence for any matter of fact which lies beyond the testimony of sense or memory is derived entirely from the relation of cause and effect; that we have no other idea of this relation than that of two objects which have been frequently *conjoined* together; that we have no argument to convince us that objects which have, in our experience, been frequently conjoined will likewise in other instances be conjoined in the same manner; and that nothing leads us to this inference but custom or a certain instinct of our nature, which it is indeed difficult to resist, but which, like other instincts, may be fallacious and deceitful.[29]

(4) *Hume's defense of causal inferences.* Hume, then, did not think he had *justified* causal inferences. He did, however, offer a weaker defense of our making causal inferences.

[28] *Enquiry concerning Human Understanding,* p. 154.
[29] *Ibid.,* p. 159. Note here that Hume does not, despite charges to the contrary, find causal inferences unjustified just because they are not "deductive" in character. Cf., for example, Stephen Toulmin, *The Uses of Argument* (Cambridge, 1958), p. 165.

This defense is based upon a crucial characteristic of causal beliefs. All men, because of their common human nature, are compelled to have them. Hume holds, that is, that it is impossible for men not to make causal inferences. Causal inferences are, unlike the propositions of mathematics and immediate awareness, not justifiable, but they are, like these other forms of cognitions, forced upon us.

> Nature, by an absolute and uncontrollable necessity has determin'd us to judge as well as to breathe and feel; nor can we any more forebear viewing certain objects in a stronger and fuller light, upon account of their customary connexion with a present impression, than we can hinder ourselves from thinking as long as we are awake, or seeing the surrounding bodies, when we turn our eyes towards them in broad sunshine.[30]

It is true that Hume does qualify this statement somewhat. He admits that sceptical reasonings can momentarily cause a suspension of judgment. However, this effect can be only momentary, for Nature soon breaks the force of such reasonings.[31]

Hume's defense of our making causal inferences is this: because men cannot avoid making them, any injunction not to do so is beside the point. The demand not to have them may be based upon having shown that causal beliefs cannot be justified, but in view of their unavoidability, it has no point. Man cannot be enjoined to combat hopelessly his essentially believing nature.

[30] *Treatise*, p. 183.
[31] *Ibid.*, pp. 218, 269; *Enquiry concerning Human Understanding*, p. 160.

. . . though a *Pyrrhonian* may throw himself or others into a momentary amazement and confusion by his profound reasonings, the first and most trivial event in life will put to flight all his doubts and scruples, and leave him the same, in every point of action and speculation, with the philosophers of every other sect or with those who never concerned themselves in any philosophical researches. When he awakes from his dream, he will be the first to join in the laugh against himself and to confess that all his objections are mere amusement, and can have no other tendency than to show the whimsical condition of mankind, who must act and reason and believe, though they are not able, by their most diligent enquiry, to satisfy themselves concerning the foundation of these operations or to remove the objections which may be raised against them.[32]

I cannot stress enough here that Hume does not equate his defense of *our making* causal inferences with a justification of the *beliefs* themselves. Nor does Hume confuse "epistemic" and "genetic" considerations; he only shows that, in the case of causal inference, the latter are relevant to the former. His essential point is that the epistemic question "Ought we to make causal inferences?" is "blocked" by the unavoidability of our having to make them. Apparently presupposing the principle (which he explicitly adopts in moral philosophy) that ought not implies able not to, he simply argues that inasmuch as we cannot help but make causal inferences, there is no point in anyone's saying we ought not.

The natural character which is the basis of Hume's final defense of causal beliefs is still their arising from

[32] *Enquiry concerning Human Understanding*, p. 160.

what is common to and inseparable from all men's imaginations. It is because the causes of these beliefs are unavoidable that the beliefs are likewise. That a belief is natural in the sense of being causally determined is not sufficient, for a belief may be causally necessary and yet be avoidable, the causes themselves being avoidable. To recur to Hume's example, someone's belief in specters in the dark may be determined by the anxious, "weak" character of his mind, but this belief is not unavoidable for that person can avoid having such a mind.[33] Thus, if one says that Hume defends causal and perceptual beliefs because they are "necessary," he must point out that this is a stronger sense of "necessity" than mere causal necessity.

Hume's defense is not an indiscriminate one, for not all beliefs have the required natural character. In addition to causal inferences, it applies only to other natural beliefs such as men's conviction that there exists a world of bodies.

> . . . [man] must assent to the principle concerning the existence of body, tho' he cannot pretend by any arguments of philosophy to maintain its veracity. Nature has not left this to his choice . . . We may well ask, *What causes induce us to believe in the existence of body?* but 'tis in vain to ask, *whether there be body or not?* That is a point, which we must take for granted in all our reasonings.[34]

Moreover, because causal inferences are unavoidable other beliefs may well be undermined. If a superstition continually conflicts with causal inferences, it may well

[33] *Treatise*, pp. 225–26, quoted above.
[34] *Ibid.*, p. 187.

be given up. Men seek to remove contradictions among their beliefs, and, inasmuch as the causal inferences are irresistible, it will be the other belief that is dropped. It will be subverted by the more powerful principles of human nature.[35]

[35] *Treatise*, pp. 225–26.

HUME, PROBABILITY, AND INDUCTION

D. STOVE

It is well known that Hume's discussion of our "reasonings concerning matters of fact" never received, from the great nineteenth-century writers on scientific inference, the attention due to it. It is also very evident that in the present century this neglect has been corrected. The correction has gone too far, in the opinion of the present writer, so that many philosophers now credit Hume with having proved far more than he in fact proved about inductive arguments.

More particularly, one finds it commonly said nowadays that Hume forestalled any attempt to justify induction which "appeals to the mathematical theory of probability." Such claims are difficult to discuss, since it is usually quite unclear what those who make them understand by an appeal to the mathematical theory of probability. Yet I think we may infer with reasonable certainty at least one thesis that such writers must suppose Hume to have forestalled.

The fundamental idea underlying the "classical" writings on probability—though one not made fully explicit before the "logical" theories of probability of

From *The Philosophical Review*, Vol. LXXIV (1965). Reprinted by permission of the author and *The Philosophical Review*.

the present century—is this. There exist arguments which, although not valid (that is, their premises do not entail their conclusions), necessitate, for any rational being of limited knowledge who knows their premises, belief, rather than disbelief or the suspension of belief, in their conclusions—belief to which, nevertheless, a degree of assurance attaches, less than that (maximal) degree which a valid argument necessitates. In short, there are probable arguments.

Now, Hume had shown that inductive arguments cannot be valid. Premises about observed instances of empirical predicates never entail generalizations or predictions about unobserved instances of those predicates. Since inductive arguments cannot attain the maximum of rationality, must we conclude that all arguments from experience are altogether irrational?

A middle way will naturally suggest itself to anyone who believes that there are arguments which are probable in the sense explained above. All we need do, it appears, in order to avoid being committed by Hume's result to inductive skepticism, is to suppose that not only are there probable arguments, but that among such arguments there are at least some inductive ones —in short, that there are probable inductive arguments.

It can only be this thesis, I suggest—arising as it does from Hume's result on the one hand and the fundamental idea of the probability theorists on the other —which modern writers have in view when they credit Hume with having forestalled even a "mitigated skepticism" about inductive arguments.

I propose to use "I. P." ("inductive probabilism") to

refer to the thesis that there are probable inductive arguments. It is the object of this article to show that Hume's refutation of I. P. is an entirely imaginary episode in the history of philosophy.

My thesis then is historical. But its interest is not only historical. For some think, as I do, that I. P. is true; many more think that its truth is at least a live issue at the present time, which it could scarcely be if, even before Laplace was born, Hume had shown I. P. to be false.

I

The following quotations and references will suffice to establish that some of the best writers in the last thirty years, on Hume or on induction, have subscribed to the view that Hume refuted I. P.:

> Some have tried to save the situation by admitting that all scientific inference is probable inference. But Hume's sceptical attack applies with equal force to probable inference.[1]

> Can we not, however, argue that while experience yields no *certainty* as to the future, it may yet instruct us as to what is *likely* to happen in the future? But this, too, as Hume points out, is "no thoroughfare."[2]

> In other words Hume points out that we get involved in an infinite regress if we appeal to experience in order to justify *any* conclusion concerning unobserved instances—*even mere probable conclusions,* as he adds

[1] A. H. Basson, *David Hume* (London, 1958), pp. 167-68.
[2] N. Kemp Smith, *The Philosophy of David Hume* (London, 1941), pp. 374-75.

in his Abstract (p. 15). For there we read: "It is evident that Adam, with all his science, would never have been able to *demonstrate* that the course of nature must continue uniformly the same. . . . Nay, I will go farther, and assert that he could not so much as prove by any *probable* arguments that the future must be conformable to the past. All probable arguments are built on the supposition that there is this conformity betwixt the future and the past, and therefore can never prove it."[3]

It deserves mention that David Hume, who was the first to see that general synthetical propositions cannot be proved *a priori*, also clearly apprehended that this result of the impossibility of foretelling the future cannot be "evaded" or "minimised" by reference to probability. He was aware of the infinite retrogression to which the introduction of probabilities in this connection leads and also of the necessity of interpreting probability as a statistical concept if it is to be of relevance to statements on future events. This clarity, in our opinion, gives the highest possible credit to the philosophical genius of Hume and strikingly contrasts him with those numberless critics of his ideas who have in the realm of probabilities found an escape from the "scepticism" he taught.[4]

It would be easy, but it is unnecessary, to cite other authorities for this opinion. It would also be easy to show that, when it comes to saying precisely *how* Hume refuted I. P., the accounts given by the writers cited above do not bear the least resemblance one to

[3] K. Popper, *The Logic of Scientific Discovery* (London, 1959), p. 369. Cf. *ibid.*, p. 265, starred addition to n. 2. And cf. the same author's *Conjectures and Refutations* (London, 1963), pp. 192–93, 289.

[4] G. H. von Wright, *The Logical Problem of Induction* (London, 1957), p. 153. Cf. *ibid.*, p. 176.

any other. But this, though instructive, is not strictly to our purpose.

Up to the present, the only protest which, to my knowledge, the ascription to Hume of a refutation of I. P. has evoked is a very recent one by Professor Flew.[5] He writes that it is historically inaccurate, and "surely too generous," of Popper to suppose (in effect) that Hume refuted I. P. Yet he seems immediately afterward to reverse this judgment. For, after having said that we cannot suppose that Hume took cognizance of (what Flew very vaguely calls) "attempts to use elaborations of probability theory here," he concludes with this surprising *volte-face:*

> But of course both the passage in the *Abstract* and that in the *Inquiry* are in general equally decisive against any such (attempts). Perhaps some of them would never have been made had their authors begun from a really close examination of Hume's own words in this demonstration.

II

Fortunately, there is no doubt as to which passages of Hume's writings contain the supposed refutation of I. P. Both Popper and von Wright expressly base their belief in this refutation on the long paragraph of page 15 of the *Abstract* (Keynes and Sraffa Edition [Cambridge, 1938]).

But the argument given there is not, as Popper

[5] A. Flew, *Hume's Philosophy of Belief* (London, 1961). All my references are to pp. 74–76.

thought, "added" in the *Abstract*. It occurs already in
the *Treatise* (Selby-Bigge Edition [Oxford, 1888], pp.
88–90). It occurs again in the first *Enquiry* (Selby-
Bigge Second Edition [Oxford, 1902], pp. 33–38). Basson and Kemp Smith could be referring to any one
or more of these three versions of the argument.

It is quite impossible, however, to understand the
argument of these passages unless we consider it as—
what it evidently is—only one stage of a longer argument. This longer argument runs, in the *Abstract*,
from the top of page 13 to near the end of the first
paragraph of page 16. In the *Treatise* it runs from page
86 to page 90; in the *Enquiry*, from page 25 to page
38.

While the entire argument is essentially the same in
all these versions, the version of the *Abstract* is the
best in every respect; and I have taken it as my main
model in giving my account of the argument.

Our task, then, seems, and indeed is, rather simple.
We have merely to study the passages in question and
satisfy ourselves as to whether they contain a successful, or any, argument against I. P.

What difficulty there is in the case is due to what
may be called the "translation problem." Hume's philosophical language is not ours, and the danger of taking his words in a sense he did not intend is acute in
the present case. Indeed, on the account I will give
of his argument, the belief that Hume refuted I. P.
must have arisen almost entirely from a certain translation error of this quite ordinary kind. But there is also
a translation problem of a less ordinary kind. The passages which concern us are woven into a general epis-

temology which, to a contemporary empiricist, is altogether unacceptable and often unintelligible. We are
here taken into that intellectual world where nothing
exists but impressions and ideas, where a bundle of
perceptions can run along a smooth series of perceptions, or spread itself on external objects, and so forth.
From those philosophical catacombs we have to rescue
arguments that are, and deserve to be, alive.

III

In all of the relevant passages—and this means, in
the case of the *Abstract,* for example, pages 13–16 and
not just page 15—Hume is discussing what he calls
"the inference from the impression to the idea"; that
is, arguments of the class of which "This is a flame,
so this is hot" is typical.

The over-all argument which Hume offers, concerning such inferences, is represented below in a
"structure-diagram"[6] to be read in accordance with the
accompanying "dictionary." The argument is given
here in its untranslated form; that is, the language of
the dictionary is substantially that of Hume himself.

---

[6] This device, and the name, are borrowed from Professor J.
L. Mackie. Some such device is nearly essential in dealing with a
problem like the present one. I think the diagram will be found
self-explanatory; but it perhaps needs to be said that "$p \rightarrow q$"
means simply that the arguer gives p as a ground for believing q.
Nothing, that is, about the *actual*, but only about the *intended*,
logical or evidential relation between p and q is to be understood
by the arrow.

Structure-Diagram of Hume's
Argument as a Whole:
for example, of pages 13-16 of the
Abstract.

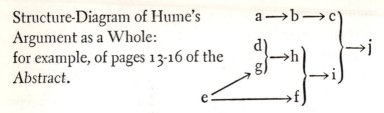

Dictionary.

(a) That the premise of an inference from the impression to the idea should be true, while its conclusion is false, is a perfectly intelligible proposition.

(b) The inference from the impression to the idea is not one which reason engages (determines) us to make.

(c) To lead us to make an inference of this kind, experience—of the conjunction of the objects (impressions) in question—is necessary.

(d) All probable arguments presuppose that the future resembles the past.

(e) That the future resembles the past is a statement concerning matter of fact.

(f) That the future resembles the past cannot be proved by any demonstrative arguments.

(g) If there are any arguments for this statement, they are probable arguments.

(h) Any probable argument for this statement would be circular.

(i) Even when we have had experience (of the appropriate constant conjunction), the inference from the impression to the idea is still not one which reason determines us to make.

(j) It is not reason at all, but custom alone, which determines us to make this inference.

This argument as a whole falls naturally into three stages:

Stage 1 is the argument from (a) through (b) to (c). Here Hume argues that reason alone—that is, unaided by experience—cannot "engage us" to infer the idea from the impression.

Stage 2 is the argument from the premises (d) and (e), through (f), (g), and (h) to (i), the conclusion that even *with* the aid of experience, reason cannot engage us to infer the idea from the impression.

Stage 3 is the argument from the conjunction of these two results (c) and (i), to the ultimate conclusion (j) that it is not reason that engages us to make these inferences at all, but only custom.

On inspection of the relevant texts, it will be immediately evident that the long paragraph of page 15 of the *Abstract,* and the *Treatise* and *Enquiry* pages which correspond to that, are represented above *just by Stage 2 of the argument as a whole.*

Now, since it is just these pages which are alleged to contain Hume's refutation of I. P., it will be sufficient to discredit this allegation if I can show that Stage 2 of this argument contains not a suggestion of any argument at all against I. P.

Consequently, it will not be necessary to translate elements of the dictionary other than those used in Stage 2; that is, we need only consider statements (d)-(i) inclusive.

At the outset of Stage 2 the setting is this. Hume has just, in Stage 1, considered inferences of the sort "This is a flame, so this is hot," and has given, in (b), his critical verdict on them. Statement (c) invites us to consider instead arguments of the sort "This is a flame, and all flames observed in the past have been hot, so this is hot." The first premise corresponds, of course, to the "impression," the second to the "experience" which, according to (c), is necessary to lead us to infer the conclusion. It is arguments of this second kind that Stage 2 is about.

Such arguments are sometimes called "predictive inductive inferences (arguments)," since their conclusions are singular rather than general. Consequently I translate the "inference from the impression to the idea, when we have had experience . . ." as "predictive inductive arguments." Thus statement (i) now reads: "Predictive inductive arguments are not ones which reason engages us to make."

In (e) I translate "is a statement concerning matter of fact" as "is a contingent statement."

The important question that next arises is how to translate Hume's "demonstrative arguments" and "probable arguments" respectively.

Hume often expresses the conclusion of his whole discussion of our arguments from experience as that we have "no reason" to draw *any* conclusion from experience.[7] This, together with the fact that Hume evidently takes this conclusion to be utterly skeptical, may easily suggest to us that by "no reason" Hume meant what we might call "no reason, demonstrative or probable." And when we find Hume himself, in the argument for this conclusion, characterizing arguments exhaustively and exclusively as "demonstrative" and

---

[7] E.g., *Treatise*, p. 139.

"probable"[8] and, moreover, speaking occasionally of knowledge and probability as "degrees of evidence,"[9] we are apt to suppose that he must at least have *contemplated* I. P. And since he appears to have established an utterly skeptical conclusion, we presume that he must en route have not only contemplated but refuted I. P.

Now whether in fact Hume contemplated I. P. or not, his use of the phrases "demonstrative argument" and "probable argument" is no ground whatever for thinking that he did. For Hume certainly does not mean what we mean by speaking of an argument either as demonstrative or as probable.

When *we* call an argument "demonstrative" we mean that it is "logically conclusive," "valid," that its premises entail its conclusion. (The correct analysis of entailment does not concern us here.) When Hume calls an argument "demonstrative," however, he means that it is an argument (all) the premises of which are necessarily true, or such as can be known independently of experience. By "probable arguments," correspondingly, he means arguments of which the premises are (all) contingent, or such as can be known by experience if at all. Moreover, he *regularly identifies "probable arguments"* with a subclass of arguments with contingent premises, namely, *with just those "arguments from experience"* which form the central topic of his theory of understanding.

It is clearly out of the question to examine here, in order to substantiate these assertions as to what Hume

[8] E.g., *Enquiry*, p. 35.
[9] E.g., *Treatise*, p. 89.

meant, the textual details of Hume's usage of these phrases. But the above interpretations are very easy to check, especially with the aid of Selby-Bigge's analytical indexes.

Our distinction between demonstrative and probable arguments is concerned with their degree of conclusiveness, not with the epistemological character of their premises: it may be called a formal or evaluative distinction. Hume's distinction is a material or descriptive one, concerned solely with the epistemological character of the premises.

No doubt, Hume tacitly added to his notion of "demonstrative arguments," as given above, the requirement that such arguments be valid. No doubt, too, no man knew better than Hume that, in all those arguments from experience with which he regularly identifies the genus "probable arguments," the conclusions we draw are all invalidly drawn. In the present passages, as we will see, the distinction between validity and invalidity is the only distinction among "degrees of evidence" that Hume takes notice of; but it is not even this distinction between "demonstrative" and "probable" arguments that is made use of in these passages. The phrases are used here by Hume just in the senses mentioned in the last paragraph but two. This is also how they have been generally taken by commentators, and indeed no other interpretation can survive familiarity with the texts.

Consequently, (f) ought to be translated as: "That the future resembles the past is not deducible from any premises (all of) which are necessarily true"; and "probable arguments" in (d), (g), and (h) as "arguments from experience" or "arguments from premises (all of) which are observational."

Stage 2 now reads (with the places at which a translation has been made being indicated by italics) as follows. (It is to be understood that predictive inductive arguments are a species of arguments from experience.)

"All *arguments from experience* presuppose that the future resembles the past (d). That the future resembles the past, however, is a *contingent* statement (e); consequently it is *not deducible from any premises (all of) which are necessarily true* (f), and if there are any arguments for this statement, they are *arguments from experience* (g). But—from (d) and (g) —any *argument from experience* for this statement would be circular (h). Hence—from (f) and (h)—no *predictive inductive inference* is one which reason engages us to make (i)."

The prospects for a substantiation of the view that Hume refuted I. P. fade markedly once Hume's use of "demonstrative" and "probable" is understood. But the argument is still too obviously undertranslated for a final decision on this view to be made. Three words or phrases still need attention.

The first of these is the word "presuppose" in (d). What can Hume possibly have meant by saying that all arguments from experience *presuppose* that the future resembles the past—or, as I will say for shortness hereafter, presuppose "the Resemblance Thesis"?

The second is the phrase "any argument" in (g), along with the phrase "any argument from experience" in (h). For it may perhaps be thought that Hume's

phrase here meant, or at least could now be made to
bear the meaning, "any argument, demonstrative (in
our sense) or probable (in the sense of I. P.)." I will
need to show that this suggestion can be positively
excluded.

The third is the phrase, used of an inference or argument in (i), that it is not "one which reason engages
(determines) us to make."

The first of these three remaining problems of
translation is the critical one, not only because it concerns the meaning of one of the two premises of Stage
2, but also because it furnishes the key to the other
two problems just mentioned.

The word "presuppose" occurs in what I gave as the
original, untranslated version of (d). This was a silent
"translation" of sorts, for Hume does not use the word.
He uses instead a wide variety of phrases for which
"presuppose" seems an apt, though unilluminating,
translation.[10]

---

[10] In the following quotations I have italicized the phrase
which I have translated as "presuppose."

"All reasonings from experience *are founded on the supposition*
that the course of nature will continue uniformly the same" (*Abstract*, pp. 14–15).

"If reason determined us, it would *proceed upon that principle*,
that instances of which we have had no experience, must resemble those of which we have had experience" (*Treatise*, pp. 88–
90).

". . . probability *is founded on the presumption of* a resemblance betwixt those objects, of which we have had experience
(etc.)" (*Treatise*, p. 90).

". . . all our experimental conclusions *proceed upon the supposition* that the future will be conformable to the past" (*Enquiry*, p. 35).

". . . all inferences from experience *suppose, as their foundation,* that the future will resemble the past" (*Enquiry*, p. 37).

But whether we consider (d) in its partially translated or in its untranslated form—as being about "arguments from experience" or about "probable arguments"—(d) is surely not a proposition which commands immediate assent, or even understanding. It is surprising, therefore, to find that writers who assert (d) in one of Hume's versions—whether by paraphrase, as Kemp Smith does, or by quotation, as Popper and von Wright do—feel under no obligation to say what it means. One would not expect to find contemporary writers introducing, without any explanation, the following thesis: "Of all the principles of association, causation alone transfers from the impression to the idea that liveliness of conception in which belief consists." Yet for Hume, it is from some such rude ancestor that (d) derives its obviousness. From what, one wonders, does (d) derive its obviousness for Popper, say?

We need, then, to translate (d) further.

There is certainly more than one sense in which we speak of an argument as presupposing something, and I suspect that there may be many senses. I will not attempt to survey all the possible ones. Some are perhaps excluded on the ground that they are senses in which what an argument presupposes is a rule or a principle of inference, whereas we have Hume's word for it that what arguments from the impression to the idea presuppose is a proposition, and one concerning matter of fact at that.

One clear and common sense in which we speak of an argument as presupposing a certain statement, and in which the statement presupposed would normally be a contingent one, can be elicited by consideration of the following argument:

"The canary is dead; it could have been killed by the gas escaping from the oven, and there is nothing else that could have caused its death. So it must have been the gas."

It is an orthodox, as well as a correct, comment on such "eliminative inductions" that they presuppose that the number of possible causes of the event in question is finite. But in what sense does the argument presuppose this? Only in the sense, I suggest, that unless it were *true* that the number of possible causes is finite, then no one could be entitled to assert the premises of the argument (in particular, of course, the third premise in the above example).

In this sense, then, an argument "*p*, so *c*" presupposes that *q* if and only if, unless *q*, no one could be entitled to assert *p*.

I do not think this is the sense in which Hume used "presuppose" in (d). In this sense of "presuppose," (d) is in fact false, or at any rate would certainly have been thought false by Hume. He would not have wanted to maintain that unless the future does resemble the past, in respect of the hotness of flames, no one could be entitled to assert even that "this is a flame and all flames observed in the past have been hot." I realize that one of the more obscure lines of criticism of Hume tries to establish something like this. But that is an additional reason for believing that this is not Hume's sense of "presuppose."

A second clear and common sense in which we speak of an argument as presupposing a statement can best be introduced by referring again to the argument about the canary.

It is an orthodox, and again a correct, comment on arguments like this one, that they presuppose that the event in question has some cause; for example, this argument presupposes that *something* killed the canary (the "deterministic postulate" of eliminative induction). But in what sense does the argument presuppose the statement that something killed the canary? Only in the sense, I suggest, that the argument is invalid as it stands, and that in order to turn it into a valid argument it is necessary to add to its premises the premise that something killed the canary.

In this sense, then, an argument "*p*, so *c*" presupposes that *q* if and only if the argument is invalid as it stands, and it is necessary, in order to turn it into a valid argument, to add *q* to its premises.

I think this *is* Hume's sense of "presuppose" in (d), although having positively excluded only one other suggestion, I cannot feel entirely certain of this.

This sense of "presuppose" not only allows but requires (at any rate according to most philosophers) that a presupposed statement be a contingent one.[11] But its positive advantages are three. First, it makes (d) true. Second, it is simple, as Hume's sense surely must have been, since he did not bother to explain it. Third, it issues in an interpretation of Stage 2 as a whole which on other grounds is very probably cor-

[11] For a defense of the minority view, that necessary premises are as necessary as any others for validity, see A. R. Anderson and N. Belnap, "Enthymemes," *Journal of Philosophy*, LVIII (1961), 713–23.

rect. (For these other grounds, see Section V below.)

The claim that (d) is true under this interpretation needs a short defense.

Now (d) is translated as: "All arguments from experience are invalid as they stand, and in order to turn them into valid arguments, it is necessary to add to their premises the Resemblance Thesis."

When I say that this is true, allowance must of course be made for the great freedom in the use of language of which Hume avails himself in the formulation of the Resemblance Thesis as everywhere else. He repeatedly treats quite different formulations as though they were equivalent (cf. note 10 above). In particular, Hume never saw the problem, so glaring to us, of so formulating the Resemblance Thesis that, without being obviously false, it is *sufficient* to turn arguments from experience into valid ones. All this notwithstanding, it is true that all arguments like "this is a flame, and all flames observed in the past have been hot, so this is hot" are invalid; and that in order to turn them into valid arguments it is necessary to add a premise *which can be very naturally described as asserting that* the future resembles the past. The simplest form of such a premise would be: "If this is a flame and all flames observed in the past have been hot, then this is hot." But even the most complicated form would, like this, be aptly describable as asserting that the future resembles the past.

The translation just adopted for "presuppose" furnishes a key to the other two remaining translation problems.

Of these the next concerns the phrase "any arguments" in (g), and the phrase "any argument from experience" in (h). It might be thought that in both these places Hume meant "any argument, demonstrative (in our sense) or probable (in the sense of I. P.)."

We can confidently exclude this suggestion with respect to (h), for it would require us to suppose that in (h) Hume introduced, without a syllable of explanation, the idea of *an argument which is probable in the sense of I. P., being circular.* How entirely foreign this would be to Hume's circle of ideas even the most superficial reading of him would establish. But this idea is not one that only Hume would have needed to explain at length. It would require most careful explanation if it were to be introduced now (as I do not think it has been, even yet). Not only is the notion unfamiliar, however. It is prima facie self-contradictory. For a circular argument, as usually understood, *could* not be probable in the sense of I. P., since (whatever its defects as a proof) it *must* be valid. Consequently, we may safely assume that in (h) "any arguments from experience" means "any valid arguments from experience," and further translate (h) as: "Any valid arguments from experience for the Resemblance Thesis would be circular."

That this translation is correct is confirmed by the fact that, so translated, (h) is actually entailed by the conjunction of (d) and (g); for (d) asserts that any argument from experience is valid only if the Resemblance Thesis is added to its premises, and (g) asserts that any argument for the Resemblance Thesis is an argument from experience. It follows that any argument from experience for the Resemblance Thesis is

valid only if it has the Resemblance Thesis added to
its premises—that is, is circular—and this is what (h)
asserts.

I cannot show positively that in (g), correspondingly, "any argument" means "any valid argument." My
grounds for supposing that it does are: (a) the fact
that there is nothing to suggest, however remotely,
that Hume meant anything other than this; (b) the
fact that Hume normally omits the qualification
"valid" in other contexts where he undoubtedly intends it. For example, he usually writes that there are
no demonstrative arguments, in his sense, for a conclusion concerning matter of fact, where clearly what
he intends is that there are no *valid* demonstrative
arguments. Consequently, I propose to translate (g)
further as: "If there are any *valid* arguments for the
Resemblance Thesis, they are arguments from experience."

It is to be noted that even if this translation is
wrong, and even if in (g) Hume did mean "any argument, valid or probable (in the sense of I. P.)," this
would be the last mention of the idea of "probable
argument" in his argument. For we have been able to
exclude positively the suggestion that he meant this
in the conclusion (h) drawn from (g), in conjunction
with (d). So even then nothing would have been
concluded about probable arguments for the Resemblance Thesis.

What, finally, did Hume mean by saying in (i) of an
inference that it is not one which reason engages or
determines us to make?

Hume's grounds for (i) are (h) and (f) taken together. The arrows in our diagram are of course not entailment arrows. Still, it is the natural presumption that if the grounds offered for a conclusion do entail it, then they were intended to entail it. Consequently, I propose as what Hume means by (i) what (h) and (f) actually entail which, given that predictive inductive arguments are a species of arguments from experience, is the following. "Predictive inductive arguments are valid only if there is added to their premises a premise which is deducible neither from necessarily true premises nor, without circularity, from observational ones."

Let us now put all the pieces of Stage 2 together. Hume's argument was as follows.

"Predictive inductive inferences are valid only if the Resemblance Thesis is added to their premises (d). But the Resemblance Thesis is a contingent statement (e), and consequently is not deducible from necessarily true premises (f) but is deducible from observational premises if from any (g). But—from (d) and (g)—it is deducible only with circularity from observational premises (h). Consequently—from (f) and (h)—predictive inductive inferences are valid only if a premise is added to them which is deducible neither from necessarily true premises nor, without circularity, from observational ones (i)."[12]

---

[12] Yet this is the passage in which von Wright finds an awareness on Hume's part of a (supposed) "necessity of interpreting probability as a statistical concept if it is to be of relevance to statements on future events"! (See his note 16 to the passage quoted earlier in this paper.) Von Wright's other assertion, that Hume was "aware of the infinite retrogression to which the introduction of probabilities in this connection leads," furnishes an equally striking instance of the tendency to ascribe all things

(A number of minor verbal changes are incorporated here. The main one is that I employ, in (g), (h), and (i), the terminology of ". . . is not deducible" rather than that of "there are no valid arguments for. . . .")

It should be said that Hume no doubt intended this argument to apply also to nonpredictive inductive inferences, for example to inductive inferences whose conclusions are general. Clearly enough, the argument does have this wider application, and can be admitted as proving of the genus "arguments from experience," whatever it proves of the species "predictive inductive arguments."

IV

Unless I have badly mistaken the nature of Hume's argument, it will by now be clear that there is simply *no* evidence for the claim that Hume refuted I. P.

On the contrary, there are in his argument—quite apart from what, in statement (i), we found to be his conception of an argument that reason can engage us

---

(thought) good to Hume. For it is based (see his note 15) on, of all things, the notorious argument of the *Treatise*, Book I, Part IV, Sect. 1, according to which the confidence that a rational man reposes in *any* argument, even a proof in mathematics, must finally decay altogether. This argument, if it were a good one, would certainly destroy, among other things, the importance which von Wright like the rest of us attaches to *deductive* inference; but fortunately it is generally recognized as being among the worst ever conceived by a man of genius. In any case, it is perfectly certain that it is not, what von Wright takes it to be, an anticipation of the infinite-regress argument advanced by von Wright himself in the pages immediately preceeding the passage I quoted in Sect. I above.

to make—three independent pieces of evidence that Hume did not even entertain I. P.

The first of these occurs in Stage 1 of the argument. Consider the transition from (a) to (b). Here Hume gives, as a sufficient ground for saying that the inference from "this is a flame" to "this is hot" is not one that reason engages us to make, the fact that it is perfectly intelligible to suppose the premise true and the conclusion false; that is, that the *inference is invalid*. What could more plainly show the absence from Hume's mind of the idea of probable reasoning in the sense of I. P.? And what could more plainly show the risk of misinterpretation involved in failing to consider the *whole* argument, of which page 15 of the *Abstract* is only the second stage?

The second and third pieces of evidence against Hume's having even contemplated I. P. both arise from a consideration of the *strategy* of Stage 2. Hume's strategy is one we often employ. In order to criticize an argument we try to show that while the argument presupposes a certain statement, this statement is, on some ground or other, "unavailable." In this way, Hume criticizes *all* predictive inductive arguments by alleging that while they all presuppose the Resemblance Thesis, this thesis is unavailable.

Now, a statement presupposed by an argument would be commonly admitted to be unavailable if it were, for example, false, or extremely improbable. A statement presupposed by an argument may be unavailable *ad hominem* if it is inconsistent with some other statement made by the arguer. No doubt there are other grounds of unavailability. But—and this is

the second piece of evidence—Hume thinks it sufficient
to establish the unavailability of the Resemblance
Thesis for predictive inductive arguments, that it is
not (without circularity) *deducible* from premises of
the type appropriate to be evidence for it. He could
not possibly have regarded this as a sufficient ground
of unavailability had he entertained the idea of probable reasoning in the sense of I. P.

The third and most important piece of evidence is
this. Hume plainly intends his argument as a *criticism*
of all predictive inductive inferences. The statement
(i) is unmistakably an *unfavorable verdict* on them.
Now, an argument has been effectively criticized only
if it has been shown to be *less conclusive than it was
intended to be.* Let us, then, waive our previous objection, and suppose that Hume has established the unavailability of the Resemblance Thesis for predictive
inductive arguments. Then his charge that they presuppose the Resemblance Thesis would, along with its
unavailability, constitute an effective *criticism* of these
arguments, *only if they were intended to be valid.* But
a man may use an argument, intending it as only a
probable argument in the sense of I. P.; and if he does,
it is not an objection to his argument to point out,
however truly, that a premise necessary to turn it into
a *valid* argument is unavailable. Thus, by taking it as
a criticism of inductive arguments that they presuppose, in his sense, an unavailable premise, Hume again
demonstrates that the idea of a probable argument, in
our sense, was absent from his mind.

V

Although the claim that Hume refuted I. P. is false in its literal sense, there may be a more relaxed sense in which it is true. That is, while no argument of Hume's was even intended to refute I. P., there may be some argument which does refute it, and which at the same time is clearly enough a descendant of some argument that Hume did employ. Nothing that I have shown excludes this possibility; nor could anything exclude it. I know of no such argument. But time, or the present article, may bring one forth.

But, matters standing as they *actually* do, who could deny that we might have been spared much that we would have been better without if, to borrow Flew's words, certain authors had "begun from a really close examination of Hume's own words in this demonstration"? Not, however, the things of which Flew was thinking. We might have been spared all the following: an entirely imaginary episode in the history of philosophy, conjured into existence by some of the best philosophers and historians; exaggerated ideas, based on this episode, of how much Hume contributed to the philosophy of induction; scores of vague pronouncements as to the impossibility of justifying induction "by an appeal to the theory of probability"; and a great many "proofs" of the impossibility of justifying induction "either deductively or inductively," "with certainty or probability," in which it is fondly imagined that these phrases echo something Hume said about "demonstrative arguments" and "probable arguments" —"proofs" which, however slipshod, are exempted from criticism on the groundless supposition that Hume has long ago done the thing properly.

HUME ON PERSONAL IDENTITY

TERENCE PENELHUM

I want in this paper to examine the arguments which Hume uses in the famous Sixth Section of Part IV of Book I of the *Treatise*, not primarily as a work of scholarship, but in order to assess how good they are and to try to learn something from them when they are mistaken as well as when they are right.[1] Hume's discussion of personal identity is the best there is; no one can feel the same about the problem after reading it as he did before; and like so much that Hume says, it is incisive, penetrating, and most unsatisfying. It also has an additional, topical, interest: it gives us, I think, an excellent example of how complex and far-reaching the consequences of a mistake in linguistic or conceptual investigation can be.

I

To consider first the general problem with which Hume deals: the problem of personal identity can be

From *The Philosophical Review*, Vol. LXIV (1955). Reprinted by permission of the author and *The Philosophical Review*.

[1] This is a revised version of a paper read to a meeting of the Pacific Division of the American Philosophical Association at the University of Washington, Seattle, September 8, 1954.

roughly described as that of trying to justify a practice which seems at first sight to be strange, and even paradoxical. This is the practice of talking about people as single beings in spite of the fact that they are constantly changing, and over a period of time may have changed completely. It almost seems a contradiction to say that John Smith at two and John Smith at fifty-two are the same person, because they are so different.

Of course the same problem could be raised in the case of other things—think of Heraclitus and the river. It might look as though the problem of personal identity were just one case of a general problem of the persistence of an object through change, and that any special interest we had in personal identity, rather than in fluminal, floral, or faunal identity, arose from the fact that the kind of thing in question is nearer home. But this last fact has had other effects as well: we are in a position to know that human beings have feelings and thoughts and images and pains, and that although these can be talked about by others, they cannot be *seen* or *had* by them, even though our bodily movements are open to public inspection. Now there has been a tendency among philosophers to do more than just recognize that people's lives *include* such private happenings—the tendency has been to regard them as forming a separate *thing* which has a purely contingent relationship to the body. This tendency to dualism has frequently restricted the way in which the problem of personal identity has been put. It has ceased to be "How are we to account for the unity we assume people to have throughout their lives?" and has become "How are we to account for the unity possessed by one *mind* throughout the changes in its (uniformly private) states?" A result of this restriction has been the invention of an entity called "the self," which Hume very properly derides. The purpose its invention serves is this: there is a certain type of solution to the problem of the identity of changing things which consists in saying that in spite of all appearances, which it is admitted are certainly to the contrary, there in fact *is* some item in the composition of changing objects, which does *not* change in any respect. A partiality to this type of solution in the case of persons might quite naturally lead to making the unchanging item a private one; but if this partiality is combined with the dualistic view of the nature of persons, then it is inevitable that the seat of personal identity should be thought to lie in the mind, and the unchanging item be mental. This is of course "the self," which Hume begins by attacking. I shall now turn to his actual argument,[2] and expound it briefly.

II

He has already maintained in the previous Section that no one has rendered intelligible the relationship of "support" which is supposed to hold between "the self" and the other components of our mental histo-

[2] All quotations in what follows are taken from the Selby-Bigge edition of Hume's *Treatise* (Oxford, 1888). I have only given page references in the case of moderately lengthy quotations.

ries. In Section 6 he opens by disposing of the view
that the existence of the self can be recognised empirically—he does this very simply by denying that anyone can find it, unless of course its defenders are differently constituted from himself. Assuming that this
is not the case, then the whole of mankind are "nothing but a bundle or collection of different perceptions"
in a constant state of change. There is none of the
simplicity or identity that the self was supposed to
provide. This means that it is a mistake to "suppose
ourselves possessed of an invariable and uninterrupted
existence through the whole course of our lives." Yet
we all do suppose it (not merely, Hume implies, the
philosophers who try to justify us). How does this
mistake arise?

It is based, Hume says, on the confusion between
two ideas: (a) that of an object which persists throughout a length of time without change or interruption
—this is the idea of identity; (b) that of a succession
of related objects—this, he says, is clearly a case of
diversity.

We confuse these two because the succession is a
succession of *related* objects, and contemplating or
imagining such a succession feels much the same as
contemplating or imagining an unchanging and uninterrupted object. Having been thus confused, we "substitute" the idea of identity for that of a related succession. And we cannot free ourselves from this confusion for long; the only result of reflecting on it is
the bogus attempt to justify it by inventing "some new
and unintelligible principle," like "substance" or "the

self," which is somehow supposed to preserve the sequence unchanged.

To prove this thesis Hume thinks he has merely to show that those things we (mistakenly) call the same even though they are changing and interrupted consist of a succession of related parts. To show this he takes various kinds of changing thing, claiming in each case that the relation of the change to the whole which changes causes us to overlook its occurrence and continue to call the object the same. (The change, for example, is small in proportion to the whole, takes place only gradually, leaves the function of the whole unaffected, etc.) The same principles are at work in the case of persons; so in their case, as in all other cases, the identity we ascribe to them is "fictitious."

Hume ends by saying that his whole examination of this question reveals that most of the disputes about identity are "merely verbal." Since, as he puts it, "identity depends on the relations of ideas, and these relations produce identity by means of that easy transition they occasion," when these relations and the ease of transition grow less, the tendency to believe in identity grows less too. He gives no example here, but the kind of thing I take it he has in mind is this (I shall take a simple and non-personal instance): if a philosopher were to take a particular case like the history of a building from its initial construction to its final demolition, and were to ask at what point what was originally a mere pile of bricks became the house, and at what point what had been the house ceased to be this and gave place to a mere pile of bricks once more (should we date these events by the laying or crumbling of the foundations, or the tiling or stripping of the roof, or the installation or removal of the plumbing? etc., etc.), the answer to give him would be that the tendency to ascribe identity to the changing and complex object is in this case based on the relationship which all the parts have to a central function, viz., the usefulness of the building for sheltering people, but that when this relationship is equivocal (e.g., when the structure could hold people, but only uncomfortably) we simply have a stretch of time when the tendency to say that this is a house rather than a heap of bricks exists, but with less force. At such a time we can decide much as we please which to say it is, and it does not really matter. Our decision would only matter if we invented some philosophical fiction to bolster it up.

III

I wish first to comment briefly on Hume's statement that the whole of mankind are "nothing but a bundle or collection of different perceptions." What is meant by this? Part of what he means is of course that human beings are not composed of something called a "self" *plus* some other, less permanent, items, but only of these latter items themselves. So much would be a mere reiteration of what he has already said. But he is clearly committing himself besides to something much stronger and stranger than this, viz., to the view that these items of which, and of nothing-else-but, the whole of mankind are composed are "perceptions."

Now this claim is clearly not of quite the same sort as the claim of some philosophers that material things are nothing but perceptions. For (a) this latter claim is usually somewhat to the effect that statements made about any material thing can somehow be construed as being in fact statements about some of the things that happen to observers when they look at it; and if this were the sort of thing that Hume meant by saying that *people* were nothing but perceptions, it would follow that according to him each person is composed of *other people's* perceptions, that every statement about a given person ought to be construed as a statement about some *other* person or persons; I feel confident that he does not mean this. (b) I feel confident also that he is using the word "perception" in a much wider sense than the sense in which it is used by philosophers who claim that material things are nothing but perceptions, since they use it to mean events which might otherwise be called "sensations," whereas he seems to include in its meaning such events as dreams, feelings, images, etc.—all those events I mentioned earlier which are not open to public view in the way in which our bodily movements are.

What Hume's claim about human beings involves, then, is that they are nothing but the series of *their own* sensations, feelings, dreams, images, and the rest. Clearly to reach this conclusion he must have been dealing not with the question "How are we justified in attributing identity to persons?" but the question "How are we justified in attributing identity to *minds?*" (where the word "mind" is understood as meaning the "theatre," to use Hume's own term, where these private events take place). It is far from trivial to notice that these two questions are not equivalent (obviously not, since the words "person" and "mind" are not); for answering the latter rather than the former restricts the discussion of personal identity considerably. It forces us to ignore, for example, that the most common way of settling practical problems of identification is by scrutinizing people's physical appearance; or that the gradualness of the changes in complex things which Hume claims to be one of the main contributing causes of our calling them identical is only a feature of human beings if one thinks of them partly in terms of their physical careers; or that the uninterruptedness which he thinks we erroneously attribute to them is in fact a feature of their physical lives.

Fortunately, however, this restriction does not affect the pertinence of his discussion as much as it might be expected to do. This is due to the fact that although he talks at various points as though the problem he is trying to answer is that of the unity of the *mind*, and refers to that of personal identity as though it were the same, the way in which he tries to illumine it is by putting forward a *general* thesis, which I have already outlined, concerning the *general* propensity to call complex and changing objects identical, a propensity of which the ascription of identity to persons is just one instance. It follows, therefore, that the objections I have just raised would apply rather to his view of what sort of thing a person *is* than to his *general* view of the *kinds* of factor at work when we ascribe identity to changing and complex things, whether they are persons or not. I am prepared to agree with him (a) that persons are changing and complex, and (b) that such features as the proportionate smallness of changes, or their gradualness, which he says consolidate our propensity, can be found in the case of persons (more easily, in fact, if we recognize that "person" means more than just "mind"), and this is all that it is necessary to agree to in order to admit that his thesis applies to the case of persons. My subsequent comments will be concerned with this central and general thesis, and are therefore independent of the foregoing criticisms of Hume's view that the life-histories of persons have merely mental components, just as the thesis itself could be stated independently of this view.

IV

Hume's thesis turns on one central point, and stands or falls with it. This point is his contention that it is, "to a more accurate method of thinking," a confusion to call an object that changes the *same*. The "idea of identity or sameness" is the idea of an object that persists *without* changing. The fact that the parts of a changing thing may be related to one another does not, after all, alter the further fact that they do change, so in this case we do *not* have identity or sameness, and it must therefore be due to some ingrained tendency of the mind that we talk as though we do. From this point, which he brings in fairly unobtrusively, the remainder of his arguments follow naturally:

(1) The puzzle that remains is a psychological one,

viz., what is it about us that makes this mistake possible?

(2) Any account of the relationships that hold between the parts of complex things will only be relevant to *this* question; they do not affect the question of whether we are *justified* in calling such objects the same, because we just aren't.

(3) Clearly the borderline cases, where we are undecided whether to say that what is before us is the same object or another one, as it were, taking over where the first one left off, are merely verbal and undecidable because *whatever* we decide will be groundless and mistaken. For the very fact that a change is taking place ought strictly to make us say it is not the same object, but the fact that other changes have preceded this one should have made us say that long before. There is no difference in *kind* between the borderline cases and the times of change during the previous history of the object. The only difference is in the degree of psychological compulsion acting on us—the propensity to misapply the notion of identity is beginning to falter when the borderline is reached, but has not done so before. The only possible *standard* is violated at *all* stages.

(4) The fictions of the self and substance have arisen because philosophers have sensed the nature of our common mistake, but have not been able to free themselves from it for long. The inevitable result of this conflict-state is that they have felt there *must*, really, underneath, out of sight, be an unchanging something-or-other which is the real object, so that our strange habit is justified after all.

All of these are natural consequences of what Hume says about the nature of identity in the early part of the Section. If it is true that we make a mistake in the first place by talking of identity through change at all, then all the rest follows. But I think it is not hard to show that *he* is making an elementary error here, not everyone else, and that the facts he brings to our notice are twisted and misapplied as a result.

It is important to keep in mind as one reads him that he does think he has uncovered a *mistake*, as his language does not always lay stress on this. For instance, when talking about persons, he says:

> I cannot compare the soul more properly than to a republic or commonwealth . . . as the same individual republic may not only change its members, but also its laws and constitutions; in like manner the same person may vary his character and disposition, as well as his impressions and ideas, without losing his identity.[3]

This does not, taken out of context, sound like the account of an alleged mistake at all, but it is quite clear from everything that has led up to it that it is, including in particular the fact that this passage is intended as a demonstration that the identity of the mind of a person is a "fictitious" one. The same applies too, of course, to the identity of a republic or commonwealth. Hume is not just saying that our common practice of attributing identity in such cases cannot be justified, or has no sound reason in its favor (as he says of our belief in the regularity of nature): he is here making the less modest claim that our common

3 *Treatise*, p. 261.

practice is wrong, that the evidence points unequivocally to the opposite. We proceed not without, but in
the face of, the evidence. But it would seem from the
tone of the above passage, as well as from his well-
known second thoughts in the Appendix, that even
Hume found this odd and paradoxical sometimes.

For odd and paradoxical it certainly is. What he is
actually claiming is that we are constantly making a
mistake in referring to a person from day to day as the
same person (in using the same proper name, for example), or in referring in this way to *anything* that
has changed in the slightest. For, strictly speaking, a
changed person would be literally *another* person.
A little effort of imagination is enough to indicate just
how much chaos would result from adopting Hume's
diagnosis as the source of a prescription and using a
different proper name whenever we noticed the slightest change, even in ourselves (or rather in the separate
people that we would be from minute to minute). If
we make a *mistake* in *not* doing this, it is a mistake we
all make *all* the time, and a mistake of which the correction would require a complete overhaul of the concepts and syntax of our language. I suppose Hume
would say this is one of the reasons why we continue
to make the mistake—to avoid the desperate awkward-
ness of trying to live up to our moments of philosophical insight all the time. But I find it hard to believe
that a mistake lies at the root of so much of our language, especially since Hume has claimed to reveal it
by a piece of linguistic analysis. I want to show that
his analysis is a bad one, that the "mistake" is not a
mistake at all, and that its supposed revelation is not

a piece of philosophical insight, but of short sight, or rather, astigmatism.

Once the basic point is located, it is not hard to see that Hume has gone wrong. Let us consider the essential three sentences:

> We have a distinct idea of an object, that remains invariable and uninterrupted thro' a suppos'd variation of time; and this idea we call that of *identity* or *sameness*. We have also a distinct idea of several different objects existing in succession, and connected together by a close relation; and this to an accurate view affords as perfect a notion of *diversity*, as if there was no manner of relation among the objects. But tho' these two ideas of identity, and a succession of related objects be in themselves perfectly distinct, and even contrary, yet 'tis certain, that in our common way of thinking, they are generally confounded with each other.[4]

It is not hard to find his error here. What he is saying is that since we would call something the same for a given length of time when it continued without any alteration, and since we would say that a succession of objects was a collection or number or series of objects, it would obviously be a contradiction to say that in the latter case we would have *one* object. In a sense this is true, but not in the sense which Hume requires. He has not noticed what is wrong because he has chosen to talk in very general terms here, and to ignore the way in which we would actually talk on particular occasions. But a rebuttal can be produced even in general terms. Let us call the unchanging single object X. X, we would say, is the same throughout. Let us call our

4 *Ibid.*, p. 253.

succession of distinct but related objects A, B, C, D, E, F, etc. Here, if we count, we obviously have several, not one. But we can quite easily produce a class-name for the series of them, say ϕ, such that a ϕ is, by definition, any group of things like A, B, C, D, E, F, etc. So there would be no contradiction in saying there are six objects and one ϕ; this is what a ϕ *is*. Quite obviously our ordinary language works this way. A succession of notes is one theme. A succession of words is one sentence. If the succession does not form a theme or sentence, it is still a *succession* or series. There is no contradiction in saying "There are six notes in this theme," or "There are six words in this sentence," though there would be in saying "There are six notes but only one," or "There are six words but only one." Naturally *this* would be absurd, but no one ever says it (for that reason).

So, in spite of Hume, there is no contradiction in saying that certain kinds of things are composed of a succession of parts, and yet are each only one thing. Whether a thing can have many parts or not depends entirely on what sort of thing it is. Most things (including people) do.

There is another, closely related, mistake which Hume has made. This is the mistake of thinking that for anything to be entitled to be called "the same" it has to remain *unchanged* from one period to the next. This is a muddle of two things that he himself distinguishes at one point, viz., the two distinct senses of the word "identical" or "the same." These are the numerical and the specific senses, as he calls them. Two things can be the same as one another in the specific sense, i.e., exactly alike in some respect, yet they will still be two things; but if they are said to be the same in the numerical sense they are being said to be not two things but one after all. These two senses are distinct from one another. Now to remain unchanged is to remain the same in the *specific* sense, i.e., to be now exactly as one was at an earlier time. But I can remain the same in the *numerical* sense without doing so in the specific sense—I can be numerically the same but changed. In fact I cannot be said to have changed unless I *am* the same in the numerical sense. The only reason for saying that something is numerically different (something else, that is) when a change occurs, is if it is by definition an unchanging thing. When a note is played, for example, as soon as the tone is raised or lowered we have another note, not the same one at all. But in the case of most things, the words we use to talk about them are words the meanings of which allow us or require us to continue to use them throughout certain changes, though not of course *any* changes. What kind of changes can occur without our having to say that the thing has ceased to exist and given place to something else depends on what *kind* of thing we are talking about. To know what such changes are is part of what it is to know the meaning of the class-term for that sort of object. A house, or a person, is something which admits of many changes before we would say it had ceased to exist. To know what these changes are is to know, in part at least, what the words "house" and "person" mean.

The rejoinder to Hume, then, consists simply in saying that the pairs of expressions, (a) "numerically the same" and "containing many parts" and (b) "numerically the same" and "changed," are not pairs of contradictories. So we have not made a mistake in saying that a succession of related objects may form a unit of a certain kind, or that the same thing may undergo radical changes. Once this is admitted, the rest of what he says appears in quite a different light.

V

(1) His *examples* point quite a different moral from what he thinks:

(a) The paragraph I quoted can hardly be said to contain an example, but if we produce examples to fit it we get quite different results from those Hume intended. There is nothing about "an object that remains invariable and uninterrupted" *per se* which requires us to say it is the same thing throughout, and nothing about a succession of different but related ones *per se* which requires the opposite. It depends entirely on what concepts we are using when we talk about each. If we heard a continuous sound we would say it was one sound and not several; but it is not hard to imagine some situation in which we would be interested in counting the number of seconds of sound, in which case we would say there were, for example, ten of them. In the case of a succession of objects, the whole series might very well be said to form a unit: a succession of men may form a march-past. There is nothing revealing in choosing a single and uninterrupted sort of thing rather than a complex thing, and

Hume has fallen into a conceptual muddle by doing so. He only makes it worse by talking of "an *object* that remains invariable" and "several *objects* existing in succession," because he is here using the same noun in each case, viz., "object"; and although this is the vaguest noun in the language, the mere fact that he uses the same one in each case suggests very easily that in the two phrases he is thinking of objects of the same kind, e.g., a single and uninterrupted note and a succession of distinct notes. This would point a contrast, though of dubious value to Hume;[5] but if we took the variable-word "object" at its face value and substituted different nouns in each phrase the contrast would disappear: where is there a contrast between "an invariable and uninterrupted arithmetical progression" and "a succession of different but related numbers"? If it is thought that I have chosen a favorable example here, the reply is that I am quite entitled to do so. I am quite ready to admit that we could find a contrast here by making different substitutions, but this just bears out the essential point that whether we get one or not depends entirely on what nouns we choose to work with, and not on the concepts of identity and diversity. Put generally, whether the result is logically absurd, or logically possible, or logically necessary, if the two phrases "the same continuing x" and "several different y's" are used of the same thing, depends entirely on what nouns we use to replace x and y. It

---

[5] It would be of dubious value to him because although if we replaced "object" by the same noun in each phrase we would get a contrast, we would quite clearly get a case where the confusion he has in mind would be altogether unlikely.

does not depend on the words "same" and "different" in themselves.

(b) There are two specific examples which Hume does offer, but misunderstands. He offers both as instances of confusion between numerical and specific identity. The first is this:

> A man, who hears a noise, that is frequently interrupted and renew'd, says it is still the same noise; tho' 'tis evident the sounds have only a specific identity or resemblance, and there is nothing numerically the same, but the cause, which produc'd them.[6]

I do not think the man in this case would be guilty of this confusion. When he says it is still the same noise, he may mean one of two things: (i) he might be using "same" in the specific sense, in which case he would be saying merely that the noise he hears now is exactly like the one he heard before; or (ii) he might be using the word "noise" as roughly equivalent to "an intermittent series of exactly similar sounds," in which case the constituent sounds of the noise, in this sense of "noise," can certainly come and go.

The second example is this:

> In like manner it may be said, without breach of the propriety of language, that such a church, which was formerly of brick, fell to ruin, and that the parish rebuilt the same church of free-stone, and according to modern architecture. Here neither the form nor materials are the same, nor is there anything common to the two objects, but their relation to the inhabitants of the parish; and yet this alone is sufficient to make us denominate them the same.[7]

[6] *Treatise*, p. 258.
[7] *Ibid.*, p. 258.

Here again the example does not bear out Hume's views at all. Of *course* the relationship of the building to the inhabitants is enough for us to call it the same, because the concept with which we are operating, say that of "the village church of Muddlehampton," is simply and solely the concept of *any* structure which has the unique purpose at any period of subserving the religious needs of the people of that parish. This is why we would use the same phrase whatever building was there, and would say, both before and after the rebuilding, that we had the same thing there; for, in the sense of the concept we would be using, we *would* have the same thing there. There is no mistake in this, as there would be in saying we had the same building, in the sense of the same pile of stones; but we would not say *that*. The village church of Muddlehampton can be pulled down and rebuilt again many times over with perfect logical propriety.

(2) But Hume's error of supposing that invariance is the standard of identity in all cases, when it is only the standard in a very few (those in which invariance is part of the concept of the thing) makes him not only misunderstand the import of his own examples, but miss the point of his otherwise very revealing account of *the relations between the parts of complex things*. Factors like the proportionate smallness of changes, or the conspiracy of the remaining parts to the same end, he claims to be factors which make us overlook the fact that changes have occurred at all. But we do not overlook this fact; we are perfectly aware of it. What Hume is actually describing here in general terms are the kinds of change that are compre-

hended under the concepts of certain sorts of things. It is true that these are often small in proportion to the whole, that they take place slowly, and so on. But it is not true always; it is not true of the concept of a river, as Hume himself says. It depends on the concept. As he puts it himself, "What is natural and essential to any thing is, in a manner, expected"; that is to say, more changes are allowed in some things than others, depending on the kind. He should have added, "and it is embodied in the concept of the thing." This might have stopped him saying that these natural and essential changes merely make us misapply the concept of identity, and revealed instead that the standards for applying the concept of identity depend entirely on the substantives it is joined onto. The rules for using nouns (and it is the *modus operandi* of nouns to which his description is relevant) are evolved by generations of language-users, and we have to decide in terms of these at what point a noun applies to whatever we may be considering and when it ceases to.

(3) This decision is not always easy, since the rules we apply are at best very general ones, learned from experience, and not able to cover every eventuality. There are inevitably times when we do not know just what term applies. These are the *borderline cases*, the occasions when the "nice and subtile" questions about identity start coming up. In deciding whether the roofless structure in front of us is a house or a heap of stones, we may have reached a point where the conventions governing neither expression are sufficient to tell us, and we just have to decide for ourselves and, in so doing, make these conventions more precise. We

can make mistakes here, like taking a decision which has unforeseen legal repercussions regarding the status of our property. But we do not make a mistake just because we are considering saying it is the same object when it has changed. Hume would have to say that in this case we are merely repeating an error which we have made many times already during the object's history, and just happen for strictly psychological reasons to be feeling uneasy about it this time. But we are uneasy because the rules for our words are not geared to meet every eventuality, not because they ought not to meet any at all. It is true that we lack a standard, but not because we have not been following one before.

(4) It is now time to consider *Hume's criticisms of other philosophers.* He pours scorn on theories of "the self" and "substance," whether they claim to be empirical or not. I do not want to dwell on his criticisms of these theories, since they seem to me to be sound ones. I am more interested in discussing his account of how such theories arise. He claims that they arise because philosophers, like the rest of us, are subject to those factors which produce the mistake of allowing numerical identity to complex and changing things, but are occasionally made aware, by the kind of argument he himself uses, that they *are* making this mistake. Being human, and unable therefore to shake off this pernicious but convenient confusion, they have eventually tried to justify it by inventing fictions like "the self" to meet the requirement of invariance that they see could not be met otherwise. I have suggested that the factors he has enumerated do not contribute to a mistake or confusion, because there is none. But I

agree that the self is a fiction. Such fictions have quite probably arisen in the way Hume describes. That is, the philosophers in question may have thought they found a contradiction between saying a thing has changed and saying it is still the same thing; and they may have tried to overcome this by saying that there is in fact some crucial respect in which the thing will *not* have changed, and inventing the self to fill the bill. But if I am right, they need not have bothered; since there is no contradiction there to be avoided, the fiction is unnecessary. What is of more interest is that Hume, in exposing the nature of their mistake, has conceded their main premise, viz., that there *is* a contradiction there, and has merely said that it is impossible to avoid it and recommended us by implication not to try to justify it. This is a sturdier course than theirs; but as it proceeds from the same starting-point, it is not surprising that Hume's solution seems to him the sort of paradoxical scepticism for which the only cure is a change of subject or a game of backgammon. This is all the result, as far as I can see, of a linguistic error, of a misdescription of the way in which certain words in the language are in fact used.

I must now try to anticipate a criticism: it might seem that I have been too severe on Hume, too keen to stress the consequences of a position which is more austere than the one he actually holds. I might appear to have missed the point of the fact (noted above) that as his discussion proceeds he does not seem to be *objecting* to the practice of calling people, for all their complexity and changingness, the same throughout their lives; in the course of several pages devoted to the psychological influences on our linguistic conventions, Hume does not seem to be *criticizing,* but only to be *describing,* the way in which we talk. He certainly says that our tendency to talk of changing things as identical is a mistake and a confusion, but he only says this at the beginning, in an attempt to discredit philosophical constructs like the self, which only occur when philosophers try to justify, or show rational ground for, a practice which is just a matter of habit and could not conceivably depend on anything *they* had to say. Hume is not trying to discredit our usage, but only to discredit misguided attempts to defend it.

This sort of view is held by Professor Kemp Smith,[8] who insists that Hume has no objection to our everyday use of the notion of identity, once this is understood to be based on custom and not on argument. It would follow from this (and Kemp Smith accepts this consequence) that when Hume refers to the identity of persons as "fictitious," he does not mean *fictitious,* but something less censorious, something more like "stretched": Kemp Smith suggests "Pickwickian." So although he begins by maintaining that "to an accurate view" talk of the changing or complex as identical is paradoxical, Hume is not himself disposed to take the accurate view, nor to urge it on others—the fact that it is a universal custom *not* to take the accurate view makes it pointless to attempt to impose it in any case.

I have no particular wish either to welcome or to

[8] N. Kemp Smith, *The Philosophy of David Hume* (London, 1941). See particularly pp. 96–98, 497–505.

resist this interpretation of Hume's position, or to discuss how far Hume is consistent if this reading of his
position is correct. For it is irrelevant to my main
contentions:

(a) Whether he is saying that our habit of talking
involves us in a paradox which we render tolerable by
certain psychological mechanisms, or that the habit is
only paradoxical when we take an overscrupulous view
of it, but justifies itself pragmatically somehow and
should therefore not distress us, he is in either case
saying that it can be shown to involve a paradox on
examination. However lightly he takes it, he believes
it is there. I have denied it is there at all, whether we
take an "accurate view" or not.

(b) Whether he thinks the use of the word "identical" with reference to complex things or changing
things is a mistaken use or merely a stretched use, he
certainly thinks the word is being at least mildly abused
on these occasions. I have denied this.

(c) Whether his account of what makes us talk of
identity in this mistaken or Pickwickian way is intended
as a description of how we hide the paradox from ourselves, or merely of what enables us to talk with a
(perfectly proper) lack of concern for it, it is in either
case misdirected, since our apparent unconcern for the
paradox is due to its nonexistence, and what he in fact
describes are the factors governing the use of substantives, and not the *mis*use of the adjective "same."

In other words, however tolerant of our linguistic
behavior Hume may be, there is nothing for him to be
tolerant about.

VI

Two points in conclusion: (1) I have not paid special attention to personal identity rather than any other kind. Here I am following Hume. While his chapter and my comments might well have been enriched by descriptions of the relationships between the various stages and facets of the life of persons, such descriptions would have been incidental to the issue which is the core of his argument, viz., the analysis of the concept of identity, and in particular its compatibility or incompatibility with the concepts of complexity and change. This question is the same whatever complex or changing objects we choose to take as examples. Admittedly persons have a greater degree of complexity and a greater tendency to change than most other things, but to explore this complexity and these changes is to illuminate the concept of a person rather than that of identity.

But there is a positive danger also in laying special emphasis on persons, a danger to which Hume is very much alive: it makes one very susceptible to the suggestion that as we are persons ourselves we are in a better position in this one case to locate the unchanging particle which carries our identity with it, since we have access to human life from the inside as well as the outside. This makes it tempting to give a term like "the self" a quasi-empirical character, as though it referred to an object of introspection. It has been suggested that when this happens it is easy to believe that certain somatic sensations are revelations of the self. If this is true it might explain some of the (otherwise very extraordinary) empirical claims of the kind Hume mentions. It is one thing to claim the self must be there, but quite another to claim you have found it. But to follow the scent of this red herring is to be diverted from recognizing that the whole purpose for which the search was instigated is misconceived.

(2) Hume's language throughout makes it clear that he thinks the error he claims to detect is committed by everyone, that is, by every user of the language, not just by philosophers. If I am right, this is not the case and the ordinary language-user is quite innocent. He clearly holds that it is the philosophers who have invented the fictions of substances and selves. Here he is right, of course. What emerges from this is that such philosophers, in inventing their fictions, are not defending the layman at all. For they concede, with Hume, that the only chance of showing there is no such paradoxical error in the layman's language is by finding the unchanging kernel within each changing thing. But the layman does not need this sort of defense, because there is no paradox there in the first place. So any claim that the doctrine of the self is a defense of the layman or that it represents the "common sense position," if this means the same, would be bogus. This point is in no way altered by the fact (and it does seem to be one) that laymen beginning philosophy tend to prefer substance-type theories. For this would be the result of unclear theorizing *about* language (quite a different activity from the mere using of language, and demanding quite·distinct

aptitudes—rather as travel and cartography differ). Someone new to linguistic theorizing could quite well think he detected a paradox where others claimed to, and fail to notice that his own daily practice did not bear this out. Once this happened, the self might very well seem the only way of evading the paradox. But at this point we are not dealing with a layman any more, but with a philosophical novice. A view which the plain-man-newly-turned-philosopher prefers is not necessarily one he is committed to beforehand.

HUME ON "IS" AND "OUGHT"

A. C. MAC INTYRE

I

Sometimes in the history of philosophy the defense of a particular philosophical position and the interpretation of a particular philosopher become closely identified. This has notoriously happened more than once in the case of Plato, and lately in moral philosophy it seems to me to have happened in the case of Hume. At the center of recent ethical discussion the question of the relationship between factual assertions and moral judgments has continually recurred, and the nature of that relationship has usually been discussed in terms of an unequivocally sharp distinction between them. In the course of the posing of this question the last paragraph of Book III, Part I, Section 1, of Hume's *Treatise* has been cited over and over again. This passage is either quoted in full or at least referred to—and with approval—by R. M. Hare,[1] A. N. Prior,[2]

From *The Philosophical Review*, Vol. LXVIII (1959). Reprinted by permission of the author and *The Philosophical Review*.

[1] R. M. Hare, *The Language of Morals* (Oxford, 1952), pp. 29 and 44.
[2] A. N. Prior, *Logic and the Basis of Ethics* (Oxford, 1949), pp. 32–33.

P. H. Nowell-Smith,[3] and a number of other writers.
Not all contemporary writers, of course, treat Hume
in the same way; a footnote to Stuart Hampshire's
paper, "Some Fallacies in Moral Philosophy,"[4] provides an important exception to the general rule. But
very often indeed Hume's contribution to ethics is
treated as if it depended largely on this one passage,
and this passage is accorded an interpretation which
has acquired almost the status of an orthodoxy. Hare
has even spoken of "Hume's Law."[5]

What Hume says is:

> In every system of morality which I have hitherto met
> with, I have always remark'd, that the author pro-
> ceeds for some time in the ordinary way of reasoning,
> and establishes the being of a God, or makes observa-
> tions concerning human affairs; when of a sudden I
> am surpriz'd to find, that instead of the usual copula-
> tions of propositions, *is*, and *is not*, I meet with no
> proposition that is not connected with an *ought*, or
> an *ought not*. This change is imperceptible; but is,
> however, of the last consequence. For as this *ought* or
> *ought not*, expresses some new relation or affirma-
> tion, 'tis necessary that it should be observ'd and
> explain'd; and at the same time that a reason should
> be given, for what seems altogether inconceivable,
> how this new relation can be a deduction from others,
> which are entirely different from it. But as authors do
> not commonly use this precaution, I shall presume to
> recommend it to the readers; and am persuaded that
> this small attention wou'd subvert all the vulgar sys-
> tems of morality, and let us see, that the distinction

[3] P. H. Nowell-Smith, *Ethics* (London, 1954), pp. 36–38.
[4] S. Hampshire, "Some Fallacies in Moral Philosophy,"
Mind, LVIII (1949), 466.
[5] R. M. Hare, "Universalisability," *Proceedings of the Aristotelian Society*, LV (1954–55), 303.

of vice and virtue is not founded merely on the relations of objects, nor is perceiv'd by reason.[6]

The standard interpretation of this passage takes
Hume to be asserting here that no set of nonmoral
premises can entail a moral conclusion. It is further
concluded that Hume therefore is a prime opponent of
what Prior has called "the attempt to find a 'foundation' for morality that is not already moral." Hume
becomes in this light an exponent of the autonomy of
morality and in this at least akin to Kant. In this paper
I want to show that this interpretation is inadequate
and misleading. But I am not concerned with this only
as a matter of historical interpretation. The thread of
argument which I shall try to pursue will be as follows.
First, I shall argue that the immense respect accorded
to Hume thus interpreted is puzzling, since it is radically inconsistent with the disapproval with which
contemporary logicians are apt to view certain of
Hume's arguments about induction. Second, I shall try
to show that if the current interpretation of Hume's
views on "is" and "ought" is correct, then the first
breach of Hume's law was committed by Hume; that
is, the development of Hume's own moral theory does
not square with what he is taken to assert about "is"
and "ought." Third, I shall offer evidence that the
current interpretation of Hume is incorrect. Finally,
I shall try to indicate what light the reinterpretation
of Hume can throw upon current controversies in
moral philosophy.

[6] Hume, A Treatise of Human Nature, ed. L. A. Selby-Bigge
(Oxford, 1888), pp. 469-70.

II

To approach the matter obliquely, how can we pass from "is" to "ought"? In Chapter IV of *The Language of Morals,* Hare asserts that a practical conclusion and a fortiori a moral conclusion is reached syllogistically, the minor premise stating "what we should in fact be doing if we did one or other of the alternatives open to us" and the major premise stating a principle of conduct. This suggests an answer to our question. If you wish to pass from a factual statement to a moral statement, treat the moral statement as the conclusion to a syllogism and the factual statement as a minor premise. Then to make the transition all that is needed is to supply another moral statement as a major premise. And in a footnote to Chapter III of *Ethics* we find Nowell-Smith doing just this. He quotes from Bishop R. C. Mortimer the following passage: "The first foundation is the doctrine of God the Creator. God made us and all the world. Because of that He has an absolute claim on our obedience. We do not exist in our own right, but only as His creatures, who ought therefore to do and be what He desires."[7] On this Nowell-Smith comments: "This argument requires the premise that a creature ought to obey his creator, which is itself a moral judgment. So that Christian ethics is not founded solely on the doctrine that God created us."[8] That is, he argues that the inference,

[7] R. C. Mortimer, *Christian Ethics* (London, 1950), p. 7.
[8] *Op. cit.,* p. 51.

"God created us, therefore we ought to obey him," is defective unless and until it is supplied with a major premise, "We ought to obey our creator."

I can only make sense of this position by supposing that underlying it there is an assumption that arguments must be either deductive or defective. But this is the very assumption which underlies Hume's skepticism about induction. And this skepticism is commonly treated as resting upon, and certainly does rest upon, a misconceived demand, a demand which P. F. Strawson has called "the demand that induction shall be shown to be really a kind of deduction."[9] This is certainly an accurate way of characterizing Hume's transition from the premise that "there can be no *demonstrative* arguments to prove, that those instances of which we have had no experience resemble those of which we have had experience" to the conclusion that "it is impossible for us to satisfy ourselves by our reason, why we should extend that experience beyond those particular instances which have fallen under our observation."[10] Part of Hume's own point is that to render inductive arguments deductive is a useless procedure. We can pass from "The kettle has been on the fire for ten minutes" to "So it will be boiling by now" (Strawson's example) by way of writing in some such major premise as "Whenever kettles have been on the fire for ten minutes, they boil." But if our problem is that of justifying induction, then this major premise itself embodies an inductive assertion that stands in

[9] P. F. Strawson, *Introduction to Logical Theory* (London, 1952), p. 250.
[10] *Treatise*, pp. 89, 91.

need of justification. For the transition which constitutes the problem has been justified in the passage
from minor premise to conclusion only at the cost of
reappearing, as question-beggingly as ever, within the
major premise. To fall back on some yet more general
assertion as a premise from which "Whenever kettles
have been on the fire for ten minutes they boil" could
be derived would merely remove the problem one
stage farther and would be to embark on a regress,
possibly infinite and certainly pointless.

If then it is pointless to present inductive arguments
as deductive what special reason is there in the case of
moral arguments for attempting to present them as
deductive? If men arguing about morality, as Bishop
Mortimer is arguing, pass from "God made us" to "We
ought to obey God," why should we assume that the
transition must be an entailment? I suspect that our
inclination to do this may be that we fear the alternative. Hare suggests that the alternative to his view is
"that although, in the strict sense of the word, I have
indeed shown that moral judgments and imperatives
cannot be *entailed* by factual premisses, yet there is
some looser relation than entailment which holds between them." I agree with Hare in finding the doctrine
of what he calls "loose" forms of inference objection-
able; although I cannot indeed find this doctrine present in, for example, S. E. Toulmin's *The Place of Reason in Ethics* [Cambridge, 1950] which Hare purports
to be criticizing. And certainly entailment relations
must have a place in moral argument, as they do in
scientific argument. But since there are important
steps in scientific argument which are not entail-

ments, it might be thought that to insist that the relation between factual statements and moral conclusions be deductive or nonexistent would be likely to hinder us in elucidating the character of moral arguments.

How does this bear on the interpretation of Hume? It might be held that, since Hume holds in some passages on induction at least that arguments are deductive or defective, we could reasonably expect him to maintain that since factual premises cannot entail moral conclusions—as they certainly cannot—there can be no connections between factual statements and moral judgments (other perhaps than psychological connections). But at this point all I am suggesting is that our contemporary disapproval of Hume on induction makes our contemporary approval of what we take to be Hume on facts and norms seem odd. It is only now that I want to ask whether—just as Hume's attitude to induction is much more complex than appears in his more skeptical moments and is therefore liable to misinterpretation—his remarks on "is" and "ought" are not only liable to receive but have actually received a wrong interpretation.

III

The approach will still be oblique. What I want to suggest next is that if Hume does affirm the impossibility of deriving an "ought" from an "is" then he is the first to perform this particular impossibility. But before I proceed to do this, one general remark is worth making. It would be very odd if Hume did affirm the logical irrelevance of facts to moral judgments, for the whole difference in atmosphere—and it is very marked—between his discussion of morality and those of, for example, Hare and Nowell-Smith springs from his interest in the facts of morality. His work is full of anthropological and sociological remarks, remarks sometimes ascribed by commentators to the confusion between logic and psychology with which Hume is so often credited. Whether Hume is in general guilty of this confusion is outside the scope of this paper to discuss. But so far as his moral theory is concerned, the sociological comments have a necessary place in the whole structure of argument.

Consider, for example, Hume's account of justice. To call an act "just" or "unjust" is to say that it falls under a rule. A single act of justice may well be contrary to either private or public interest or both.

> But however single acts of justice may be contrary, either to public or to private interest, 'tis certain, that the whole plan or scheme is highly conducive, or indeed absolutely requisite both to the support of society, and the well-being of every individual. 'Tis impossible to separate the good from the ill. Property must be stable, and must be fix'd by general rules. Tho' in one instance the public be a sufferer, this momentary ill is amply compensated by the steady prosecution of the rule, and by the peace and order, which it establishes in society.[11]

Is Hume making a moral point or is he asserting a causal sociological connection or is he making a logical point? Is he saying that it is logically appropriate to

[11] *Ibid.*, p. 497.

justify the rules of justice in terms of interest or that to observe such rules does as a matter of fact conduce to public interest or that such rules are in fact justified because they conduce to public interest? All three. For Hume is asserting both that the logically appropriate way of justifying the rules of justice is an appeal to public interest and that in fact public interest is served by them so that the rules are justified. And that Hume is clearly both justifying the rules and affirming the validity of this type of justification cannot be doubted in the light of the passage which follows.

> And even every individual person must find himself a gainer on ballancing the account; since, without justice, society must immediately dissolve, and everyone must fall into that savage and solitary condition, which is infinitely worse than the worst situation that can possibly be suppos'd in society.

Moreover, this type of argument is not confined to the *Treatise*; elsewhere also Hume makes it clear that he believes that factual considerations can justify or fail to justify moral rules. Such considerations are largely appealed to by Hume in his arguments in the essay "On Suicide" that suicide is morally permissible.

To return to the justification of justice: Hume clearly affirms that the justification of the rules of justice lies in the fact that their observance is to everyone's long-term interest; that we ought to obey the rules because there is no one who does not gain more than he loses by such obedience. But this is to derive an "ought" from an "is." If Hare, Nowell-Smith, and Prior have interpreted Hume correctly, Hume is contravening his own prohibition. Someone might argue, however, that Hume only appears to contravene it. For, if we ignore the suggestion made earlier in this paper that the attempt to present moral arguments as entailments may be misconceived, we may suppose that Hume's argument is defective in the way that Bishop Mortimer's is and attempt to repair it in the way Nowell-Smith repairs the other. Then the transition from the minor premise, "Obedience to this rule would be to everyone's long-term interest," to the conclusion, "We ought to obey this rule," would be made by means of the major premise, "We ought to do whatever is to everyone's long-term interest." But if this is the defense of Hume, if Hume needs defense at this point, then he is indefensible. For the locution offered as a candidate for a major premise, "We ought to do what is to everyone's long-term interest," cannot function as such a premise for Hume since in his terms it could not be a moral principle at all, but at best a kind of compressed definition. That is, the notion of "ought" is for Hume only explicable in terms of the notion of a consensus of interest. To say that we ought to do something is to affirm that there is a commonly accepted rule; and the existence of such a rule presupposes a consensus of opinion as to where our common interests lie. An obligation is constituted in part by such a consensus and the concept of "ought" is logically dependent on the concept of a common interest and can only be explained in terms of it. To say that we ought to do what is to the common interest would therefore be either to utter an aphoristic and misleading truism or else to use the term "ought" in a sense quite other than that understood by Hume. Thus the locution "We ought to do what is to everyone's long-term interest" could not lay down a moral principle which might figure as a major premise in the type of syllogism which Hare describes.

The view which Hume is propounding can perhaps be illuminated by a comparison with the position of J. S. Mill. On the interpretation of Mill's ethics for which J. O. Urmson has convincingly argued,[12] Mill did not commit the naturalistic fallacy of deriving the principle that "We ought to pursue the greatest happiness of the greatest number" from some statement about what we ourselves or all men desire. He did not commit this fallacy for he did not derive his principle at all. For Mill "We ought to pursue the greatest happiness of the greatest number" is the supreme moral principle. The difference between Mill's utilitarianism and Hume's lies in this: that if we take some such statement as "We ought to do whatever is to the advantage of most people," this for Mill would be a moral principle which it would be morally wrong to deny, but which it would make sense to deny. Whereas for Hume to deny this statement would be senseless, for it would detach "ought" from the notion of a consensus of interest and so evacuate it of meaning. Roughly speaking, for Mill such a principle would be a contingent moral truth; for Hume it would be a necessary truth underlying morality.

Moreover, Hume and Mill can be usefully contrasted in another respect. Mill's basic principle is a moral affirmation independent of the facts: so long as some

[12] J. O. Urmson, "The Interpretation of the Philosophy of J. S. Mill," *Philosophical Quarterly*, III (1953), 33.

course of action will produce more happiness for more people than alternative courses will, it provides at least some sort of effective moral criterion. But at any rate, so far as that part of his doctrine which refers to justice is concerned, it is quite otherwise with Hume. We have moral rules because we have common interests. Should someone succeed in showing us that the facts are different from what we conceive them to be so that we have no common interests, then our moral rules would lose their justification. Indeed the initial move of Marx's moral theory can perhaps be best understood as a denial of the facts which Hume holds to constitute the justification for social morality. Marx's denial that there are common interests shared by the whole of society in respect of, for instance, the distribution of property meets Hume on his own ground. (We may note in passing that the change from Hume's characterization of morality in terms of content, with its explicit reference to the facts about society, to the attempt by later writers to characterize morality purely in terms of the form of moral judgments is what Marxists would see as the significant change in philosophical ethics. Since I would agree with Marxists in thinking this change a change for the worse—for reasons which I shall indicate later in the argument—I have been tempted to retitle this paper "Against Bourgeois Formalism in Ethics.")

One last point on the contrast between Hume and Mill: since Mill's basic principle in ethics is a moral principle, but Hume's is a definition of morality, they demand different types of defense. How does Hume defend his view of the derivation of morality from interest? By appeal to the facts. How do we in fact induce someone to do what is just? How do we in fact justify just actions on our own part? In observing what answers we have to give to questions like these, Hume believes that his analysis is justified.[13]

IV

What I have so far argued is that Hume himself derives "ought" from "is" in his account of justice. Is he then inconsistent with his own doctrine in that famous passage? Someone might try to save Hume's consistency by pointing out that the derivation of "ought" from "is" in the section on justice is not an entailment and that all Hume is denying is that "is" statements can entail "ought" statements, and that this is quite correct. But to say this would be to misunderstand the passage. For I now want to argue that in fact Hume's positive suggestions on moral theory are actually an answer to a question posed in the "is" and "ought" passage, and that that passage has nothing to do with the point about entailment at all. The arguments here are twofold.

First, Hume does not actually say that one cannot pass from an "is" to an "ought" but only that it "seems altogether inconceivable" how this can be done. We have all been brought up to believe in Hume's irony so thoroughly that it may occasionally be necessary to remind ourselves that Hume need not necessarily

13 J. O. Urmson, "The Interpretation of the Philosophy of J. S. Mill," *Philosophical Quarterly*, III (1953), 498.

mean more or other than he says. Indeed the rhetorical and slightly ironical tone of the passage renders it all the more ambiguous. When Hume asks how what seems altogether inconceivable may be brought about, he may be taken to be suggesting either that it simply cannot be brought about or that it cannot be brought about in the way in which "every system of morality which I have hitherto met with" has brought it about. In any case it would be odd if Hume thought that "observations concerning human affairs" necessarily could not lead on to moral judgments since such observations are constantly so used by Hume himself.

Second, the force of the passage as it is commonly taken depends on what seems to be its manifest truth: "is" cannot entail "ought." But the notion of entailment is read into the passage. The word Hume uses is "deduction." We might well use this word as a synonym for entailment, and even as early as Richard Price's moral writings it is certainly so used. But is it used thus by Hume? The first interesting feature of Hume's use of the word is its extreme rarity in his writings. When he speaks of what we should call "deductive arguments" he always uses the term "demonstrative arguments." The word "deduction" and its cognates have no entry in Selby-Bigge's indexes at all, so that its isolated occurrence in this passage at least stands in need of interpretation. The entries under "deduction" and "deduce" in the Oxford English Dictionary make it quite clear that in ordinary eighteenth-century use these were likely to be synonyms rather for "inference" and "infer" than for "entailment" and "entail." Was this Hume's usage? In the essay entitled

"That Politics may be Reduced to a Science," Hume writes, "So great is the force of laws, and of particular forms of government, and so little dependence have they on the humours and tempers of men, that consequences almost as general and certain may sometimes be deduced from them as any which the mathematical sciences afford us."[14] Clearly, to read "be entailed by" for "deduced from" in this passage would be very odd. The reference to mathematics might indeed mislead us momentarily into supposing Hume to be speaking of "entailment." But the very first example in which Hume draws a deduction makes it clear how he is using the term. From the example of the Roman republic which gave the whole legislative power to the people without allowing a negative voice either to the nobility or the consuls and so ended up in anarchy, Hume concludes in general terms that "Such are the effects of democracy without a representative." That is, Hume uses past political instances to support political generalizations in an ordinary inductive argument, and he uses the term "deduce" in speaking of this type of argument. "Deduction" therefore must mean "inference" and cannot mean "entailment."

Hume, then, in the celebrated passage does not mention entailment. What he does is to ask how and if moral rules may be inferred from factual statements, and in the rest of Book III of the *Treatise* he provides an answer to his own question.

[14] Hume, *The Philosophical Works*, ed. T. H. Green and T. H. Grose, 4 vols. (London, 1874–75), III, 99.

V

There are, of course, two distinct issues raised by this paper so far. There is the historical question of what Hume is actually asserting in the passage under discussion, and there is the philosophical question of whether what he does assert is true and important. I do not want to entangle these two issues overmuch, but it may at this point actually assist in elucidating what Hume means to consider briefly the philosophical issues raised by the difference between what he actually does say and what he is customarily alleged to say. Hume is customarily alleged to be making a purely formal point about "ought" and "is," and the kind of approach to ethics which makes such formal analyses central tends to lead to one disconcerting result. The connection between morality and happiness is made to appear purely contingent and accidental. "One ought to . . ." is treated as a formula where the blank space might be filled in by almost any verb which would make grammatical sense. "One ought occasionally to kill someone" or "One ought to say what is not true" are not examples of moral precepts for more than the reason that they are at odds with the precepts by which most of us have decided to abide. Yet if ethics is a purely formal study any example ought to serve. If a philosopher feels that the connection between morality and happiness is somehow a necessary one, he is likely to commit, or at least be accused of, the naturalistic fallacy of defining moral words in factual terms. It is obvious why philosophers should seem to be faced with this alternative of committing the naturalistic fallacy or else making the connection between morality and happiness contingent and accidental. This alternative is rooted in the belief that the connections between moral utterances and factual statements must be entailments or nothing. And this belief arises out of accepting formal calculi as models of argument and then looking for entailment relations in nonformal discourse.

To assert that it is of the first importance for ethics to see that the question of the connection between morality and happiness is a crucial one is not, of course, to allow that Hume's treatment of it is satisfactory. But at least Hume did see the need to make the connection, whereas the "is" and "ought" passage has been interpreted in such a way as to obscure this need.

Second, the reinterpretation of this passage of Hume allows us to take up the whole question of practical reasoning in a more fruitful way than the formalist tradition in ethics allows. If anyone says that we cannot make valid inferences from an "is" to an "ought," I should be disposed to offer him the following counterexample: "If I stick a knife in Smith, they will send me to jail; but I do not want to go to jail; so I ought not to (had better not) stick a knife in him." The reply to this may be that there is no doubt that this is a valid inference (I do not see how this could be denied) but that it is a perfectly ordinary entailment relying upon the suppressed major premise "If it is the case that if I do x, the outcome will be y, then if I don't want y to happen, I ought not to do *x*." This will certainly make the argument in question an entailment; but there seem to me three good reasons for not treating the argument in this way. First, inductive arguments could be rendered deductive in this way, but, as we have already noted, only a superstitious devotee of entailment could possibly want to present them as such. What additional reason could there be in the case of moral arguments that is lacking in the case of inductive arguments? Moreover, a reason akin to that which we have for not proceeding in this way with inductive arguments can be adduced in this use also, namely, that we may have made our argument into an entailment by adding a major premise; but we have reproduced the argument in its non-entailment form as that premise, and anything questionable in the original argument remains just as questionable inside the major premise. That premise itself is an argument and one that is not an entailment; to make it an entailment will be to add a further premise which will reproduce the same difficulty. So whether my inference stands or falls, it does not stand or fall as an entailment with a suppressed premise. But there is a third and even more important reason for not treating the transition made in such an inference as an entailment. To do so is to obscure the way in which the transition within the argument is in fact made. For the transition from "is" to "ought" is made in this inference by the notion of "wanting." And this is no accident. Aristotle's examples of practical syllogisms typically have a premise which includes some such terms as "suits" or "pleases." We could give a long list of the concepts which can form such bridge notions between "is" and "ought": wanting, needing, desiring, pleasure, happiness, health—and these are only a few. I think there is a strong case for saying that moral notions are unintelligible apart from concepts such as these. The philosopher who has obscured the issue here is Kant whose classification of imperatives into categorical and hypothetical removes any link between what is good and right and what we need and desire at one blow. Here it is outside my scope to argue against Kant; all I want to do is to prevent Hume from being classified with him on this issue.

For we are now in a position to clarify what Hume is actually saying in the "is" and "ought" passage. He is first urging us to take note of the key point where we do pass from "is" to "ought" and arguing that this is a difficult transition. In the next part of the *Treatise* he shows us how it can be made; clearly in the passage itself he is concerned to warn us against those who make this transition in an illegitimate way. Against whom is Hume warning us?

Hume himself identifies the position he is criticizing by saying that attention to the point he is making "wou'd subvert all the vulgar systems of morality." To what does he refer by using this phrase? The ordinary eighteenth-century use of "vulgar" rules out any reference to other philosophers and more particularly to Wollaston. Hume must be referring to the commonly accepted systems of morality. Nor is there any ground for supposing Hume to depart from ordinary eighteenth-century usage on this point. Elsewhere in the *Treatise*[15] there is a passage in which he uses inter-

---

[15] *Treatise*, Book I, Part IV, Sect. 2.

changeably the expressions "the vulgar" and "the generality of mankind." So it is against ordinary morality that Hume is crusading. And for the eighteenth century ordinary morality is religious morality. Hume is in fact repudiating a religious foundation for morality and putting in its place a foundation in human needs, interests, desires, and happiness. Can this interpretation be further supported?

The only way of supporting it would be to show that there were specific religious moral views against which Hume had reason to write and which contain arguments answering to the description he gives in the "is" and "ought" passage. Now this can be shown. Hume was brought up in a Presbyterian household and himself suffered a Presbyterian upbringing. Boswell records Hume as follows: "I asked him if he was not religious when he was young. He said he was, and he used to read the *Whole Duty of Man*; that he made an abstract from the Catalogue of vices at the end of it, and examined himself by this, leaving out Murder and Theft and such vices as he had no chance of committing, having no inclination to commit them."[16] *The Whole Duty of Man* was probably written by Richard Allestree, and it was at once a typical and a popular work of Protestant piety, and it abounds in arguments of the type under discussion. Consider, for example, the following: "Whoever is in distress for any thing, wherewith I can supply him, that distress of his makes it a duty on me so to supply him and this

[16] James Boswell, "An Account of My Last Interview with David Hume, Esq.," reprinted in *Dialogues concerning Natural Religion*, ed. N. Kemp Smith, 2nd ed. (London, 1947).

in all kinds of events. Now the ground of its being a
duty is that God hath given Men abilities not only for
their own use, but for the advantage and benefit of
others, and therefore what is thus given for their use,
becomes a debt to them whenever their need requires
it . . ."[17] This is precisely an argument which runs
from "the being of a God" or "observations concerning human affairs" into affirmations of duty. And it
runs into the difficulty which Hume discusses in the
section preceding the "is" and "ought" passage, that
what is merely matter of fact cannot provide us with
a reason for acting—unless it be a matter of those facts
which Hume calls the passions, that is, of our needs,
desires, and the like. Interestingly enough, there are
other passages where Allestree provides his arguments
with a backing which refers to just this kind of matter.
"A second Motive to our care of any thing is the
USEFULNESS of it to us, or the great Mischief we
shall have by the loss of it . . . 'Tis true we cannot
lose our Souls, in one sense, that is so lose them that
they cease to Be; but we may lose them in another
. . . In a word, we may lose them in Hell . . ."[18] That
is, we pass from what God commands to what we ought
to do by means of the fear of Hell. That this can provide a motive Hume denies in the essay "Of Suicide":
obviously in fact, though he does not say so very
straightforwardly, because he believes that there is no
such place.

The interpretation of the "is" and "ought" passage
which I am offering can now be stated compendiously.

[17] Sunday XIII: Sect. 30.
[18] Preface.

Hume is not in this passage asserting the autonomy of morals—for he did not believe in it; and he is not making a point about entailment—for he does not mention it. He is asserting that the question of how the factual basis of morality is related to morality is a crucial logical issue, reflection on which will enable one to realize how there are ways in which this transition can be made and ways in which it cannot. One has to go beyond the passage itself to see what these are; but if one does so it is plain that we can connect the facts of the situation with what we ought to do only by means of one of those concepts which Hume treats under the heading of the passions and which I have indicated by examples such as wanting, needing, and the like. Hume is not, as Prior seems to indicate, trying to say that morality lacks a basis; he is trying to point out the nature of that basis.

VI

The argument of this paper is incomplete in three different ways. First, it is of a certain interest to relate Hume's argument to contemporary controversies. On this I will note only as a matter of academic interest that there is at least one recent argument in which Hume has been recruited on the wrong side. In the discussion on moral argument between Hare and Toulmin,[19] Hare has invoked the name of Hume on the side

[19] R. M. Hare, *The Language of Morals*, p. 45; Review of Toulmin, *The Place of Reason in Ethics*, *Philosophical Quarterly*, I (1950–51), 372; and Review of Nowell-Smith, *Ethics*, *Philosophy*, XXXI (1956), 89 ff.

of his contention that factual statements can appear in moral arguments only as minor premises under the aegis of major premises which are statements of moral principle and against Toulmin's contention that moral arguments are nondeductive. But if I have reread Hume on "is" and "ought" correctly, then the difference between what Hume has been thought to assert and what Hume really asserted is very much the difference between Hare and Toulmin. And Hume is in fact as decisively on Toulmin's side as he has been supposed to be on Hare's.

Second, the proper elucidation of this passage would require that its interpretation be linked to an interpretation of Hume's moral philosophy as a whole. Here I will only say that such a thesis of Hume's as that if all factual disagreement were resolved, no moral disagreements would remain, falls into place in the general structure of Hume's ethics if this interpretation of the "is" and "ought" passage is accepted; but on the standard interpretation it remains an odd and inexplicable belief of Hume's. But to pursue this and a large variety of related topics would be to pass beyond the scope of this paper.

Finally, however, I want to suggest that part of the importance of the interpretation of Hume which I have offered in this paper lies in the way that it enables us to place Hume's ethics in general and the "is" and "ought" passage in particular in the far wider context of the history of ethics. For I think that Hume stands at a turning point in that history and that the accepted interpretation of the "is" and "ought" passage has obscured his role. What I mean by this I can indicate only in a highly schematic and speculative way. Any attempt to write the history of ethics in a paragraph is bound to have a "1066 and All That" quality about it. But even if the paragraph that follows is a caricature it may assist in an understanding of that which it caricatures.

One way of seeing the history of ethics is this. The Greek moral tradition asserted—no doubt with many reservations at times—an essential connection between "good" and "good for," between virtue and desire. One cannot, for Aristotle, do ethics without doing moral psychology; one cannot understand what a virtue is without understanding it as something a man could possess and as something related to human happiness. Morality, to be intelligible, must be understood as grounded in human nature. The Middle Ages preserves this way of looking at ethics. Certainly there is a new element of divine commandment to be reckoned with. But the God who commands you also created you and His commandments are such as it befits your nature to obey. So an Aristotelian moral psychology and a Christian view of the moral law are synthesized even if somewhat unsatisfactorily in Thomist ethics. But the Protestant Reformation changes this. First, because human beings are totally corrupt their nature cannot be a foundation for true morality. And next because men cannot judge God, we obey God's commandments not because God is good but simply because He is God. So the moral law is a collection of arbitrary fiats unconnected with anything we may want or desire. Miss G. E. M. Anscombe has recently suggested that the notion of a morality of law was

effectively dropped by the Reformers;[20] I should have
thought that there were good grounds for asserting
that a morality of law-and-nothing-else was introduced
by them. Against the Protestants Hume reasserted the
founding of morality on human nature. The attempt
to make Hume a defender of the autonomy of ethics is
likely to conceal his difference from Kant, whose moral
philosophy is, from one point of view, the natural outcome of the Protestant position. And the virtue of
Hume's ethics, like that of Aristotle and unlike that of
Kant, is that it seeks to preserve morality as something
psychologically intelligible. For the tradition which up-
holds the autonomy of ethics from Kant to Moore to
Hare, moral principles are somehow self-explicable;
they are logically independent of any assertions about
human nature. Hume has been too often presented
recently as an adherent of this tradition. Whether we
see him as such or whether we see him as the last representative of another and older tradition hinges
largely on how we take what he says about "is" and
"ought."

[20] G. E. M. Anscombe, "Modern Moral Philosophy," *Philosophy*, XXXIII (1958), 1–19.

HUME ON "IS" AND "OUGHT": A REPLY TO MR. MacINTYRE

R. F. ATKINSON

I

In a recent paper in the *Philosophical Review*,[1] Mr. A. C. MacIntyre criticizes what he takes to be the current interpretation of a celebrated passage in Hume's *Treatise*[2] and suggests an alternative for which he claims the important merit that it makes Hume's ethical views self-consistent. The main point that I wish to make in this discussion is the general one that MacIntyre's treatment of the question whether Hume did or did not affirm the "autonomy of morality" is vitiated by a failure to make clear what he understands by that phrase; but I shall also contend more particularly that MacIntyre's arguments against the received interpretation are less than conclusive, and suggest that even on MacIntyre's interpretation Hume's views are by no means wholly consistent with themselves.

From *The Philosophical Review*, Vol. LXX (1961). Reprinted by permission of the author and *The Philosophical Review*.

[1] Reprinted in this volume, pp. 240–64 above.
[2] Book III, Part 1, Sect. 1; ed. L. A. Selby-Bigge (Oxford, 1888), pp. 469–70. (Quoted above, pp. 241–42.)

II

According to MacIntyre, the "standard" interpretation of this passage is that Hume is asserting that no set of nonmoral premises can entail a moral conclusion, from which it is held to follow that Hume is opposed to any attempt to supply a nonmoral "foundation" for morality and accordingly that he is an exponent of "the autonomy of morality."

It is important to get clear what we are to understand by the phrase "autonomy of morality." It is by no means self-explanatory, nor unfortunately is it used with much precision, and it would perhaps be conducive to clarity if its application could be confined to a thesis of Kant's. Nevertheless the phrase is, I believe, nowadays quite frequently used as a convenient label for the view that moral conclusions cannot be entailed by nonmoral premises. I shall call this Autonomy$_1$. This view itself is often confused with or unclearly related to the view that *evaluative* conclusions cannot be deduced from nonevaluative (by which is usually intended factual) premises—no doubt because it is often held that moral judgments are a species of value judgments and hence that if value judgments are not, then neither can moral judgments be deducible from nonevaluative premises. There is a real need for a thorough attempt to disentangle the various views that have been or could be maintained in this field, but it could hardly be started within the scope of the present discussion. For the present purpose it is enough to remark that MacIntyre cannot, or cannot consistently, be using "autonomy of morality" in the sense I have distinguished as Autonomy$_1$, for while he makes it very clear that he is opposed to Autonomy, he nevertheless writes that factual statements "certainly cannot" entail moral conclusions.[3] In fact, the version of autonomism MacIntyre rejects—call it Autonomy$_2$—seems to be the view that factual statements are logically irrelevant to (in a sense stronger than that of "do not entail") moral judgments. The two versions of autonomism are clearly different and are related in the following way: Autonomy$_2$ entails Autonomy$_1$, but not conversely. Autonomy$_2$ is, however, deducible from Autonomy$_1$ *together with* the additional and independent thesis that, as MacIntyre succinctly expresses it, arguments are "either deductive or defective."

If we are concerned to deny that Hume, either generally or in the particular passage under discussion, was an autonomist, it is obviously essential to make clear whether we are denying that he was an autonomist in sense 1 or in sense 2. It is clear that MacIntyre denies that he was an autonomist$_2$, but somewhat unclear whether he also denies that he was an autonomist$_1$; my impression, for what it is worth, is that he does not. But if this is the case, then it would seem very hard for him to maintain that Hume was a *consistent* repudiator of Autonomy$_2$. For MacIntyre admits that in his treatment of induction, Hume does assume that arguments are either deductive or defective—and we

[3] *Op. cit.*, p. 246. Somebody might, but so far as I can see MacIntyre does not, hold that while factual premises cannot, some other sort of nonmoral premises can entail moral conclusions.

shall see in Section III below that he also does so in
at least one place in his ethical writings.

These general remarks have a bearing on the interpretation of the "ought/is" passage in particular. For
if, as I suggest, Hume elsewhere maintains Autonomy$_1$
or $_2$, there is so much the less reason for denying in
order to save his consistency that he maintained
either or both of these views in the passage in question.
Because of this there seems to me to be comparatively
little force in two of the general points MacIntyre
makes against the standard interpretation of the passage.

The first of these is his "general remark" (pp. 246–
47) to the effect that it would be very odd indeed if
Hume did affirm the logical irrelevance of facts to
moral judgments, that is, Autonomy$_2$—odd because
his work is full of anthropological and sociological remarks which have a necessary place in the whole structure of his argument, for instance in his treatment of
justice. The second point, which partly overlaps with
the first, is MacIntyre's observation (p. 248) that
Hume in his justification of justice clearly does derive
an "ought" from an "is"—"derive" apparently here being used in such a way that one can consistently say
both that an "ought" can be derived from an "is" and
that an "ought" is never entailed by an "is."[4]

It is, moreover, only in the light of MacIntyre's apparent assumption that the standard interpretation of
the "ought/is" passage is that Hume is there maintaining Autonomy$_2$—an assumption partly determined

[4] Book III, Part I, Sect. 1; ed. L. A. Selby-Bigge (Oxford,
1888), p. 252.

no doubt by his unclear or ambiguous use of the phrase "autonomy of morality"—that these points seem to have any force at all. For if Hume were maintaining Autonomy$_1$ only—and this I am sure is the standard interpretation, if there is one—he could quite consistently allow that "ought's" can, in some sense, be derived from "is's," that facts are logically relevant to moral judgments. MacIntyre, at any rate, is in no position to deny the consistency of this since he holds such a view himself.

There is a further general point made by MacIntyre (p. 262) against the received interpretation, namely, that it fails to accommodate Hume's thesis that if all factual disagreements were resolved no moral disagreements would remain. I am not sure whether MacIntyre means to suggest that this thesis is actually incompatible with autonomism in either sense, or merely that it is a rather uncongenial associate for these views. I am, however, quite sure that the thesis is not incompatible with autonomism. An autonomist (sense 1 or sense 2) certainly can *consistently* maintain that people fully informed on all factual matters will agree in their moral judgments with regard to a given situation. They will so agree if they make the same fundamental moral judgments or accept the same ultimate moral principles. Whether people do so or not is, of course, a question of fact, but an open question so far as the autonomist is concerned. In the particular case of Hume, I think that Stevenson's exegesis is highly plausible, namely that Hume holds that there will be no moral disagreement between factually fully informed people because he assumes, in Stevenson's view falsely or rashly, that all people are inclined to approve the same sorts of thing.[5] For Hume morality is indeed founded on sentiment, but he also holds that the sentiments of mankind are uniform to a high degree.[6]

III

So much in general terms. Consider now MacIntyre's more particular objections to the received interpretation of the passage in question. (a) The first of these is that Hume does not assert that we *cannot* pass from "is" to "ought" but only that it is very difficult to see how we can (pp. 252–53). We are informed that "We have all been brought up to believe in Hume's irony so thoroughly that it may occasionally be necessary to remind ourselves that Hume need not necessarily mean more or other than he says" (pp. 252–53). "Pass from" is perhaps ambiguous as between "deduce" in the modern narrow sense which is tied to entailment and the more general "infer" or "derive." MacIntyre, however, clearly intends it to be used in the latter, wider sense, for he goes on to observe that (b) Hume is not even asserting that "is" cannot entail "ought."

[5] C. L. Stevenson, *Ethics and Language* (New Haven, Conn., 1944), Ch. XII, Sect. 5. Stevenson perhaps slightly overstates Hume's claim. It might be nearer the mark to say that Hume held that *most* people approve *very much the same* sorts of thing. Cf. A. Stroll, *The Emotive Theory of Ethics* (Berkeley, 1954), p. 77.

[6] See *Treatise*, p. 547 n; *Enquiry concerning the Principles of Morals*, ed. L. A. Selby-Bigge, 2nd ed. (Oxford, 1902), p. 272. The most useful source for Hume's views on this topic is the *Dialogue* printed at the end of the Selby-Bigge edition of the *Enquiries*.

Entailment is read into the passage. Hume's word is "deduce," which in his day and in his writings had the meaning of the modern "infer" (pp. 253–54).

In other words, MacIntyre is denying that Hume in the passage in question is maintaining either Autonomy₂ —objection (a) —or Autonomy₁ —objection (b). Before going on to consider what MacIntyre thinks Hume *is* maintaining, it is perhaps worth observing that neither of his objections is wholly convincing. With regard to (a), while it is clearly true that there are many places where Hume is not writing ironically, I cannot think that this is one of them, though I grant that opinions are likely to differ on points of this nature. Further, on the suggestion that entailment is read into the passage from which objection (b) derives, it seems to me that even if it be true it does not, without the at best dubious support of objection (a), do much to help MacIntyre's case. Certainly if Hume was not talking about entailment because he had not got the concept of entailment as we now understand it, he cannot have been maintaining Autonomy₁ explicitly and in contradistinction from Autonomy₂. But this does not exclude the possibility, indeed it rather suggests, that he was maintaining Autonomy₂. All this apart, I am not sure that it is really plausible to suggest that entailment is simply read into the passage. For, as Professor Flew[7] has pointed out to me, Hume thinks it worthy of remark that the relations expressed by "ought" and "ought not" are "entirely different" from those expressed by "is" and "is not." And this,

---

[7] To whom, and to my colleague Mr. Montefiore, I am indebted for a number of valuable comments.

so far as it goes, suggests that it is something akin to entailment or deduction (narrow sense) that Hume has in mind rather than inference in the wide sense— the crucial difference between entailment and inference being just this, that we may speak of *inferring* conclusions differing from or going beyond, and hence not *entailed by*, the premises. Moreover Reid, a contemporary of Hume and one very much on the lookout for any departure from the common usage of his day, interprets the "ought/is" passage as if it concerned the entailment or deduction (narrow sense) of moral conclusions.[8] He does not deny that "ought" expresses a different relation (though he will not have it that there is anything unfamiliar or unintelligible about it), nor does he suggest that this relation can be deduced or in some other sense derived or inferred from other relations entirely different from it. He is content to insist that the first principles of morals are not deductions at all but, like axioms in other fields, self-evident truths, and that moral truths which are not self-evident are deduced from the first principles of morals and not from relations entirely different from them.

We have seen what, in MacIntyre's opinion, Hume is *not* trying to show in the "ought/is" passage. What, then, is he supposed to be doing? The suggestion is that he is first urging us to take note of the key point where we pass from "is" to "ought" and arguing that it is a difficult transition. He is not arguing that it cannot be made, only that it can be made legitimately or

---

[8] Thomas Reid, *Essays on the Active Powers of Man* (Edinburgh, 1788), Essay V, Ch. vii, pp. 480–82. Cf. A. N. Prior, *Logic and the Basis of Ethics* (Oxford, 1949), p. 33.

illegitimately. And in the next part of the *Treatise*, he shows how it can legitimately be done. In fact what Hume is warning us against is not the attempt to provide a basis for morality—he himself goes on to supply one—but against those who try to supply a particular sort of basis, namely, a religious one. Given the ordinary eighteenth-century use of the term "vulgar" the "vulgar systems" he expects to subvert cannot be philosophical systems (for example Wollaston's), but they very well could be religious systems (pp. 258–60).

I do not think very much weight can be attached to the ordinary eighteenth-century use of the term "vulgar," for in the *Enquiry concerning the Principles of Morals* Hume refers to the "vulgar dispute" concerning the respective degrees of benevolence and self-love in human nature and this surely was a dispute which figured in philosophical writings.[9] And, incidentally, the "ought/is" passage itself opens with a reference to *every* system of morality, which surely suggests that the term "vulgar" when it is introduced later on is being used in a pejorative rather than a purely classificatory sense. But even if Hume did not have *philosophical* systems in mind when he wrote the passage it does not follow that he was not there maintaining Autonomy$_1$ or Autonomy$_2$. The most natural approach is, it seems to me, to take the passage in the context of the section of which it forms the last paragraph—the section headed "Moral Distinctions not deriv'd from Reason." Viewed in this light, Hume's position would seem to have been this: that he thought that he had disposed of the philosophical systems in the earlier part of the

[9] P. 270.

section by showing that virtue and vice consist neither in "relations of ideas" nor in "matters of fact." (This surely amounts to Autonomy$_1$ at least, even though it may be anachronistic to suppose that Hume's distinction exactly coincides with the analytic-a priori synthetic-a posteriori distinction as it is commonly drawn today, and even though Hume tends to write as if he—inconsistently—regarded moral judgments not as expressing approval, but rather as statements to the effect that the speaker or others approve certain things.) And then, thinking very reasonably that what has upset the philosophical systems will upset the vulgar too, Hume in the concluding paragraph of the section in effect summarizes his arguments and directs them at the vulgar. The last few lines of the paragraph seem to me very clearly to support this interpretation. The "small attention" recommended is held not merely to "subvert all the vulgar systems of morality," but also to make clear to us—what Hume has labored to show in the preceding parts of the section —"that the distinction of vice and virtue is not founded merely on the relations of objects, nor is perceiv'd by reason."

Be all this as it may, it is instructive to refer to Hume's discussion of Wollaston, whom he takes to have maintained that an action's tendency to cause a false judgment in others is "the first spring or original source of all immorality."[10] Against this he argues that such an attempt to supply a nonmoral foundation for morality is either circular or invalid. The point that it

[10] *Treatise*, p. 461 and n.

is, on one interpretation, circular is made in paragraphs 6 and 7 of the footnote:

> Besides, we may easily observe, that in all those argu-
> ments there is an evident reasoning in a circle. A
> person who takes possession of *another's* goods, and
> uses them as his *own*, in a manner declares them to be
> his own; and this falsehood is the source of the im-
> morality of injustice. But is property, or right, or
> obligation, intelligible, without an antecedent moral-
> ity?
>
> A man that is ungrateful to his benefactor, in a
> manner affirms that he never received any favours
> from him. But in what manner? Is it because 'tis his
> duty to be grateful? But this supposes, that there is
> some antecedent rule of duty and morals . . .

The alternative charge of invalidity is made in paragraph 8:

> But what may suffice entirely to destroy this whimsi-
> cal system is, that it leaves us under the same diffi-
> culty to give a reason why truth is virtuous and false-
> hood vicious, as to account for the merit or turpitude
> of any other action. I shall allow, if you please, that
> all immorality is derived from this supposed false-
> hood in action, provided you can give me any plausible
> reason, why such a falsehood is immoral. If you con-
> sider rightly of the matter, you will find yourself in
> the same difficulty as at the beginning.

Hume has, of course, a variety of arguments against
Wollaston, but one of them, which I have tried to
illustrate by the above quotations, is that Wollaston's
arguments either lack a moral premise and hence are
defective, *or*, if they have a moral premise and so are
deductive, that they are circular and fail to supply a
(nonmoral) foundation for morality. Hume, in fact,

commits himself to the view I have labeled Autonomy$_2$. It is no doubt partly for this reason that MacIntyre takes the trouble to remark (p. 258) that Hume would not have counted Wollaston's "whimsical system" among the vulgar. But even so there is surely little reason to suppose that Hume intended to retract what he had said against Wollaston when criticizing the vulgar in the "ought/is" passage. Nor, clearly, could he have consistently done so. At the very best, MacIntyre's Hume would not appear to be markedly more consistent than the Hume of the so-called standard interpretation.

To conclude: I do not want to be taken as suggesting that MacIntyre's points are unworthy of serious consideration, but only that they are not conclusive against the received interpretation whether that be that Hume is maintaining Autonomy$_1$ or Autonomy$_2$. I think further that proponents of one or other version of the received interpretation ought to be grateful to MacIntyre for arousing it from "the deep slumber of a decided opinion." So much on the interpretation of the "ought/is" passage in particular. On the topic of Hume's ethical views as a whole, I quite agree with MacIntyre that it would be grossly misleading to represent him as taking a view of the same general type as, say, Hare's, and I do not doubt that a Toulmin-type view can fairly readily be constructed out of Humean materials—but so can a Stevenson-type view for that matter. On no such interpretation or re-interpretation, it seems to me, can Hume be made wholly consistent. This is no doubt to a large extent due to his immense subtlety, insight, and open-mindedness. As for Hume's place in the history of ethics, I agree that he belongs to the Aristotelian rather than the Kantian camp, though I find a bit extravagant the suggestion that Hume was the *last* representative of the Aristotelian tradition.

ON THE INTERPRETATION OF HUME

ANTONY FLEW

(1) In his "Hume on *Is* and *Ought*" (*Philosophy*, XXXVII [1962], 148–52), Mr. Geoffrey Hunter discusses the now famous passage on *is* and *ought* (*Treatise*, Book III, Part I, Section 1). (It is perhaps worth underlining, parenthetically, that *now*. For in *Principia Ethica* Moore did not even mention the passage; indeed, there is no reference at all to Hume in the Index.) Hunter challenges what he calls "the Brief Guide interpretation" (BGI). This consists in asserting that Hume here was "claiming or implying that propositions about what men ought to do are radically different from purely factual propositions, and that they cannot ever be entailed by any purely factual propositions."

Hunter begins by referring to an article by his former colleague A. C. MacIntyre; and explains, "my aim here is only to show more shortly and more simply than he does that the Brief Guide interpretation is wrong." This article had the same title as Hunter's, and it was published in *The Philosophical Review*. Since I believe that my colleague R. F. Atkinson dealt very faithfully with MacIntyre's arguments in his own reply, published in the same journal, I shall follow

From *Philosophy*, Vol. XXXVIII (1963). Reprinted by permission of the author and the Editor of *Philosophy*.

Hunter in making no further reference to MacIntyre.[1]

Hunter's basic idea is that the BGI cannot be correct, because Hume himself elsewhere offers analyses of moral utterances which construe these as being themselves statements of fact. Hunter, for instance, points out that, in the equally famous paragraph which precedes the one under discussion, Hume insists: "So that when you pronounce any action or character to be vicious, you mean nothing but that, from the constitution of your nature, you have a feeling or sentiment of blame from the contemplation of it." Hunter's conclusion runs: "Since he thinks that *ought*-propositions are logically equivalent to certain *is*-propositions, it is absurd to attribute to him the view that no *is*-proposition can by itself entail an *ought*-proposition, or that no statement of fact can by itself entail a moral judgment. Thus, the celebrated passage about *is* and *ought* must be interpreted very differently from the way in which it has often been taken during the last ten years."

I want here to do two things. First, in Section (2), to argue: both, particularly, that Hunter has given us no good reason for abandoning the BGI; and, generally, that his fundamental principle of interpretation is illegitimate. Second, in Sections (3) and (4), to try to show: both, more particularly, how we can come to terms with the apparent contradiction which so disturbs Hunter; and, more generally, how the sorts of misinterpretation to which he and others are here and elsewhere inclined may in part result from a common

---

[1] The MacIntyre and Atkinson articles are both reprinted in this volume, pp. 240–64 and 265–77 above, respectively.

contemporary failure to take account of Hume's own main stated interests.

(2) The principle which Hunter is following is one which is often, but tacitly, employed by the more devout sort of Kant or Plato scholar, unwilling ever to allow that his hero actually made mistakes. It is also favored by those philosophers of religion—not by any means always themselves believers—who assume that the philosophical analyst is professionally committed: not just to producing analyses which are in fact correct; but to assuming that no analysis can possibly be correct unless it will allow the belief so analysed to count as rational, or at least as not positively irrational. It is unusual, and in a way refreshing, to find this unsound principle being employed in the defense of Hume; a philosopher who has very rarely been accorded such privileged treatment. Nevertheless, as a principle, it is unsound. It consists simply in insisting that where two passages in an author appear to be inconsistent, one of these passages has to be so interpreted that the apparent inconsistency is resolved. Let us label this, rudely, the Infallibility Assumption.

Now this Infallibility Assumption is quite different from the entirely sound and proper rule that we should always employ all the resources of scholarship in the attempt to show, what may of course turn out not to be true, that any apparent absurdities or apparent inconsistencies in our author are when properly understood neither absurdities nor inconsistencies. The temptation, to which Hunter seems to have succumbed, is to confuse these two principles; and to replace the second, which really is a fundamental rule of sympathetic scholarship, by the first, which has only to be formulated to be seen to be preposterous. This aetiological suggestion is, of course, speculative. But that Hunter's whole argument for forcing some fresh interpretation on to the famous *ought/is* paragraph depends upon the Infallibility Assumption is, surely, certain. Consider again the presuppositions and implications of the sentences already quoted. "Since he [Hume] thinks that ought-propositions are logically equivalent to certain is-propositions, *it is absurd* to attribute to him the view that no is-proposition can by itself entail an ought-proposition, or that no statement of fact can by itself entail a moral judgment. Thus, the celebrated passage about is and ought *must* be interpreted very differently from the way it has often been taken during the last ten years" (the italicizing is, this time, mine).

(3) But, though we may dismiss this insistence that *it is absurd* to hold that Hume contradicted himself as being itself absurd; and though we may reject as preposterous the Infallibility Assumption, which alone could justify the conclusion that this passage *must* be reinterpreted; still there remains the question of what is to be said about the apparent contradiction to which Hunter is pointing. The answer, I think, is: not that we ought to be surprised if we find Hume being slightly, or even very seriously, inconsistent here; but that it would be perfectly extraordinary had he contrived not to be inconsistent at all.

Hunter maintains that "it is a central part of Hume's moral theory that moral judgments *are* statements of fact . . . namely statements to the effect that there is a

causal relation between the speaker's contemplation of
some actual or imagined state of affairs and his feeling
certain 'peculiar' . . . 'feelings' or 'sentiments.'" Now
—waiving the point that in the second *Enquiry* "a
spectator" replaces "the speaker"—it may possibly have
to be allowed that this is perhaps strictly correct. But
it quite certainly gets the emphasis wrong. It would
be so much better to say that Hume's central insight
was: that moral judgments are *not* statements of *either*
logically necessary truths *or* facts about the natural (or
Supernatural) universe around us; *and, hence,* that
"All morality depends upon our sentiments" (*Treatise,*
Book III, Part II, Section 5).

It is the disturbing implications of this fundamental
anthropocentricity which raised the questions about
which Hume was consulting Hutcheson in that letter
of 1740 to which Hunter refers: "I wish from my heart
I could avoid concluding that since morality, according
to your opinion as well as mine, is determined merely
by sentiment, it regards only human nature and human life. This has often been urged against you, and
the consequences are very momentous."[2] The point is
that Hume's first concern was: not with the idea that
moral judgments report some sort of fact about us; but
rather with the contention that they cannot be analysed in terms simply of any sort of statement about
some objective reality entirely independent of human
sentiments and human desires.

Now if this is right, as surely it is, then Hume is to
be regarded as the first parent of all those tough-

2 *The Letters of David Hume,* ed. J. Y. T. Greig, 2 vols.
(Oxford, 1932), I, 40.

minded and this-worldly moralists who are characterized by their opponents as, in an admittedly very broad
sense, subjectivists, and who might, in America at any
rate, label themselves as, in an equally broad and quite
un-Moorean sense, naturalists: such writers as F. P.
Ramsey, Ayer, Stevenson, Hare, Nowell-Smith, Ed-
wards, *et hoc genus omne*. Once we have seen Hume
in this perspective we no longer have any business to
be surprised if we should find that he fails perfectly
and systematically to reconcile what he has to say about
ought and *is* with either of his two positive accounts of
the nature of moral judgment. (It is, nevertheless,
worth underlining that Hume's "observation . . . of
some importance" about *ought* and *is* meshes in perfectly with his primary rejection of the idea that such
judgments are reducible to assertions *either* of logical
necessities *or* of facts about the natural (or Supernatural) world quite independent of all human interest.) No doubt he ought to have said, boldly and consistently, something like: that when we say *This is
wrong* we are not stating anything, not even that we
have certain feelings, but rather we are giving vent to
our feelings; or that when we say *He ought to resign*
we are again not stating anything, but instead uttering
some rather devious sort of crypto-command. But
years of labor and ingenuity have been needed fully
to develop such fashionable and sophisticated moves.

What is remarkable is that he should ever have got
as near to this as he sometimes did. Take, for instance,
the penultimate paragraph of the first *Enquiry*, the
paragraph which serves as a "trailer" for the second
Enquiry; the work which he described in his autobi-

ography as "of all my writings, historical, philosophical, or literary, incomparably the best." This reads: "Morals and criticism are not so properly objects of the understanding as of taste and sentiment. Beauty, whether moral or natural, is felt more properly than perceived. Or if we reason concerning it, and endeavour to fix the standard, we regard a new fact, to wit, the general taste of mankind, or some such fact which may be the object of reasoning and inquiry."

(4) One final point, with implications extending over the whole field of Hume interpretation. The *Treatise* and the two *Enquiries* seem often to be read as if they had been written for submission to the journal *Analysis*. But to understand Hume it is necessary always to remember that he thought of himself as contributing in these works to a would-be Newtonian science of man; or, failing that, to some sort of mental geography. (See, for instance, both the subtitle and the whole Introduction of the *Treatise*; and compare Section I of the first *Enquiry*. Compare too J. A. Passmore, *Hume's Intentions* [Cambridge, 1952], especially Chapter III.) In Hume's view the second *Enquiry* is thus a sort of *Prolegomena to the Mechanics of Morals:* and hence it is entirely appropriate that most of what it contains in the way of philosophy, in the narrowest modern sense, is stowed away in the Appendices.

The present implication of this is that we need to be much more cautious in construing Hume's famous definitions of the meaning of prescriptive moral utterances than Hunter, and many others, have been. Thus, in the first Appendix to the second *Enquiry*, Hume writes: "The hypothesis which we embrace is plain. It maintains that morality is determined by sentiment. It defines virtue to be *whatever mental action or quality gives to a spectator the pleasing sentiment of approbation*; and vice the contrary. We then proceed to a plain matter of fact—to wit, what actions have this influence." Even from the rather limited context which we are able to quote it must surely be clear that Hume's main concern here is not with a question of logical analysis but with issues of psycho-social fact. Consider too, from the same Appendix: "But after every circumstance, every relation, is known the understanding has no further room to operate, nor any object on which it could employ itself. The approbation or blame which then ensues cannot be the work of the judgment but of the heart; and it is not a speculative proposition or affirmation, but an active feeling or sentiment." Or again, and perhaps still more striking, consider, from later in the same paragraph: "And when we *express* that detestation against him [Nero] . . . it is not that we see any relations of which he was ignorant, but that, . . . we *feel* sentiments against which he was hardened" (italics supplied). These passages are all no doubt wearisomely familiar. But they are not being adequately appreciated when Hunter can bluntly assert: "In short, it is a central part of Hume's moral theory that moral judgments *are* statements of fact" (italics original).

The other famous "definition" is that of the *Treatise:* "So that, when you pronounce any action or character to be vicious, you mean nothing but that, from the constitution of your nature, you have a feeling or

sentiment of blame from the contemplation of it. Vice
and virtue, therefore, may be compared to sounds,
colours, heat and cold, which . . . are not qualities in
objects, but perceptions in the mind. And this discovery in morals, like that other in physics, is to be regarded as a considerable advancement of the speculative sciences. . . ." Once again this "definition" too,
when taken in context, does not seem to be intended
by Hume in quite the way in which a contemporary
philosophical moralist might offer a definition epito-
mising his analytical investigations. The emphasis is
all on the alleged psychological and other non-linguis-
tic facts; rather than on what the words, as currently
used, actually mean. The young Hume's choice of
phrase is also, surely, significant. These are the phrases
of the harsh debunker: "You pronounce . . ." but
"you mean nothing but that . . ." When phrases of
this sort are employed the point usually is: not that
this is what your actual words do actually mean; but
rather that this is what, if you would only face the facts
and be entirely honest, you would have to admit. It is
this sort of brilliant harshness which sometimes makes
one want to describe the *Treatise* as Hume's *Language, Truth and Logic.*

REPLY TO PROFESSOR FLEW

GEOFFREY HUNTER

In my original note[1] I did not present the case against the BGI as well as it could have been presented. Let me try again, this time profiting from the criticisms of Professor Flew and others, and especially from the comments of Mr. Bernard Williams.

(1) The Brief Guide interpretation of the remarks about *is* and *ought* in the last paragraph of *Treatise*, Book III, Part I, Section 1, is logically incompatible with what Hume says about moral judgments elsewhere, and in particular with what he says in the paragraph immediately before, in which he makes it clear that for him moral judgments are statements of fact, in the Brief Guide's sense of "statements of fact" (the whole of that preceding paragraph supports my case, and not just the few words I quoted from it in my original note).

(2) The case for the BGI rests solely on the last paragraph of *Treatise*, Book III, Part I, Section 1.

(3) In the last paragraph of *Treatise*, Book III, Part I, Section 1, Hume does not say that no *ought*-proposi-

From *Philosophy*, Vol. XXXVIII (1963). Reprinted by permission of the author and the Editor of *Philosophy*.
[1] Geoffrey Hunter, "Hume on *Is* and *Ought*," *Philosophy*, XXXVII (1962), 148–52.

tion can be validly deduced from any set of *is*-proposi-
tions. Taken in conjunction with (2), this means that
there is no sure textual foundation for the BGI.

(4) The BGI is a quite recent and parochial interpretation of the passage, perhaps only to be found
among some British philosophers and only during the
last fifteen years: these philosophers have themselves
been much concerned with "the logical gulf between
is and *ought*." Take this in conjunction with (3), and
it begins to look as though the BGI has its source as
much in present-day concern with the gulf between *is*
and *ought* as in the careful reading of Hume.

(5) "But if the BGI is wrong, what does the famous
paragraph mean?" Here my original note was inadequate: I had all the pieces in my hands but I did not
fit them together properly. In that note I said that
what Hume was objecting to in earlier writers was their
failure to explain how *ought* can be deduced from *is*,
and that Hume himself set out to repair this deficiency.
But, as Bernard Williams pointed out to me, to draw
attention to earlier writers' failure to explain something that could be explained would scarcely "subvert
all the vulgar systems of morality": at most it would
show them to be incomplete. If Hare's interpretation
("Earlier writers deduced *ought* from *is*, and this is
never legitimate") is too strong, mine ("Earlier writers
failed to explain how *ought* can be deduced from *is*")
is too weak. Hume must have meant something more
than I attributed to him.

(6) For what seems to me obviously the right answer I am indebted to Williams. What Hume is objecting to in this passage is, not the deduction-in-

general of *ought*-propositions from *is*-propositions, and
not the mere failure to explain how such deductions
are possible, but the unjustified and unjustifiable deduction of *ought*-propositions from *is*-propositions
that refer merely to relations of reason or of external
objects and say nothing about human sentiments.
Hume is saying: "*Ought*-propositions involve essentially reference to human sentiments or feelings, and
sentiments are the objects of feeling, not of reason or
the understanding. *Ought*-propositions cannot therefore be validly deduced from propositions that refer
merely to objects of reason or the understanding. The
vulgar systems of morality fail to take account of this.
They all involve a move from propositions that according to them refer merely to objects of reason, such
as eternal fitnesses and unfitnesses of things, or else
from propositions that refer merely to relations between external objects, i.e. that refer merely to objects
of the understanding, to propositions about how men
ought to live. But propositions about how men ought
to live refer to human sentiments and cannot be deduced from propositions that are merely about the
relations of objects or are merely about what can be
perceived by reason, i.e. from propositions that do not
refer to human sentiments (cf. the last words of the
famous paragraph: ". . . this small attention wou'd
subvert all the vulgar systems of morality, and let us
see, that the distinction of vice and virtue is not
founded merely on the relations of objects, nor is perceiv'd by reason"). So all these systems involve an unjustified and unjustifiable move from some set of *is*-
propositions in which no reference is made to human

sentiments to *ought*-propositions, which by their very nature do refer to human sentiments." "Earlier writers have failed to explain how the deduction of *ought* from *is* is possible": so far my earlier interpretation was right. But I should have added: "and if you think about what I [Hume] have shown about *ought*-propositions, and if you consider also the nature of those earlier writers' premisses, you will see that in their case the deduction is not legitimate."

It seems to me that there was a good deal of agreement between Flew's reply to my original note and the note itself (see especially p. 151 of my note), and I wonder now whether there is anything in this new and improved version that he really wants to quarrel with. What I was, and am, attacking is the BGI, i.e. the claim that in the last paragraph of *Treatise*, Book III, Part 1, Section 1, Hume said that no *ought*-proposition can be validly deduced from any set of *is*-propositions. Hume did not say this. Does Flew think he did?

"NOT PROVEN"—AT MOST

ANTONY FLEW

I wish I could accept the reconciling project of Hunter's final paragraph.[1] But he has succeeded neither at his first nor at this his second attempt in showing either the need for some fresh interpretation or the adequacy of any particular candidate. I will follow Hunter in his numbering, albeit, I am afraid, in little else.

(1) It is, as I have already suggested (see my (3) above), not right to say of Hume that, without qualification, "for him moral judgments are statements of fact." It is precisely because Hume is uneasy about the implications of saying this that he is himself reluctant to speak here of judgments at all. Thus, in the paragraph immediately following our present bone of contention, he urges: "Morality . . . is more properly felt than judged of; though this feeling or sentiment is commonly so soft and gentle, that we are apt to confound it with an idea . . ."

(2) Hume certainly does present his point about *is* and *ought* as an isolated addendum rather than by making it integral to the development of his account of morality: "I cannot forebear adding . . . an obser-

[1] P. 290 above.

vation . . ." (*Treatise*, Book III, Part I, Section 1).
But one ought not to forget that the next Section includes his distinction of three senses of *natural*, followed by the splendid dismissal: "Nothing can be more
unphilosophical than those systems, which assert, that
virtue is the same with what is natural, and vice with
what is unnatural."

(3) Hunter's bald assertion here would seem to be
true only if to say the same thing one has to say the
very same words. The key sentence is: "For as this
ought, or *ought not*, expresses some new relation or
affirmation, 'tis necessary that it should be observed
and explained; and at the same time that a reason
should be given, for what seems altogether inconceivable, how this new relation can be a deduction from
others, which are entirely different from it"; and this,
surely, has to be construed as an ironically modest way
of putting the point that it *is* altogether inconceivable,
and hence that a reason *could not* be given.

(4) It is indeed only fairly recently that it has become commonplace for philosophers to concede "some
importance" to Hume's observations about *is* and
ought, and to accept his own assessment of the difference between the one and the other as "of the last
consequence." But a belated recognition of the importance of a passage is no sufficient reason for doubting
that it means what it does mean.

(5) and (6) I am at a loss as to how Hunter thinks
that his revised interpretation, or anything like it, is
to be derived from the actual words of the disputed
paragraph. He asserts: "Hume is saying: '*Ought*-prop-
ositions involve essentially reference to human senti-

ments or feelings . . .'" The only passage here which
even suggests any such essential reference is the final
clause, urging that if readers will take Hume's tip they
will see "that the distinction of vice and virtue is not
founded merely on the relations of objects, nor is perceived by reason." Yet the most that this clause can
reasonably suggest is that a reader willing to follow
Hume's present advice will come to realize that sentiments are somehow involved in all moral discrimina-
tions; and this, of course, is a conclusion for which
Hume has been arguing in other ways throughout the
whole Section containing this concluding paragraph.
A suggestion so modest is, however, quite inadequate
to the Hunter-Williams interpretation. For this apparently requires a far more drastic and specific realization; namely, that the *ought*-conclusions, which cannot
be deduced from *is*-propositions stating either the relations of ideas or matters of fact about non-human nature, can be so deduced if we summon in aid as further
premises suitable *is*-propositions about human sentiments. I insert the *apparently* because Hunter never
quite gets around to stating outright that this is what
he thinks Hume is actually saying. It is nevertheless
essential to the Hunter-Williams interpretation that
Hume should be committed to the notion that such
deduction is at the very least not ruled out. For without this possible exception they would be reduced to
the intolerably commonplace view that Hume is really
saying what we might uninstructedly have taken him
to be saying: that *ought*-conclusions generally and
without exception cannot be deduced from exclusively
is-premises.

It should not go entirely unremarked, although this is not by itself a decisive objection against an interpretation *qua* interpretation, that, if Hume had been saying what Hunter and Williams maintain that he was saying, his statement would have been false. A more direct objection is that they are committed to reading Hume's references to *is*-propositions in the second sentence of the battleground paragraph as being tacitly restricted to two sorts; and for this crucial restriction there is here no positive textual warrant whatsoever. Are we really supposed to know that none of the books Hume had read had used any proposition of the other sort in such a context? And do we then have tacitly to supply the appropriate qualifications which Hume himself so improvidently neglected to insert? This would have been indeed a curious oversight, considering their crucial importance for what Hunter and Williams claim that Hume not merely ought to be but is not simply suggesting but saying.

In sum, my answer to Hunter's question is, obviously, "Yes obviously." Furthermore, though this is not an argument but a confession, it is hard for me to discern any compelling reason other than the obviousness of the accepted reading why MacIntyre, Hunter, Williams, and others should find it necessary so to labor to excogitate new interpretations. However, to interpretations also the famous maxim for Balliol men applies: "Even a truism may be true."

HUME ON *IS* AND *OUGHT*

W. D. HUDSON

The famous passage in Hume's *Treatise* concerning "is" and "ought" (quoted above, pp. 241–42) has recently come in for some re-interpretation. Contemporary philosophers were accustomed to interpret Hume as condemning any attempt to deduce *ought* from *is*. But A. C. MacIntyre[1] and Geoffrey Hunter,[2] amongst others, have assured us that he was doing no such thing. So far from condemning this move, he was in fact intent upon making it himself. In the famous passage he was simply complaining "that earlier writers have failed to explain how this deduction is possible" (Hunter's interpretation), or rejecting the way in which religious moralists make the move, that is, "repudiating a religious foundation for morality and putting in its place a foundation in human needs, interests, desires, and happiness" (MacIntyre's interpretation). MacIntyre thinks that Hume's attempt to make the move "shows us how it can be made"

From *The Philosophical Quarterly*, Vol. XIV (1964). Reprinted by permission of the author and *The Philosophical Quarterly*.

[1] A. C. MacIntyre, "Hume on 'Is' and 'Ought,'" reprinted in this volume, pp. 240–64 above.

[2] Geoffrey Hunter, "Hume on *Is* and *Ought*," *Philosophy* XXXVII (1962), 148–52.

(p. 258); Hunter, on the other hand, says that Hume was "mistaken" (p. 151). But, in the view that he was attempting to make it, they are at one. I do not think that they have proved their point. Two issues are involved here, of course: (i) what was Hume's opinion in this matter of *is* and *ought?* and (ii) what is the correct view? I shall try not to confuse them.

I

Hunter calls attention to a paragraph, immediately before the famous one, in which Hume says:

> . . . when you pronounce any action or character to be vicious, you mean nothing, but that from the constitution of your nature you have a feeling or sentiment of blame from the contemplation of it.

The crucial word here is "mean." Hunter's interpretation of this passage runs as follows: "This is no casual statement. . . . What Hume is saying here is that 'This action is vicious' just means 'Contemplation of this action causes a feeling or sentiment of blame in me.' Now the statement 'Contemplation of this action causes a feeling or sentiment of blame in me' *is a statement of fact.* . . . And Hume obviously thinks that a similar sort of analysis holds good for all moral judgments . . ." Hunter brings out explicitly what he takes the force of Hume's "mean" to be: "In short, it is a central part of Hume's moral theory that moral judgments *are* statements of fact" (p. 149). But was it Hume's concern here to maintain that moral

judgments are statements of fact? He was certainly intent upon maintaining that they are not matters of
fact "which can be discover'd by the understanding"
(*Treatise*, Book III, Part i, Sect. 1). If his moral philosophy is set in its historical context, it will be seen
that its purport was to rebut the doctrine of rational
intuitionists, such as Cudworth, Clarke or Richard
Price, that moral attributes are non-natural, objective
properties, apprehended by reason. The only matters
of fact involved, when moral judgments are made,
Hume asserts, are "certain passions, motives, volitions
and thoughts." "You never can find it (*sc.* the viciousness of wilful murder) till you turn your reflexion into
your own breast, and find a sentiment of disapprobation, which arises in you, towards this action" (*ibid.*).
It is now that Hume makes his remark that, when we
pronounce an act to be vicious, we "mean nothing but"
that we have a sentiment of blame towards it. What
shall we take his point to be: (*a*) the positive one that
"X is vicious" is equivalent to "I have a sentiment of
blame towards X," or (*b*) the negative one that "X is
vicious" is not equivalent to "X has a non-natural, objective property of viciousness, apprehended by reason"? In support of taking it to be the latter, the fact
may be adduced that Hume's whole section is headed
"Moral distinctions not deriv'd from reason."

Professor A. Flew argues that Hume's contention in
his "mean nothing but" is not that the words "X is
vicious" do actually mean "I have a sentiment of
blame towards X," but rather that this is what "if you
would only face the facts and be entirely honest, you

would have to admit."[3] But just why did Hume want his readers to admit this? There are two conceivable answers.

(i) He might conceivably have wished to establish the psychological thesis that, when we say "X is vicious," we are experiencing, or have experienced in the past, a particular sort of feeling about X. The purport of the word "mean" is not infrequently that some such inference can be drawn. For instance, "He said that he was going home; that meant he was bored." Whether, when we say "X is vicious," we mean that we have a sentiment of blame towards X in this sense is not a logical, but an empirical question, to be answered, not by analysis, but observation. But is it really credible that Hume's contention was simply that certain psychological inferences can be drawn from the fact that we make the moral judgments which we do? If it was simply this, then it was irrelevant to the debate in which it was a contribution, for any of the rationalists would have conceded that investigation might conceivably show that moral judgments were always accompanied by certain feelings. This, however, was entirely beside their point, which was that moral judgments have a certain logical character, namely that of being statements of objective, non-natural fact.

(ii) This brings us to the second conceivable answer to our question. Hume may have wished us to admit that moral judgments are subjective, i.e. that, when we say "X is vicious," we are voicing our own reaction to it, not stating some fact about it, as the

[3] Antony Flew, "On the Interpretation of Hume," reprinted in this volume, p. 286.

proponents of moral objectivism maintained. Hume
writes: "To have the sense of virtue, is nothing but to
feel a satisfaction of a particular kind from the contemplation of a character" (*op. cit.*). Now feeling, or
rather giving vent to feeling, is not the same logical or
linguistic activity as saying that you are having a feeling. Hume, it is true, did not draw this distinction as
sharply as a contemporary philosopher would; but it
cannot be doubted that, however confused he was
about it, it was his concern to make a logical point
about moral judgments against the rationalists, rather
than to advance a thesis in psychology. It is with this
in mind that his "mean nothing but" should be interpreted. His contention, to use contemporary terms,
was that moral judgments are emotive or subjective.
But moral judgments even if emotive—one might say
particularly if emotive—are logically distinct from statements of psychological fact, and I do not think that it
can be shown to follow, from the indisputable fact that
Hume made much of the feeling element in moral
judgment, that he intended to equate "X is vicious"
with "I have such-and-such a feeling for X." He tells
us that he has been listening carefully to the uses made
of *is* and *ought* (see the passage cited at the beginning of this discussion) and has been puzzled as to
how men get from one to the other. But what was he
puzzled about? If one could take the view that he was
intent solely upon subverting religious morality, or
some other particular system, then one could perhaps
assume that his puzzlement had to do with how men
could credit the particular set of is-statements concerned, e.g. "God gave ten commandments," etc. But

against this, notice that he speaks of "every system of morality," of moralists whose is-statements make "observations concerning human affairs" as well as of those who speak of the being of a God. It is difficult to see what could have been puzzling Hume, if he had not been of the opinion that, when people pass moral judgments, they are doing something logically different from stating psychological or sociological facts.

II

Some contemporary writers, notably Sir David Ross (see *The Right and the Good* [Oxford, 1930], p. 121), have spoken of the logical relationship between is-statements and ought-statements in terms of constitutive attributes, which are empirical, and consequential ones, which are moral. Act X, for instance, has the constitutive characteristic of being wilful murder, and, because of this, the consequential characteristic of being wrong. Without of course endorsing Ross's intuitionism, R. M. Hare (see *The Language of Morals* [Oxford, 1952], pp. 80 f., 153, *et al.*) has the same sort of distinction in mind when he speaks of the "supervenient" character of moral terms. Is there any indication of such a view in Hume? In the following passage, notice the distinction which is drawn between *observing that* something *is* the case and *justice taking place:*

> When therefore men have had experience enough to observe, that whatever may be the consequence of any single act of justice, perform'd by a single person, yet the whole system of actions, concurr'd in by the

whole society, is infinitely advantageous to the whole, and to every part; it is not long before justice and property take place (*Treatise,* Book III, Part II, Sect. 2).

According to Hume here, when we observe that X serves the common interest, then "not long" afterwards, the judgment "X is just" takes place. Whether this can be substantiated or not, as an empirical claim, is not the point. What matters is that observing that something is the case is differentiated from, yet connected with, pronouncing the moral judgment that it is just. Hume certainly does not make the distinction between constitutive and consequential characteristics explicitly. Nor would one claim that he was as clear about it as modern writers. But that nothing of this kind is in his mind is hard to credit. Here, as elsewhere in Hume, adumbrations of modern theory are distorted by his failure to differentiate clearly and explicitly logical from psychological or sociological issues.

The interpretation which MacIntyre puts on such a passage in Hume as that just quoted is as follows: ". . . the notion of 'ought' is for Hume only explicable in terms of the notion of a consensus of interest. To say that we ought to do something is to affirm that there is a commonly accepted rule; and the existence of such a rule presupposes a consensus of opinion as to where our common interests lie. An obligation is constituted in part by such a consensus and the concept of 'ought' is logically dependent on the concept of a common interest and can only be explained in terms of it" (p. 249). A number of doubts arise about all this. (i) I do not think there is anything in Hume which demands the interpretation that "to say we ought to do something is to affirm that there is a commonly accepted rule." Hume, of course, makes much of commonly accepted rules in connection with obligation; and to say that one ought to do something is undoubtedly to *use* or *apply* a rule. But that is not logically identical with saying that there is one. (ii) Does Hume say that the *existence* of a commonly accepted rule presupposes a consensus of opinion as to where our interests lie? He makes much of the fact (if indeed it is a fact) that when we see that a rule is in our interest we are ready to *accept* it; but again that is a different matter. (iii) In what way is obligation taken by Hume to be "logically dependent" on the concept of a common interest? Does he take "X is in the common interest" by itself to entail "X is obligatory"? The close connection which he undoubtedly draws between the notions of obligation and common interest need not be interpreted in this way. R. F. Atkinson[4] suggests that MacIntyre is not denying that Hume would have objected to this way of interpreting it. Be that as it may, there is an alternative open. "X is obligatory" can be taken to be entailed *in part* by "X is in the common interest." If whatever is in the common interest is obligatory, and X is in the common interest, then X is obligatory. It is true that, where there is a consensus of opinion that X is in the common interest, there is likely to be agreement that it is obligatory. If Hume maintains that this is more than likely, then that, Atkinson, following Stevenson, suggests (p. 270),

[4] R. F. Atkinson, "Hume on 'Is' and 'Ought': A Reply to Mr. MacIntyre," reprinted in this volume, p. 267.

is "because he assumes . . . that all people are inclined to approve the same sorts of thing." The important point here is that the particular moral judgment, "X is obligatory," is, on this interpretation, logically dependent on a statement of fact in conjunction with a general moral principle. There is, therefore, an "ought" in the premises as well as in the conclusion. But this can hardly be the logical dependence which MacIntyre has in mind, or takes Hume to have had in mind, because it is perfectly compatible with the customary interpretations of Hume on *is-ought*, in Hare, Nowell-Smith, etc., which MacIntyre claims to be refuting. But I do not see why Hume should not be taken to have had this, however vaguely, in mind, especially in the light of his criticism of Wollaston. Against the latter, he points out (*Treatise*, Book III, Part I, Sect. 1, note) that, from the fact that X is, in a given sense, a lie, it does not follow that X ought not to be done, unless there is "some antecedent rule of duty and morals" to the effect that acts, which are in the given sense lies, ought not to be done.

MacIntyre contrasts Hume and Mill, claiming that Mill's greatest-happiness principle is a moral principle which stands "independent of the facts," whereas Hume's rules of justice would lose their justification "should someone succeed in showing us that the facts are different from what we conceive them to be so that we have no common interests" (p. 251). But is there really any difference here between Mill and Hume? Not if we have been correct in claiming that Hume does not identify saying that something is in the common interest with judging it morally to be just. Mill's principle is "Seek the greatest happiness," Hume's is "Seek the common interest." Both would lose their justification if the facts were different: if, that is, there were no such thing as that which they commend. If there were no such thing as the greatest happiness, this would certainly "evacuate . . . of meaning" Mill's principle, just as MacIntyre says that it would "evacuate . . . of meaning" Hume's, if there were no consensus of interest.

III

Hume writes:

> And thus justice establishes itself by a kind of convention or agreement; that is, by a sense of interest, suppos'd to be common to all, and where every single act is perform'd in expectation that others are to perform the like. Without such a convention, no one wou'd ever have dream'd, that there was such a virtue as justice, or have been induc'd to conform his actions to it . . . 'tis only upon the supposition, that others are to imitate my example, that I can be induc'd to embrace that virtue; since nothing but this combination can render justice advantageous, or afford me any motives to conform my self to its rules (*Treatise*, Book III, Part II, Sect. 2).

The thing to notice here is the distinction which is drawn between a convention or agreement and the circumstances in which it is made. Hume's point is that the convention or agreement by which justice "establishes itself" is made by those who expect others to do the same. But notice that he writes of "motives

to conform . . . to its rules": he differentiates induce-
ments to enter an agreement from the agreement itself. To enter an agreement, for Hume as much as
anyone, it would appear, is to do something which
can be distinguished from expecting other people to
enter it. It is to commit oneself: in this case to "such
a virtue as justice." Hume is quite right: apart from
this agreement or commitment, justice cannot be
dreamed of. It is logically and empirically possible that
no one would commit himself, unless he expected others to do so too or unless they had already done so.
But the circumstances which attend a commitment are
logically distinct from the commitment itself. Surely
it is doing less than justice to Hume to suggest that he
did not realize this! And if he did realize it, then there
are no grounds for supposing that he identified saying
that we ought to do something with saying that there
is a commonly accepted rule.

In support of this theory that the inference from *is*
to *ought* is "in fact made" by Hume, and legitimately
made, MacIntyre speaks of "bridge notions between
'is' and 'ought': wanting, needing, desiring, pleasure,
happiness, health—and these are only a few" (p. 258).
He goes on: "I think there is a strong case for saying
that moral notions are unintelligible apart from concepts such as these." It is undoubtedly the case that
moral judgments are made in situations where we
want, need, etc., and Hume is aware of this; but it does
not follow that he was, or thought he was, deducing
ought from *is*. To say that a game is played in certain
circumstances is not to say that the circumstances are
part of the game; football is played in winter, enter-

tains great crowds, gives many people their living, but
these are not rules of the game. If you score, you may
win a bonus at football, and your motive in trying so
hard may be desire, or need, for the extra money; but
what "scoring" means in this game is logically distinct
from the motives which induce men to try to do it or
the profits they reap by doing it. If by "moral notions
are unintelligible" apart from wanting, needing, etc.,
MacIntyre means that we find it hard to believe that
men without passions would play the moral language-
game, then perhaps he is right. Similarly, one might
say that football would not go on unless men got some
pleasure or other reward from the game. But this does
not mean that, apart from pleasure or reward, the rules
of the game do not make sense.

IV

MacIntyre says that in the famous *is-ought* passage
Hume is "asserting that the question of how the factual basis of morality is related to morality is a crucial
logical issue, reflection on which will enable one to
realize how there are ways in which this transition can
be made and ways in which it cannot" (p. 261).
Hume's main point, he tells us, was that notions such
as the will of God will not bridge the gap, but passions, such as wanting, needing, etc., will. Well, the
gap is certainly bridged. But it is bridged by what
those philosophers whom MacIntyre purports to refute would call "reason-giving sentences" which "turn
out to be practical from the start" (P. H. 'Nowell-

Smith, *Ethics* [London, 1954], p. 82). Hume no doubt believed that "It satisfies the desire for happiness" was a better such reason-giving sentence than "It is the will of God." But this does not mean that he was, or thought he was, bridging the gap between *is* and *ought* in the way which he is generally believed to have condemned.

What Hume says concerning common interests or passions can be subsumed under two heads, viz. (i) that moral judgments are made only in situations where there are common interests or where passions are felt; (ii) that the satisfaction of certain passions, say for security or happiness, is the highest good.

MacIntyre, at the beginning of his article, finds it remarkable that modern philosophers have (*a*) rejected Hume's doubts about induction because they are based on the belief that arguments must be either deductive or defective, and (*b*) at the same time accepted his putative view that *ought* cannot be deduced from *is*, which has the same mistaken basis. But would it not be even more remarkable if, as MacIntyre seems to think, *Hume himself* had (*a*) suspected induction because he thought that arguments must be deductive or defective, and (*b*) at the same time been content to make the move from *is* to *ought*, even though that move is clearly *not* deductive? We might have to conclude that, though remarkable, such was the case, if it were impossible to harmonize what Hume says about interests and passions in their relation to moral judgments with the customary interpretation given to his famous *is-ought* passage. But I have tried to show that this is not impossible.

HUME'S ACCOUNT OF OBLIGATION

BERNARD WAND

It has often been held that Hume's ethical theory is a theory of good and evil rather than one of duty and obligation.[1] In a certain sense this view is quite correct, particularly if one pays attention solely to the *Enquiry*. Yet it may, and often does, suggest that Hume has no worked-out account concerning the nature of our duties and obligations. And this inference is quite erroneous. For Hume does not merely wish to discover the foundation of our moral appraisals; he also desires to discern the reasons for our moral actions. Although the two tasks are intimately related it is necessary, for purposes of clarity, to keep them distinct. Once this is done, and interest focused on the latter, a persuasive account of obligation will be discovered.

I

Hume's account of the motives which prompt men to moral actions is quite complex and it is important

From *The Philosophical Quarterly*, Vol. VI (1956). Reprinted by permission of the author and *The Philosophical Quarterly*.

[1] Cf. E. A. Shearer, *Hume's Place in Ethics* (Bryn Mawr, Pa., 1915), p. 9; C. D. Broad, *Five Types of Ethical Theory* (London, 1930), p. 116; D. Daiches Raphael, *The Moral Sense* (London, 1947), p. 97.

to make several preliminary distinctions if confusion is to be avoided. In the course of his treatment of the nature of moral motivation Hume distinguishes two basic types of action: (1) Those actions which, it may be claimed, men will perform without the aid or influence of reason or custom. The motives to these actions Hume terms "natural." (2) Those actions which it can be expected men will normally perform with the aid or influence of reason or custom. The motives to these actions Hume terms "artificial."

Each of these two types of action may be further distinguished in terms of the specifically moral nature of their motive, viz., whether or not the action is done from a sense of duty. Thus, for Hume, there are four classes of actions: (1*a*) those actions prompted by natural, non-moral motives; (1*b*) those actions prompted by natural, moral motives; (2*a*) those actions prompted by artificial, non-moral motives; (2*b*) those actions prompted by artificial, moral motives.

Hume's purpose must always be kept in mind in any consideration of his account of moral motivation. For removed from their context, and stated in isolation, many of his statements may appear to be misleading. In dealing with actions of type (1*a*) Hume's ultimate intention is to show that it cannot be a natural duty to carry out certain types of obligation such as being just or keeping our promises. As a consequence, he examines the basis of our duties prior to the influence of social custom; and, on his view, apart from the influence of custom, men are invariably determined by the natural partiality of their passions.

According to Hume, in any situation in which only the natural affections of a person operate we expect

that he should be influenced by the motive appropriate to that situation.[2] The action which such a motive
leads to constitutes his duty. But it would never be a
duty unless there were in human nature some natural
inclination prompting a man to perform that action.[3]
The content of our duties, then, in our natural state,
is determined by our spontaneous inclinations. Indeed,
Hume occasionally calls not only the action itself but
its prompting motive a duty.[4]

Moreover, it is the "*natural* and *usual* force"[5] of
these inclinations which determine their appropriate-
ness. It is equally usual and natural for us to prefer our
children to our nephews, our nephews to our cousins,
and our cousins to strangers.[6] And the respective degrees for these preferences are, Hume claims, due to
the original constitution of our natures.

Hume here seems to be assuming that there is a
common human nature in terms of which the "defect
or unsoundness"[7] of our passions or inclinations is to
be judged. But it is not altogether impossible that
these relations themselves may be cultural or social
products. In a matrilinear society, for example, the degree of attention towards our several relations would
be quite differently orientated than it is within west-
ern society.

It should be noted that, in this particular context,

[2] Hume, *A Treatise of Human Nature*, ed. L. A. Selby-Bigge
(Oxford, 1888), p. 477.
[3] Cf. *ibid.*, pp. 478, 518.
[4] Cf. *ibid.*, p. 478.
[5] *Ibid.*, p. 483.
[6] Cf. *ibid.*, p. 483.
[7] *Ibid.*, p. 488.

Hume is giving a quite different account of the origin of our moral appraisals from the one which is normally attributed to him. For the source of our moral appraisals, here, is certainly not a disinterested sympathy with an action's utility or agreeableness. Nevertheless it would be erroneous to impute any inconsistency on Hume's part. For the two different accounts of our moral valuations are intended by him to apply to two distinct situations. The first account purports to give a description of the basis of our moral appraisals in which only the spontaneous affections operate and in which there is as yet no stable social environment. Whether or not such a state exists is, of course, a moot point. But, on Hume's view, in such a state we should expect that our moral appraisals would be determined solely by the passions' "general force in human nature."[8] The second account purports to give a description of the foundation of morals in a stable social environment with which we are all familiar. Here, indeed, our appraisals are impartial and, for Hume, this is due to our disinterested sympathy. But in a state of nature such disinterested sympathy cannot be expected to operate.[9]

If, however, it is the case that in our natural state our duties are determined by the usual force of our inclinations, then it can never be required of us, as our natural duty, to be just or keep promises. For the usual force of these passions is essentially partial or selfish in its nature, whereas the characteristics of being just

[8] *Ibid.*, p. 483.
[9] Cf. *ibid.*, p. 481.

or keeping promises are impartiality and disinterested-ness.[10] Indeed,

> . . . our natural uncultivated ideas of morality, in-stead of providing a remedy for the partiality of our affections, do rather conform themselves to that par-tiality, and give it additional force and influence.[11]

Hume, of course, does not assert that these natural duties cease to function in a stable society. They do function. And both in the *Treatise* and in the essay "Of the Original Contract" he classifies actions, arising from the natural inclinations of men, such as "love of children, gratitude to benefactors, pity to the unfortu-nate,"[12] as moral duties. But his point is that an appeal to such natural propensities cannot possibly explain the obligation which we think we have to be just or to keep promises. As has been seen, he claims that this class of duties may even be antagonistic to the performance of such actions.

The preceding analysis is essentially psychological in its nature. But its acceptance would imply not only that it can never be a natural duty to perform impartial actions, such as being just, but that these actions can never be performed from a natural sense of duty. For since our duties, in our natural state, are always deter-mined by the partiality of our passions, our sense of duty must equally follow their partiality. Conse-quently, Hume's analysis of the foundation of our duties as relative to the normal partiality of our pas-

---

10 Cf. Hume, *A Treatise of Human Nature*, ed. L. A. Selby-Bigge (Oxford, 1888), pp. 488, 518.

11 *Ibid.*, p. 489.

12 Hume, *The Philosophical Works*, ed. T. H. Green and T. H. Grose, 4 vols. (London, 1874–75), III, 454.

sions leads him to preclude, on these grounds, the possibility of our performing impartial actions from a
sense of duty, i.e. of our performing actions of type
(1*b*).

However, Hume puts forth another argument which
is logical rather than psychological in its nature, to
show the impossibility of a sense of duty functioning
as a natural motive to action. It is a type of argument
which has become familiar recently through the work
of Sir David Ross.[13] Hume begins on the assumption
that the moral worth of any action is always determined by the nature of its prompting motive.[14] But
this means, Hume contends, that an action prompted
by a virtuous motive is itself virtuous before any moral
judgment can be passed on it.[15] Hence, a regard for
the moral worth of an action can only be a secondary
consideration.[16] Moreover, to argue that the recognition of the moral worth of an action can serve as its
prompting motive is to argue in a circle. For if a regard
for the moral worth of an action—a sense of duty—
must always include reference to its prompting motive,
then to say that we perform a particular action from a
regard for its moral worth is to say that our prompting
motive to that action is a regard for its prompting motive. Consequently, in view of this logical, or as Hume
himself prefers to call it, "metaphysical," argument, actions of type (1*b*) are ultimately impossible. A sense
of duty can never be a natural motive of actions.

[13] W. D. Ross, *The Right and the Good* (Oxford, 1930),
pp. 4–6.
[14] Cf. *Treatise*, pp. 349, 411, 477, 575.
[15] Cf. *ibid.*, pp. 478, 518.
[16] Cf. *ibid.*, p. 478.

The only condition under which Hume will allow that a person may act from a natural sense of duty is when that person feels a hatred towards himself for lacking a motive which is "common in human nature."[17] In such an event he may perform his duty, not through the impelling passion which normally induces men to perform it, but rather

> . . . from a *certain* sense of duty, in order to acquire by practice, that virtuous principle, or at least, to disguise to himself, as much as possible, his want of it.[18]

Now, it will be noted that Hume does not even here hold that a sense of duty, the mere regard for the moral worth of the action, induces such a person to act dutifully. There must also be some other passion prompting him to do it. In this case it is a hatred which the person has towards himself and the consequent desire to act in the required way in order that he may either eventually gain a disposition which is common to others or no longer regard himself as lacking it.

It cannot be too strongly emphasized that Hume's rejection of any appeal to either the natural operation of our passions or a natural sense of duty as a valid explanation for impartial conduct in no way implies a denial that such conduct is possible. Men may obey certain rules concerning the property of total strangers; they may keep their promises; they may attend the commands of their magistrates; and, finally, despite contrary inclinations, their women folk may re-

[17] *Treatise*, p. 479.
[18] *Ibid.*, p. 479 (italics mine).

main chaste. Hume is merely insisting that none of these activities can be accounted for on a theory of motivation which limits its account solely to a consideration of men's natural passions or a presumed natural sense of duty. And it is in an attempt to explain these types of conduct that Hume is led to incorporate into his own account of motivation the function of reason, custom and convention. These latter concepts lead to the consideration of Hume's analysis of actions of type (2a) and (2b).

Actions of type (2a)—those actions which are prompted by artificial, non-moral motives—have received the most attention in Humean criticism. For it is in this context that Hume considers the relationship which he believes to hold between reason and the passions. A full discussion of this problem would lead well beyond the limited purview of the present study. Instead, an attempt will be made to clarify the meaning of the term "obligation" as it is used by Hume in describing these actions.

The most succinct account of them is to be found in the essay, "Of the Original Contract." In that essay, after having listed those duties of inclination which form one part of our "moral duties," Hume states:

> The *second* kind of moral duties are such as are not supported by any original instinct of nature, but are performed entirely from a sense of obligation, when we consider the necessities of human society, and the impossibility of supporting it, if these duties were neglected. It is thus *justice,* or a regard to the property of others, *fidelity,* or the observance of promises,

become obligatory and acquire authority over man-kind.[19]

In the *Treatise*, Hume terms such actions "natural obligations."[20] It is important to stress that they never constitute for him a moral obligation although, as will be seen, there is an intimate connection between the two kinds of obligation.

Actions of type (1*a*) and (2*a*), both of which are classified by Hume as moral duties, are differentiated by the nature of the motive which prompts them. As has been seen, the former type of action is always prompted by some natural motive, some impelling passion, like that of benevolence. The latter type of action is always prompted by an artificial motive, one which is brought about through the aid of reason or custom. But neither of them is ever prompted by a regard for the moral worth of the action itself. The morality of these actions has reference only to their moral approval, and not to their motivation. And it is because they are considered meritorious that they become duties.

We must not be misled by Hume's employment of the phrase "from a sense of obligation" in his description of those duties prompted by artificial motives. For an examination of the text, as well as a consideration of his usage of the term "obligation," will reveal that Hume does not imply that these actions are ever prompted by considerations of their moral worth. For the phrase "from a sense of obligation" in the above quoted passage is descriptively qualified not by any

[19] *Op. cit.*, p. 455.
[20] Cf. pp. 498, 545.

reference to the recognition of the moral worth of any action as to its possible motive, but by reference solely to the social consequences which would ensue upon our failure to observe the rules of justice or fulfil our promises.

Furthermore, in considering the origin of justice, in the *Treatise*, Hume had declared that moral considerations in no way enter in the establishment of the rules of justice. Only the "degrees of men's sagacity or folly" in discerning the effects of the unrestrained exercise of their passions are relevant. It is reason, not morality, which inhibits the natural operations of men's passions for the sake of a more constant, a more permanent, self-interest.[21]

Now, what makes such actions obligatory, according to Hume, is the recognition, on the part of the agent, of the necessity to perform them when he desires to attain the satisfaction of himself and his family. Granted that this end is desired, it becomes incumbent upon, or obligatory for, a person to be just and to fulfil his promises. Here the obligation does not hold beyond this end so that a person would not be obliged in those cases in which the satisfaction of the interests of oneself or of one's family could be better attained through violating the rules of justice or breaking promises.

Hume's denial that a sense of duty can ever be an original or natural motive to just action or the keeping of promises in no way precludes the possibility of his claim that such action may be done from some artificial, moral motive. Nor, indeed, does it preclude the

21 *Treatise*, p. 492.

possibility of his maintaining that, even though the average man may *think* that he does these actions quite spontaneously from a sense of duty, careful analysis shows that he can never really perform them in this way.

It is in giving an account of those actions which we believe ourselves to be specifically morally obliged to perform that Hume develops his own positive account concerning actions of type (2*b*)—those actions which are prompted by moral, artificial motives.

Hume takes it as a datum of our moral life that we often do behave disinterestedly from a sense of duty. He never denies that such is the case. What he denies is only the claim that the motive to such action can ever be explained as being either an original or natural one. His own explanation is, indeed, quite complicated and the tendency to simplify his account has resulted in some misapprehension about it.[22]

In essence, what Hume is attempting to do in his account of the moral motives which prompt us to act in a certain way is to isolate and analyze the many factors which, taken together, constitute what we normally call "moral obligation." As might be expected, his account is a genetic one; i.e. he begins with a description of the first and fundamental element of the complex and shows how additions must have been made to it.

An act of justice is originally an interested act and, as such, it is a natural obligation. However, it can only be seen as an interested action provided that the society in which it is performed is sufficiently small to

[22] See below Sect. III.

allow the agent readily to discern for himself the advantages to be gained from acting justly. Similarly, the advantage of fulfilling one's promise is only readily seen in such a small society. But the growth of society prevents the agent from seeing the disadvantages which would follow from the breach of the rules of justice as would be the case "in a more narrow and contracted society."[23] Nevertheless, although the agent himself may lose sight of the advantages to be gained in being just and instead follow a "more present interest" he is quick to see the disadvantage to himself in someone else's act of injustice towards him. And, indeed, when an unjust act affects someone other than himself he immediately disapproves of it as a harmful act and considers it vicious. At the same time, an act of justice on the part of another is immediately approved as a useful act and is considered virtuous.[24]

Furthermore, both through the application of the general rule beyond actual instances of acts of justice and his sympathy with the valuations of others, the agent recognizes that an act of justice is the *kind* of act which is virtuous whether it be done by himself or others.[25]

It should be noted that on the above view our emotional reaction is no longer merely aroused by a *single* act of justice, but it is now extended to all acts of justice as a *class*, whether they be performed by the agent himself or by others. Hence it is possible to have a certain feeling towards them once they have been com-

---

[23] *Treatise*, p. 499.
[24] *Ibid.*, p. 499.
[25] *Ibid.*, p. 499.

mitted although it would be impossible to have any attitude towards them until some single, individual action had been performed.

Taken by itself, this feeling is insufficient to account
for our moral obligation to perform just actions and
must be sustained by other means. For, arising from
sympathy, its psychological status is that of extensive
benevolence which must, on Hume's theory of human
nature, give way to any challenge by either our own
private interest or that of some immediate friend or
relative. It is therefore necessary that our emotional
reaction towards just actions be reinforced by other
influences.

Habit plays a significant part. After having performed
acts of justice or fulfilled promises for some time
merely through a natural obligation to do so a "new
obligation" arises to perform these acts irrespective of
the advantage which might accrue to the agent. In
this case the feeling of compulsion still remains although its original ground—that of self-interest—has
disappeared; and the agent merely acts through
habit.[26]

Our attitude of favor towards just acts, and disfavor
towards unjust ones, is further strengthened by the
"artifice of politicians."[27] It should be noted, however, that although Hume insists that our attitudes
may be so artifically influenced, they cannot be arti-
ficially created, at least not completely. There must
first be some natural emotional reaction towards acts
of justice, or their opposite, which will lead us to have

[26] Cf. *Treatise*, pp. 522, 551.
[27] *Ibid.*, p. 500; cf. also *Treatise*, p. 523.

a certain feeling towards these actions. For without there being a natural distinction between what is virtuous and what is vicious, all talk about honorable or dishonorable on the part of politicians would be "unintelligible."[28]

The esteem which we have towards acts of justice is further strengthened by the education which we received as children from our parents. Our parents, observing that the more honest men are the more useful they are to themselves and to others, and seeing that honesty has a greater force when sustained by custom and education, not only inculcate into us from our earliest childhood an observance of the rules of justice but teach us to regard such observance "as worthy and honourable and (its) violation as base and infamous."[29] In this way our attitude towards these acts is established in early childhood and gains such strength as to have almost the status of an original and natural principle of our natures.[30]

Consequently, a sense of duty or moral obligation is, for Hume, partly natural and partly artificial. It is natural in the sense that the original distinction between what is right and what is wrong depends upon a natural emotional reaction to certain kinds of actions. It is artificial in the sense that this original emotional reaction must be developed into a set attitude by such social forces as customs, the artifice of politicians, education, if it is to be at all effective as a prompting motive.

[28] *Ibid.*, p. 500.
[29] Cf. *ibid.*, p. 500.
[30] *Treatise*, p. 501.

Hume was quite willing to accept "a regard to justice and abhorrence of villainy (as) sufficient reasons" for the performance of just actions, or the fulfilment of promises, *provided that* the person who is said to perform these actions for such reasons is one who has been affected by social and cultural influences, who has been, to use Hume's own words, "trained up according to a certain discipline and education."[31]

It may be thought by some philosophers, and perhaps most ordinary folk, that such a person is acting from a "natural conscience" or a "natural sense of duty" but in terms of Hume's account what that person calls his conscience or what he believes to be a natural sense of duty or obligation is essentially a complex social product.[32]

The above interpretation of Hume's position is ambiguous in one important aspect: it fails sufficiently to distinguish between an emotion or feeling, such as the sentiment of moral approval, and an attitude which is not merely affective but also conative. This failure, however, is in turn due to an ambiguity within Hume's account itself. The moral sentiment, taken by itself, is affective only; as a species of love, its psychological status is that of an emotion. It is true that it is accompanied by extensive benevolence but again Hume is not too clear whether this benevolence is merely a feeling or an active desire as well. Even if it were an active desire it could not be expected to operate against private benevolence or self-interest.[33]

---

[31] Cf. *Treatise*, p. 479.
[32] Cf. *ibid.*, p. 310.
[33] Cf. *ibid.*, p. 586.

On the above view, then, Hume is taken to mean that although the moral sentiment is originally only an emotion, having no conative status, it can, through certain social forces, become an attitude which is so strong as even to be considered an original principle of human nature, leading us to just actions. And unless this interpretation is accepted, Hume's references to the necessity of social conditioning, discipline, education, and political indoctrination to perform these actions from a sense of duty, become meaningless.[34]

II

Hume's appeal to moral obligation as a motive to just actions has been challenged more than once. But in view of the specific criticisms which have been levelled against it, it may well be that they rest on some misapprehension of his position. I. Hedenius, for example, has claimed that Hume's admission that we may perform just actions from a sense of duty involves him in an internal contradiction. For the moral worth of an act of justice is determined by its tendency to promote the public interest. Yet, according to Hume's own psychology, a regard for the public interest cannot be a motive to just conduct. Hence a sense of duty cannot be a motive to acts of justice.[35]

However, this criticism fails to pay sufficient attention to the artificial character of the sense of duty when it serves as a prompting motive to action. It is

[34] Cf. *ibid.*, pp. 310, 479.
[35] I. Hedenius, *Studies in Hume's Ethics* (Uppsala and Stockholm, 1937), pp. 418 ff.

quite true that a sense of duty can be neither an original nor a natural motive to action. It is also true that public benevolence, taken as a natural motive, is an insufficient stimulus to moral actions. And it is further true that the moral worth of just action is derived, for Hume, from the fact that it advances the public interest. But when we act from a sense of duty, in observing the rules of justice, we do not do so from any natural motive. We regard ourselves as being obliged to act justly only because, according to Hume, we have in the past been sufficiently indoctrinated, disciplined and habituated. Were these latter influences lacking we should, indeed, never be able to act from a sense of duty. Hume can be accused of this particular internal inconsistency only if his own emphasis on the artificiality of our sense of duty is ignored.

But since a sense of duty, as a motive, cannot be abandoned, Hedenius, following T. H. Green,[36] maintains that it must be

> . . . chiefly a regard for the sentiments of the spectator that causes the individual, as a member of society, to restrain his passions.[37]

Consequently, the only possible interpretation of Hume's position is a hedonistic one. We act from a sense of duty because we want to enjoy the pleasure of another's approval. And ultimately, to use Green's phrase, "It is only respectability that (Hume's theory) will explain."[38]

[36] Cf. T. H. Green, *Works* (London, 1918), Vol. I, Sect. 61 f., pp. 366 f.
[37] *Op. cit.*, p. 421.
[38] *Op. cit.*, p. 370.

Now it is not to be gainsaid that there is an element of truth in this charge. Hume would be the last to say that a desire for respectability, a desire to stand in good grace with one's neighbor, does not influence our actions. But he would also be the last to say that such a desire for reputation alone enters into our minds in performing dutiful actions. Indeed, both in the *Treatise* and in the essay, "Of the Dignity or Meanness of Human Nature," he says quite explicitly that a consideration of another's approval is only a *further* influence prompting us to act virtuously and not the sole, or indeed chief, influence.[39] But to admit, as Hume does, that our motives even when acting dutifully are often mixed in no way entails that Hume is committed to a purely hedonistic position.

Nevertheless, severe criticisms can be made of Hume's account of moral obligation even as it is here interpreted. First, moral obligation on this view has no distinctively moral function. It comes into play, according to Hume, only because men have not sufficient insight into the consequences of their unjust actions in a relatively large society. In a small group in which every one of its members can immediately discern that his unjust action is detrimental to the group's interest and, as a consequence, deleterious to his own well being, moral obligation as a prompting motive is entirely unnecessary. Its necessity arises only when the utility of a just action can no longer be seen. Theoretically, any person who was sufficiently rational or calculative could see the consequences of his contem-

[39] Cf. Hume, *The Philosophical Works, op. cit.*, III, 155, and *Treatise*, p. 501.

plated injustice and hence desist. It is only because very few of us, as a matter of fact, are ever so rational that Hume considers an appeal to moral obligation as a motive to just action.

In effect, this view destroys a basic belief about the nature of moral conduct. We do not seem to think that omniscience can supplant morality. We never consider that the function of moral obligation is to serve as a substitute for narrow self-interest. In short, we consider that when we act from moral motives, the nature of our motives is radically different from that of self-interest. And when we endow a deity with perfection we include among his characteristics not only infinite wisdom but infinite goodness.

Secondly, if it is granted that moral obligation is a product of custom, habit, and social conditioning, there is always the possibility that there will be certain persons who, in given circumstances, will abandon their moral obligation to be just once they recognize that it is no longer to their advantage to perform just actions. And yet we should not think that their obligation would thereby cease.[40]

So stated, however, it is quite possible for Hume to provide a reply to this objection. He could claim that we tend to overlook the force which custom has upon us. We are so habituated to performing just actions that even when we recognize that it is no longer in our interest on certain occasions to perform them we will continue to do so. We have become creatures of habit and are controlled by it even where the original ground of observing the rules of justice, our enlarged self-

[40] Cf. D. Daiches Raphael, *op. cit.*, p. 94.

interest, no longer obtains. If, after repeatedly performing acts from a moral obligation to do so, we discover that we are continually going against our own interests, then, and only then, would we abandon our moral obligation. Consequently, Hume could argue that we might occasionally be just from the motive of moral obligation, despite our recognition that it is to our disadvantage, because of the force of custom and habit upon us.[41]

Nevertheless, Hume's account of the nature of moral obligation breaks down at one very crucial point. As an attitude which has been developed by habit and social conditioning, Hume's view of moral obligation precludes the possibility of our recognizing, after deliberate reflection, that within any specific situation a certain action is right, and that our failure to carry it out makes us morally responsible for it. For Hume, moral obligation is passively determined upon us by others. It is true that we approve quite spontaneously the just actions of others, but we cannot perform these actions by ourselves. If we are sagacious enough we may do so through enlarged self-interest but this motive, as Hume recognizes, is a natural, not a moral obligation. Our performance of these actions from a moral obligation is possible only if we have received the necessary training and discipline, i.e. only if others have shaped within us the attitude to perform them from moral motives. But if this is so, then there can be no grounds upon which we could be held morally responsible either for their performance or their non-performance. Instead of being agents, on Hume's view

41 Cf. *Treatise*, pp. 551 f.

we are creatures. And to accept the view that every act of moral obligation must be due to the influence of others upon us is to deny the fundamental moral fact of responsibility.

III

No discussion of Hume's account of obligation would be complete unless it considered an oft-quoted definition of "obligation" which is to be found in his account of the motives to fulfil promises. The definition is as follows:

> All morality depends upon our sentiments; and when any action, or quality of the mind, pleases us *after a certain manner*, we say it is virtuous; and when the neglect, or non-performance of it, displeases us *after a like manner*, we say that we lie under an obligation to perform it.[42]

It is important to note that the above definition of obligation appears in the course of Hume's exposition of our natural duties—i.e. actions of type (1*a*)—and that Hume's purpose is to show that the fulfilment of promises, like the performance of just actions, cannot be considered, apart from the influence of reason or custom, either a duty, or as being done from a natural sense of duty.

[42] *Treatise*, p. 517. Cf. Hutcheson's definition of obligation: "When we say one is obliged to an action, we . . . mean . . . That every spectator, or he himself upon reflection, must approve his action, and disapprove his omitting it, if he considers fully all its circumstances" (from *Illustrations upon the Moral Sense*, in *The British Moralists*, ed. L. A. Selby-Bigge, 2 vols. [Oxford, 1897], I, 408).

As it stands, the above definition states that to lie under an obligation to perform an action is to have a feeling of a certain kind, a feeling which has been occasioned by the omission of an action appropriate to that situation. But if this be the case, it is impossible that in making a promise we should ever will a new obligation. For to will a new obligation is, on Hume's view of obligation in this context, to will a new feeling, a new sentiment. And to will a new sentiment is impossible. Consequently,

> . . . there could not *naturally* . . . arise any obligation from a promise, even supposing the mind could fall into the absurdity of willing that obligation.[43]

It will be seen, then, that one argument which Hume advances against the creation of an obligation in making a promise is that we cannot will a new sentiment, upon the experience of which we would be said to lie under an obligation to fulfil our promise.

Hume advances another argument against the possibility of our fulfilment of a promise being due to any natural duty. As he himself states, it is an argument of the same order as that in which he purported to show that our obedience to the rules of justice could not be either a natural duty or due to a natural sense of duty. He begins by recounting that any claim that a sense of duty can be an original and natural motive prompting us to the fulfilment of a promise must be discounted, since there must first be some motive prompting us to act before there can be any recogni-

43 *Ibid.*, p. 518 (italics mine).

tion of the merit of the action.[44] Furthermore, he
again notes that unless there is some natural passion
leading us to act that action cannot be required of us
as our duty, provided of course that only the natural
operation of the passions is considered. But he states
this point in a negative manner which serves to relate
it to the above-given definition of obligation.

> . . . where an action is not requir'd by any natural
> passion, it cannot be requir'd by any natural obliga-
> tion; since it may be omitted without proving any
> defect or imperfection in the mind and temper, and
> consequently without any vice.[45]

But, in terms of Hume's psychology, there is no natural inclination, no untutored impulse, to keep promises, and since there is no such inclination, it cannot
be, in our natural state, a duty to keep them. At the
same time failure to fulfil a promise cannot put us
under any obligation. For the omission of the act of
promise-keeping does not indicate the lack of any natural passion, which circumstance alone can arouse the
sentiment of disapproval in our natural state. And
Hume makes this point quite explicit. For, in contrast-
ing benevolence to promise-keeping, he notes that "if
no human creature had that inclination (i.e. benevolence) no one could lie under such an obligation."[46]

From the above account it should be quite evident
that this particular definition of obligation is used by
Hume to show that we cannot be expected to perform
such duties as keeping our promises or being just apart

[44] Cf. *Treatise*, p. 518.
[45] *Ibid.*, p. 518.
[46] *Ibid.*, p. 519.

from the influence of reason or custom upon the natural and normal operation of our passions. This, of course, does not deny that the obligation to fulfil promises, or to be just, cannot be a motive to such actions. Hume's point is that the moral obligation to perform these acts can only be properly understood if it is considered an artificial virtue.

Care has been taken to establish this definition of obligation within its proper context because there is a tendency to treat it as an isolated statement. This tendency can readily lead to a misleading interpretation of it. One such instance of misinterpretation is to be found in Rachael Kydd's book, *Reason and Conduct in Hume's Treatise.* Mrs. Kydd, after quoting the definition in isolation, interprets it as follows:

> Moral obligations are related to the thought of virtuous acts. The idea of failing to do those acts which we approve of is itself displeasing to us, and to say that we are morally obliged is to say that we are prompted to perform an action by the peculiar displeasure in its omission.[47]

She admits that in giving this interpretation of Hume she is "guilty of a slight emendation." For, on her view, "to be obliged is to be moved" to do the act, and not merely to feel a certain emotion. She justifies the emendation on the grounds that Hume had elsewhere maintained, in refuting Clarke, that our recognition of the merit of an act and our being moved to perform it are distinct so that it becomes necessary to show some connection between the two.[48] And, ac-

[47] Rachael M. Kydd, *Reason and Conduct in Hume's Treatise* (Oxford, 1946), p. 167.
[48] Cf. *Treatise*, pp. 465 f.

cording to Mrs. Kydd, we are now moved to act because the "thought of omitting an act displeases us."[49]
Furthermore, this interpretation is possible only if, as
she admits, we take Hume to mean that it is not the
motive of the act which is ultimately approved, or its
omission disapproved, but the act taken by itself.[50]
Otherwise, as she recognizes, we are immediately
plunged into the circular reasoning which has been
noted above.[51]

Now, Mrs. Kydd's interpretation is plausible only
if Hume's statement is taken in isolation and divorced
from its particular context. For once the context is
examined it will be seen that Hume makes this definition of obligation in order to serve as the very foundation of his argument that a promise cannot create an
obligation to its performance, that it cannot be fulfilled as a natural duty. As has been seen, on Hume's
view unless there is a natural passion prompting us to
perform an action, its omission does not occasion, in
our natural state, any disapproval. And it is in this way
that he wishes to show that the keeping of promises
cannot be a natural duty. But if this is so it is evident
that, apart from the influence of custom or reason, not
all actions, or their omission, will be reacted to in the
same way; and the way in which they will be reacted
to will depend on the nature of their prompting motives. Consequently, to accept Mrs. Kydd's emendation—in which the nature of the motive is entirely
ignored—is to reject Hume's view that the fulfilment

---

[49] *Op. cit.*, p. 168.
[50] *Ibid.*, pp. 190 f.
[51] See above, Sect. I.

of promises cannot be a natural duty. And surely this is highly paradoxical in the light of Hume's original purpose in putting forth this definition of obligation, viz. that because of it promise-keeping cannot be a natural duty.

Again, Hume's argument that we cannot will a new obligation in making a promise depends directly on accepting the view that a natural obligation is identifiable with a felt emotion.[52]

Finally, it is scarcely plausible to believe, with Mrs. Kydd, that Hume would have accepted her emendation. For it implies a rejection of his whole theory of artificial virtues. That theory would not have been needed if the thought that our failure to be just or to fulfil promises could serve, by merely arousing our displeasure, as an effective prompting motive to such actions. It is precisely because we have not, and indeed cannot have, a natural sense of duty that Hume develops his theory of artificial motivation.

There may, perhaps, be little doubt that Mrs. Kydd's emendation of Hume's position is much more in accord with common usage of the phrase "to lie under an obligation" than the original definition. Nevertheless, it is only Hume's own purport that there concerns us.

The ultimate source of Mrs. Kydd's misunderstanding is probably due to her failure to distinguish between acts of type (1*b*)—those acts which are prompted by *natural*, moral motives—and acts of type

---

[52] Cf. Hume's remark, "It wou'd be absurd, therefore, to will any new obligation, that is, any new sentiment of pain or pleasure" (*Treatise*, p. 517).

(2*b*)—those acts which are prompted by *artificial,* moral motives. That Mrs. Kydd has fused the two together becomes quite evident once it is noted that she makes no distinction between obligations determined within a natural setting and those determined within the context of social and cultural influences.[53] For Hume never denies that moral obligation can lead to the performance of just actions or the fulfilment of promises. All that he denies is that this motive can ever be an original or natural one; i.e. he denies that the mere thought, on the part of the agent, of the moral worth of an action can lead him to perform it even though that thought *may* arouse an emotion in him.

[53] *Loc. cit.,* p. 187.

THE LEGAL AND POLITICAL PHILOSOPHY OF DAVID HUME

F. A. HAYEK

It is always misleading to label an age by a name which suggests that it was ruled by a common set of ideas. It particularly falsifies the picture if we do this for a period which was in such a state of ferment as was the 18th century. To lump together under the name of "Enlightenment" (or *Aufklärung*) the French philosophers from Voltaire to Condorcet on the one hand, and the Scottish and English thinkers from Mandeville through Hume and Adam Smith to Edmund Burke on the other, is to gloss over differences which for the influence of these men on the next century were much more important than any superficial similarity which may exist. So far as David Hume in particular is concerned, a much truer view has recently been expressed when it was said that he "turned against the enlightenment its own weapons" and undertook "to whittle down the claims of reason by the use of rational analysis."[1]

A public lecture delivered at the University of Freiburg on July 18, 1963 and published in *Il Politico*, Vol. XXVIII (1963). Reprinted by permission of the author and the Editor of *Il Politico*.

[1] S. S. Wolin, "Hume and Conservativism," *American Political Science Review*, XLVIII (1954), 1001.

The habit of speaking of the *Aufklärung* as if it represented a homogeneous body of ideas is nowhere so strong as it is in Germany, and there is a definite reason for this. But the reason which has led to this view of 18th-century thought has also had very grave and, in my view, regrettable consequences. This reason is that the English ideas of the time (which were, of course, mainly expounded by Scotsmen—but I cannot rid myself of the habit of saying English when I mean British) became known in Germany largely through French intermediaries and in French interpretations— and often misinterpretations. It appears to me to be one of the great tragedies of intellectual and political history that thus the great ideals of political freedom became known on the Continent almost exclusively in the form in which the French, a people who had never known liberty, interpreted traditions, institutions and ideas which derived from an entirely different intellectual and political climate. They did this in a spirit of constructivist intellectualism, which I shall briefly call rationalism, a spirit which was thoroughly congenial to the atmosphere of an absolute state which endeavored to design a new centralized structure of government, but entirely alien to the older tradition which ultimately was preserved only in Britain.

The 17th century, indeed, had on both sides of the Channel been an age in which this constructivist rationalism dominated. Francis Bacon and Thomas Hobbes were no less spokesmen of this rationalism than Descartes or Leibniz, and even John Locke could not entirely escape its influence. It was a new phenomenon which must not be confused with ways of thought of earlier times which are also described as rationalism. Reason was for the rationalist no longer a capacity to recognize the truth when he found it expressed, but a capacity to arrive at truth by deductive reasoning from explicit premises.[2] The older tradition which had been represented by the earlier theorists of the law of nature survived chiefly in England in the works of the great common lawyers, especially Sir Edward Coke and Mathew Hale, the opponents of Bacon and Hobbes, who were able to hand on an understanding of the growth of institutions which was elsewhere displaced by the ruling desire deliberately to remake them.

But when the attempt to create also in England a centralized absolute monarchy with its bureaucratic apparatus had failed, and when what in Continental eyes appeared as a weak government coincided with one of the greatest upsurges of national strength and prosperity known to history, the interest in the prevailing undesigned, "grown" institutions led to a revival of this older way of thinking. While the Continent was dominated during the 18th century by constructivist rationalism, there grew up in England a tradition which by way of contrast has sometimes been described as "anti-rationalist."

[2] John Locke seems to have been clearly aware of this change in the meaning of the term "reason." In his recently published *Essays on the Law of Nature*, ed. W. von Leyden (Oxford, 1954), p. 111, he wrote: "By reason, however, I do not think is meant here the faculty of understanding which forms trains of thought, but certain definite principles of action from which spring all virtues and whatever is necessary for the proper moulding of morals."

The first great 18th-century figure in this tradition was Bernard Mandeville, originally a Dutchman, and many of the ideas I shall have to discuss in connection with David Hume can be found *in nuce* in his writings.[3] That Hume owes much to him seems beyond doubt. I shall discuss these ideas, however, in the fully developed form which only Hume gave them.

Almost all these ideas can be found already in the Third Book of the *Treatise of Human Nature*, which he published at the age of 28 in 1739 and which, though it was almost completely overlooked at first, is today universally acknowledged as his greatest achievement. His *Essays*, which began to appear in 1741, the *Enquiry concerning the Principles of Morals*, in which he attempted to restate those ideas in briefer and more popular form, and his *History of England*, contain sometimes improved formulations and were much more effective in spreading his ideas; but they added little that is new to the first statement.

Hume is of course known mainly for his theory of knowledge, and in Germany largely as the author who stated the problems which Immanuel Kant endeavored to solve. But to Hume the chief task was from the beginning a general science of human nature for which morals and politics were as important as the sources of knowledge. And it would seem probable that in those fields he awoke Kant as much from his "dogmatic slumber" as he had done in epistemology. Certainly Kant, but also the two other great German liberals, Schiller and Humboldt, still knew Hume bet-

---

[3] See C. Nishiyama, *The Theory of Self-Love: An Essay on the Methodology of the Social Sciences, and Especially of Economics, with Special Reference to Bernard Mandeville*, University of Chicago Ph.D. Thesis, Mineographed (Chicago, 1960).

ter than did later generations, which were entirely dominated by French thought, and particularly by the influence of Rousseau. But Hume as a political theorist and as a historian has never been properly appreciated on the Continent. It is characteristic of the misleading generalizations about the 18th century that even today it is still largely regarded as a period which lacked historical sense, a statement which is true enough of the Cartesian rationalism that ruled in France, but certainly not of Britain and least of all of Hume, who could describe his as "the historical age and [his] as the historical nation."[4]

The neglect of Hume as a legal and political philosopher is, however, not confined to the Continent. Even in England, where it is now at last recognized that he is not merely the founder of the modern theory of knowledge but also one of the founders of economic theory, his political and still more his legal philosophy is curiously neglected. In works on jurisprudence we will look in vain for his name. The systematic philosophy of law begins in England with Jeremy Bentham and John Austin, who were both indebted mainly to the Continental rationalist tradition —Bentham to Helvetius and Baccaria, and Austin to German sources. But the greatest legal philosopher whom Britain produced before Bentham and who, incidentally, was trained as a lawyer, had practically no influence on that development.[5]

[4] *The Letters of David Hume*, ed. J. Y. T. Greig, 2 vols. (Oxford, 1932), II, 444.
[5] My attention was first directed to these parts of Hume's works many years ago by Professor Sir Arnold Plant, whose development of the Humean theory of property we are still eagerly awaiting.

This is the more remarkable as Hume gives us probably the only comprehensive statement of the legal and political philosophy which later became known as liberalism. It is today fairly generally recognized that the program of 19th-century liberalism contained two distinct and in some ways even antagonistic elements, liberalism proper and the democratic tradition. Of these only the second, democracy, is essentially French in origin and was added in the course of the French revolution to the older, individualistic liberal tradition which came from England. The uneasy partnership which the two ideals kept during the 19th century should not lead us to overlook their different characters and origins. The liberal ideal of personal liberty was first formulated in England, which throughout the 18th century had been the envied land of liberty and whose political institutions and doctrines served as models for the theorists elsewhere. These doctrines were those of the Whig party, the doctrines of the Glorious Revolution of 1688. And it is in Hume and not, as is commonly believed, in Locke, who had provided the justification of that revolution, that we find the fullest statement of these doctrines.

If this is not more widely recognized, it is partly a consequence of the erroneous belief that Hume himself was a Tory rather than a Whig. He acquired this reputation because in his *History*, as an eminently just man, he defended the Tory leaders against many of the unfair accusations brought against them—and, in the religious field, chided the Whigs for the intolerance which, contrary to their own doctrine, they showed towards the Catholic leanings prevalent among the Tories. He himself explained his position very fairly when he wrote, with reference to his *History*, that "my views of *things* are more conformable to Whig principles; my representations of *persons* to Tory prejudices."[6] In this respect such an archreactionary as Thomas Carlyle, who once described Hume as "the father of all succeeding Whigs,"[7] saw Hume's position more correctly than most of the democratic liberals of the 19th and 20th centuries.

There are of course some exceptions to the common misunderstanding and neglect of Hume as the outstanding philosopher of liberal political and legal theory. One of those is Friedrich Meinecke who, in his *Entstehung des Historismus*, clearly describes how for Hume

> der Sinn der englischen Geschichte [war], von einem *government of men* zu einem *government of law* zu werden. Diesen unendlich mühsamen, ja hässlichen, aber zum Guten endenden Prozess in seiner ganzen Komplikation und in allen seinen Phasen anschaulich zu machen, war oder wurde vielmehr sein Vorhaben. . . . Eine politische Grund- und Hauptfrage wurde so zum Generalthema seines Werkes. Nur von ihm aus ist es, was bisher immer übersehen wurde, in seiner Anlage und Stoffauswahl zu verstehen.[8]

It was not Meinecke's task to trace this interpretation of history back to Hume's philosophical work

---

[6] E. C. Mossner, *The Life of David Hume* (London, 1954), p. 311. For a survey of Hume's relations to Whigs and Tories see Eugene Miller "David Hume: Whig or Tory?" *New Individualist Review*, I (1962).

[7] Thomas Carlyle, "Boswell's Life of Johnson."

[8] Friedrich Meinecke, *Die Entstehung des Historismus*, 2 vols. (Berlin, 1938), I, 234.

where he could have found the theoretical foundation of the ideal which guided Hume in the writing of his *History*. It may be true that through his historical work Hume did more to spread this ideal than through his philosophical treatment. Indeed, Hume's *History* did probably as much to spread Whig liberalism throughout Europe in the 18th century as Macaulay's *History* did in the 19th. But that does not alter the fact that if we want an explicit and reasoned statement of this ideal, we must turn to his philosophical works, the *Treatise* and the easier and more elegant exposition in the *Essays* and *Enquiries*.

It is no accident that Hume develops his political and legal ideas in his philosophical works. These ideas are most intimately connected with his general philosophical conceptions, especially with his sceptical views on the "narrow bounds of human understanding." [His concern was human nature in general, and his theory of knowledge was intended mainly as a step towards an understanding of the conduct of man as a moral being and a member of society.] What he produced was above all a theory of the growth of human institutions which became the basis of his case for liberty and the foundation of the work of the great Scottish moral philosophers, of Adam Ferguson, Adam Smith and Dugald Stewart, who are today recognized as the chief ancestors of modern evolutionary anthropology. His work also provided the foundation on which the authors of the American constitution built[9]

[9] Douglass Adair, "That Politics may be Reduced to a Science: David Hume, James Madison and the Federalist," *Huntington Library Quarterly*, XX (1957).

and in some measure the basis for the political philosophy of Edmund Burke, which is much closer to, and more directly indebted to Hume, than is generally recognized.[10]

Hume's starting point is his anti-rationalist theory of morals which shows that, so far as the creation of moral rules is concerned, "reason of itself is utterly impotent" and that "the rules of morality, therefore, are not conclusions of our reason."[11] He demonstrates that our moral beliefs are neither natural in the sense of innate, nor a deliberate invention of human reason, but an "artifact" in the special sense in which he introduces this term, that is, a product of cultural evolution, as we would call it. In this process of evolution what proved conducive to more effective human effort survived, and the less effective was superseded. As a recent writer put it, somewhat pointedly:

> Standards of morality and justice are what Hume calls "artifacts"; they are neither divinely ordained, nor an integral part of original human nature, nor revealed by pure reason. They are an outcome of the practical experience of mankind, and the sole consideration in the slow test of time is the utility each moral rule can demonstrate towards promoting human welfare. Hume may be called a precursor of Darwin in the field of ethics. In effect, he proclaimed a doctrine

[10] H. B. Acton, "Prejudice," *Revue Internationale de Philosophie*, No. 21 (1952).

[11] *The Philosophical Works of David Hume*, ed. T. H. Green and T. H. Grose, 4 vols. (London, 1874–75), II, 235. (Subsequent references to philosophical works of Hume will be to this edition; Vols. I and II contain the *Treatise*, Vols. III and IV the *Essays Moral, Political and Literary*. References to Hume's *History of England* will be to the first collected edition, 6 vols. [London, 1762].)

of the survival of the fittest among human conventions—fittest not in terms of good teeth but in terms
of maximum social utility.[12]

It is, however, in his analysis of the circumstances
which determined the evolution of the chief legal institutions, in which he shows why a complex civiliza-
tion could grow up only where certain types of legal
institutions developed, that he makes some of his most
important contributions to jurisprudence. In the discussion of these problems his economic and his legal
and political theory are intimately connected. Hume
is indeed one of the few social theorists who are
clearly aware of the connection between the rules
men obey and the order which is formed as a result.

The transition from explanation to ideal does not,
however, involve him in any illegitimate confusion of
explanation and recommendation. Nobody was more
critical of or explicit about the impossibility of a logical
transition from the *is* to the *ought*,[13] about the fact
that "an active principle can never be founded on an
inactive" one.[14] What he undertakes is to show that
certain characteristics of modern society which we
prize are dependent on conditions which were not created in order to bring about these results, yet are
nevertheless their indispensable presuppositions. They
are institutions "advantageous to the public though
. . . not intended for that purpose by the inven-
tors."[15] Hume shows, in effect, that an orderly soci-

---

[12] C. Bay, *The Structure of Freedom* (Stanford, Calif., 1958),
p. 33.
[13] II, 245.
[14] II, 235.
[15] II, 296.

ety can develop only if men learn to obey certain rules of conduct.

The section of the *Treatise* which treats "Of the Origin of Justice and Property" and which examines "the manner in which rules of justice are established by the artifice of men"[16] is his most significant contribution in this field. It sets out from the fact that it is life in society which alone gives that weak animal, man, his exceptional powers. He concisely describes the advantages of the "partition of employment"[17] (what Adam Smith was to make popular under the Mandevillian term "division of labor") and shows how the obstacles to union in society are gradually overcome. The chief ones among these are, first, every individual's predominant concern with the needs of his own or of his immediate associates, and second, the scarcity (Hume's term!) of means, i.e. the fact that "there is not a sufficient quantity of them to supply everyone's desires and necessities."[18] It is thus "the concurrence of certain *qualities* of the human mind with the *situation* of external objects"[19] which forms the obstacles to smooth collaboration: "The qualities of mind are selfishness and *limited generosity:* And the situation of external objects is their *easy change,* joined to their *scarcity* in comparison of the wants and desires for them."[20] Were it not for those facts, no laws would ever have been necessary or have been

16 II, 258–73. Note Hume's acknowledgment of his indebtedness to H. Grotius, IV, 275.
17 II, 259.
18 II, 261.
19 II, 266.
20 II, 266–67.

thought of: "if men were supplied with everything in the same abundance, or if *everyone* had the same affection and tender regard for *everyone* as for himself, justice and injustice would be equally unknown among mankind."[21] "For what purpose make a partition of goods, when everyone has already more than enough? . . . Why call this object *mine*, when, upon seizing of it by another, I need but stretch out my hand to posess myself of what is equally valuable? Justice, in that case, being totally useless, would be an idle ceremonial."[22] It is thus "only from the selfishness and confined generosity of men, along with the scanty provision nature has made for his wants, that justice derives its origin."[23]

It is thus the nature of the circumstances—what Hume calls "the necessity of human society"—that gives rise to the "three fundamental laws of nature,"[24] those of "the stability of possession, of its transference by consent, and of the performance of promises,"[25] of which the whole system of law is merely an elaboration. These rules, however, were not deliberately invented by men to solve a problem which they saw (though it has become a task of legislation to improve them). Hume takes great pains to show for each of these rules how self-interest will lead to their being

[21] II, 267.
[22] IV, 180.
[23] II, 267-68. The whole passage is in italics.
[24] Cf. II, 258: "Though the rules of justice be *artificial*, they are not *arbitrary*. Nor is the expression improper to call them *Laws of Nature*; if by natural we understand what is common to any species, or even if we confine it to mean what is inseparable from the species."
[25] II, 293.

increasingly observed and finally enforced. "The rule concerning the stability of possession," he writes for instance, "arises gradually, and acquires force by slow progression, and our repeated experience of the inconvenience of transgressing it."[26] Similarly, "it is evident that if men were to regulate their conduct [as regards the keeping of promises] by the view of particular *interest*, they would involve themselves in endless confusion."[27] He points out that as rules of justice arise so "are languages gradually established by human conventions without any promise. In like manner gold and silver become the common measure of exchange."[28] Law and morals, like language and money, are, as we would say, not deliberate inventions but grown institutions or "formations." To guard against the impression that his emphasis on proven utility means that men adopted these institutions because they foresaw their utility, he stresses that in all his references to utility he "only suppose[s] those reflections to be formed at once which in fact arise insensibly and by degrees."[29]

Rules of this sort must be recognized before people can come to agree or bind themselves by promise or contract to any form of government. Therefore, "though it be possible for men to maintain a small uncultivated society without government, it is impossible they should maintain a society of any kind without justice, and the observance of those three funda-

[26] II, 263.
[27] II, 318.
[28] II, 263; cf. IV, 275.
[29] II, 274.

mental laws concerning the stability of possession, its translation by consent, and the performance of promises. These are, therefore, *antecedent to government*, though government, *upon its first establishment*, would naturally be supposed to derive its obligation from those laws of nature," and in particular from that concerning the performance of promises.[30]

Hume's further concern is chiefly to show that it is only the universal application of the same "general and inflexible rules of justice" which will secure the establishment of a general order, that this and not any particular aims or results must guide the application of the rules if an order is to be the result. Any concern with particular ends of either the individuals or the community, or a regard for the merits of particular individuals, would entirely spoil that aim. This contention is intimately bound up with Hume's belief in the short-sightedness of men, their propensity to prefer immediate advantage to distant gain, and their incapacity to be guided by a proper appreciation of their true long-run interest unless they bind themselves by general and inflexible rules which in the particular case are applied without regard to consequences.

These ideas, first developed in the *Treatise* (from which I have so far quoted exclusively), become more prominent in Hume's later writing, in which they are also more clearly connected with his political ideals. The most concise statement of them will be found in Appendix III to the *Enquiry concerning the Principles*

[30] II, 306, first group of italics added.

of Morals.[31] I would recommend that all who wish to become acquainted with Hume's legal philosophy begin with those six pages (272–78 of Volume IV of the Green-Grose edition of Hume's *Philosophical Works*) and work backwards from them to the fuller statements in the *Treatise*. But I shall continue to quote mainly from the *Treatise*, where the individual statements often have greater freshness, even though the exposition as a whole is sometimes rather prolix.

The weakness of men's minds (or the "narrow bounds of human understanding" as Hume would say, or their inevitable ignorance, as I should prefer to express it) would, without fixed rules, have the result that they

> would conduct themselves, on most occasions, by particular judgments, and would take into consideration the characters and circumstances of the persons, as well as the general nature of the question. But it is

[31] Cf. II, 301: men "prefer any trivial advantage that is present to the maintenance of order in society which so much depends on the observance of justice. . . . You have the same propension that I have, in favour of what is contiguous above what is remote"; and II, p. 303: "Here then is the origin of civil government and society. Men are not able radically to cure, either in themselves or others, that narrowness of soul which makes them prefer the present to the remote. They cannot change their natures. All they can do is to change their situation, and render the observance of justice the immediate interest of some particular persons. . . . But this execution of justice, though the principal, is not the only advantage of government. . . . not contented to protect men in those conventions they make for their mutual interest, it often obliges them to make such conventions, and forces them to seek their own advantage, by a concurrence in some common end or purpose. There is no quality in human nature which causes more fatal errors in our conduct, than that which leads us to prefer whatever is [304] present to the distant and remote."

easy to observe that this would produce an infinite confusion in human society, and that the avidity and partiality of men would quickly bring disorder into the world, if not restrained by some general and inflexible principles.[32]

The rules of law, however, "are not derived from any utility or advantage which either the *particular* person or the public may reap from his enjoyment of any *particular* goods. . . . Justice in her decisions never regards the fitness or unfitness of objects to particular persons, but conducts herself by more extensive views."[33] In particular: "The relation of fitness or suitableness ought never to enter into consideration, in distributing the properties of mankind."[34] A single act of justice is even

> frequently contrary to the *public interest*; and were it to stand by itself, without being followed by other acts, may, in itself, be very prejudicial to society. . . . Nor is every single act of justice, considered apart, more conducive to private interest than to public. . . . But, however single acts of justice may be contrary, either to public or to private interest, it is

[32] II, 298–99. Cf. also II, 318: "It is evident that if men were to regulate their conduct in this particular [the appointment of magistrates], by the view of a particular *interest*, either public or private, they would involve themselves in endless confusion, and would render all government, in a great measure, ineffectual. The private interest of everyone is different; and though the public interest is always one, yet it becomes the source of great dissension, by reason of the different opinions of different persons concerning it. . . . were we to follow the same advantage, in assigning particular possessions to particular persons, we should disappoint our end, and perpetuate the confusion which that rule is intended to prevent. We must, therefore, proceed by general rules, and regulate ourselves by general interests."
[33] II, 273.
[34] II, 287.

certain that the whole plan or scheme is highly conducive, or indeed absolutely requisite, both to the
support of society and the welfare of the individuals.[35]

Or as Hume puts it in the Appendix to the *Enquiry*

the benefit resulting from [the social virtues of justice and fidelity] is not the consequence of every
individual single act, but arises from the whole
scheme or system, concurred in by the whole, or the
greater part of society . . . The result of the individual act is here, in many instances, directly opposite to
that of the whole system of actions; and the former
may be extremely hurtful, while the latter is, to the
highest degree, advantageous. . . . Its benefit arises
only from the observance of the general rule; and it
is sufficient, if compensation is thereby made for all
the ills and inconveniences which flow from the particular character and situation.[36]

Hume sees clearly that it would be contrary to the
whole spirit of the system if individual merit rather
than those general and inflexible rules of law were to
govern justice and government: were mankind to exe-
cute

a law which assigned the largest possession to the most
extensive virtue, and gave everyone the power of doing good according to his inclinations, . . . so great
is the uncertainty of merit, both from its natural ob-

[35] II, 269. This passage shows particularly clearly that Hume's
utilitarianism was what is now called a "restricted" and not an
"extreme" utilitarianism. Cf. J. J. C. Smart, "Extreme and Restricted Utilitarianism," *Philosophical Quarterly*, VI (1956), and
H. J. McCloskey, "An Examination of Restricted Utilitarianism,"
Philosophical Review, LXVI (1957).

[36] IV, 273.

scurity, and from the self-conceit of every individual,
that no determinate rule of conduct would ever follow from it, and the total dissolution of society
must be the immediate consequence.[37]

This follows necessarily from the fact that law can
deal only with "the external performance [which] has
no merit. [While] we must look within to find the
moral quality."[38] In other words, there can be no
rules for rewarding merit, or no rules of distributive
justice, because there are no circumstances which may
not affect merit, while rules always single out some circumstances as the sole relevant ones.

I cannot here pursue further the extent to which
Hume elaborates the distinction between the general
and abstract rules of justice and the particular and
concrete aims of individual and public action. I
hope what I have already said will suffice to show how
central this distinction is for his whole legal philosophy, and how questionable therefore is the prevalent
view that, as it is tersely expressed in an otherwise excellent work, "Die moderne Geschichte des Begriffes
des allgemeinen Gesetzes beginnt mit Kant."[39] What
Kant had to say about this seems to derive directly
from Hume. This becomes even more evident when we
turn from the more theoretical to the more practical
part of his discussion, especially his conception of the
government of laws and not of men[40] and his general
idea of freedom under the law. It contains the fullest

[37] IV, 187.
[38] II, 252.
[39] Konrad Huber, *Massnahmegesetz und Rechtsgesetz* (Berlin, 1963), p. 133.
[40] III, 161.

expression of the Whig or liberal doctrines which were made familiar to Continental thinking by Kant and the later theorists of the *Rechtsstaat*. It is sometimes suggested that Kant developed his theory of the *Rechtsstaat* by applying to public affairs his conception of the categorical imperative.[41] It was probably the other way round: Kant probably developed his theory of the categorical imperative by applying to morals the concept of the rule of law which he found ready-made.

I cannot deal here with Hume's political philosophy in the same detail in which I have considered his legal philosophy. It is extremely rich, but also somewhat better known than the latter. I will completely pass over his important and characteristic discussion of how all government is guided by opinion, of the relations between opinion and interest, and of how opinion is formed. The few points I will consider are those where his political theory rests directly on his legal theory and particularly his views on the relations between law and liberty.

In Hume's last statements on these problems, the essay "On the Origin of Government" which he added in 1770 to his *Essays*, he defines

> the government which, in common appellation, receives the appellation of free [as] that which admits of a partition of power among several members whose united authority is no less, or is commonly greater, than that of a monarch, but who, in the usual course of administration, must act by general and equal laws, that are previously known to all members, and

41 K. Huber, *loc. cit.*

to all their subjects. In this sense, it must be owned that liberty is the perfection of civil society.[42]

Earlier he had in the same series of essays described how in such a government it is necessary "to maintain a watchful *jealousy* over the magistrates, to remove all discretionary powers, and to secure every one's life and fortune by general and inflexible laws. No action must be deemed a crime, but what the law has plainly determined to be such . . ."[43] Nonetheless, he granted that

all general laws are attended with inconveniences, when applied to particular cases; and it requires great penetration and experience, both to perceive that these inconveniences are fewer than what results from full discretionary powers in every magistrate; and also to discern what general laws are, upon the whole, attended with the fewest inconveniences. This is a matter of so great a difficulty that men have made some advances, even in the sublime art of poetry and eloquence, where a rapidity of genius and imagination assists their progress, before they have arrived at any great refinement in their municipal laws, where frequent trials and diligent observation can alone direct their improvements.[44]

[42] III, 116.

[43] III, 96; cf. also *History*, V, 110: "in a monarchical constitution . . . an eternal jealousy must be preserved against the sovereign, and no discretionary power must ever be entrusted to him by which the property or personal liberty of any subject can be affected."

[44] III, 179; cf. also 185: "To balance a large state . . . on general laws, is a work of so great difficulty that no human genius, however comprehensive, is able, by the mere dint of reason and reflection, to effect it. The judgment of many must unite in this work: Experience must guide their labours, time must bring it to perfection: And the feeling of inconveniences must correct the mistakes which they inevitably fall into, in their first trials and experiments."

And in his *History of England*, speaking of the Revolution of 1688, he tells us proudly how

> No government, at that time, appeared in the world, nor is perhaps to be found in the records of any history, which subsisted without the mixture of some arbitrary authority, committed to some magistrate; and it might reasonably, beforehand, appear doubtful, whether human society could ever arrive at such a state of perfection, as to support itself with no other control, than the general and rigid maxims of law and equity. But the parliament justly thought, that the King was too eminent a magistrate to be trusted with discretionary power, which he might so easily turn to the destruction of liberty. And in the event it has been found, that, though some inconveniences arise from the maxim of adhering strictly to law, yet the advantages so much overbalance them, as should render the English for ever grateful to the memory of their ancestors, who, after repeated contests, at last established that noble principle.[45]

I must not tire your patience by more quotations, though the temptation is strong to show in detail how he endeavored sharply to distinguish between "all the laws of nature which regulate property, as well as all civil laws [which] are general, and regard alone some essential circumstance of the case, without taking into consideration the characters, situations, and connexions of the persons concerned, or any particular consequences which may result from the determination of these laws, in any particular case which offers,"[46] and those rules which determine the organization of au-

[45] *History*, V, 280.
[46] IV, 274.

thority,[47] and how even in the preserved manuscript corrections of his printed works he is careful to substitute "rules of justice" for "laws of society"[48] where this seemed advisable to make his meaning clear. I want in conclusion rather to turn to another point to which I referred earlier, the general significance of his "evolutionary" account of the rise of law and other institutions.

I spoke then of Hume's doctrine as a theory of the growth of an order which provided the basis of his argument for freedom. But this theory did more. Though his primary aim was to account for the evolution of social institutions, he seems to have been clearly aware that the same argument could also be used to explain the evolution of biological organisms. In his posthumously published *Dialogues concerning Natural Religion* he more than hints at such an application. He points out there that "matter may be susceptible to many and great revolutions, through the endless periods of eternal duration. The incessant changes to which every part of it is subject, seem to indicate some such general transformation."[49] The apparent design in the "parts in the animals or vegetables and their curious adjustment to each other" does not seem to him to require a designer, because he "would fain know how an animal could subsist unless its parts were so adjusted? Do we not find that it

[47] Cf. G. H. Sabine, *A History of Political Theory*, rev. ed. (New York, 1950), p. 604.

[48] Cf. the Appendix by R. Klibansky to Hume, *Theory of Politics*, ed. F. Watkins, (London, 1951), p. 246, note to p. 246, and note to p. 88.

[49] II, 419.

perishes wherever this adjustment ceases, and that its matter corrupting tries some new form?"[50] And "no form can subsist unless it possess those powers and organs necessary for its subsistence: some new order or economy must be tried, and so on, without intermission; till at last some order which can support and maintain itself, is fallen upon."[51] Man, he insists, cannot "pretend to an exemption from the lot of all living animals. . . . [the] perpetual war. . . . kindled among all living creatures"[52] affects also his evolution. It was still another hundred years until Darwin finally described this "struggle for existence." But the transmission of ideas from Hume to Darwin is continuous and can be traced in detail.[53]

Let me conclude this discussion of Hume's teaching with a glance at its fate during the last two hundred years. Let me focus particularly on the year 1766, which happens to be the year when the elder Pitt for the last time defended the old Whig principles in support of the demands of the American colonies, and the year before Parliament, with the assertion of its claim to omnipotence, not only brought the most glorious period of the development of political principles to an abrupt close but also produced the cause for the eventual break with the American colonies. In this year David Hume, who by then had essentially completed his work and at the age of fifty-five had become one

[50] II, 428.
[51] II, 429.
[52] II, 436.
[53] The most direct channel seems to be Erasmus Darwin, who was clearly influenced by Hume and whose influence on his grandson is unquestioned.

of the most celebrated figures of his age, out of sheer
goodness, brought from France to England an equally
famous man who was only a few months his junior but
who had lived in misery and, as he thought, was generally persecuted: Jean Jacques Rousseau. This encounter between the serene and even placid philosopher, known to the French as "le bon David," and the
emotionally unstable, unaccountable and half-mad
idealist who in his personal life disregarded all moral
rules, is one of the most dramatic episodes of intellectual history. It could not but end in a violent clash and
there can be no question today, for anyone who reads
the full story, who of the two was the greater intellectual and moral figure.

In a way their work had been directed against the
same dominant rationalism of their age. But while
Hume, to repeat a phrase I have already quoted, had
attempted to "whittle down the claims of reason by
rational analysis," Rousseau had only his uncontrolled
emotion to oppose to it. Who then, observing this encounter, would have believed that it would be the
ideas of Rousseau and not those of Hume which would
govern the political development of the next two hundred years? Yet this is what happened. It was the
Rousseauesque idea of democracy, and his still thoroughly rationalistic conceptions of the social contract
and of popular sovereignty, which were to submerge
the ideals of liberty under the law and of government
limited by law. It was Rousseau and not Hume who
fired the enthusiasm of the successive revolutions
which created modern government on the Continent

and guided the decline of the ideals of the older liberalism and the approach to totalitarian democracy in the
whole world. How did this development come about?

I believe the explanation lies largely in an accusation
which with some justice has often been levelled against
Hume, the accusation that his philosophy was essentially negative. The great sceptic, with his profound
conviction of the imperfection of all human reason
and knowledge, did not expect much positive good
from political organization. He knew that the greatest
political goods, peace, liberty, and justice, were in
their essence negative, a protection against injury
rather than positive gifts. No man strove more ar-
dently for peace, liberty, and justice. But Hume clearly
saw that the further ambitions which wanted to establish some other, positive justice on earth were a
threat to those values. As he put it in the *Enquiry:*
"Fantastics may suppose, that *domination is supported
by grace,* and *that saints inherit the earth;* but the civil
magistrate very justly puts these sublime theorists on
the same footing with common robbers, and teaches
them by the severest discipline, that a rule, which in
speculation, may seem the most advantageous, may yet
be found in practice, totally pernicious and destructive."[54] It was not from the goodness of men but from
institutions which "made it the interest even of bad
men, to act for the public good"[55] that he expected
peace, liberty, and justice. He knew that in politics
"every man must be supposed a knave"; though, as he

[54] IV, 187.
[55] III, 99.

adds, "it appears somewhat strange, that a maxim should be true in *politics* which is false in fact."[56]

He was far from denying that government also had positive tasks. Like Adam Smith later, he knew that it is only thanks to the discretionary powers granted to government that "bridges are built, harbors opened, ramparts raised, canals formed, fleets equipped, and armies disciplined; everywhere, by the care of government, which, though composed of men subject to all human infirmities, becomes, by one of the finest and most subtle inventions imaginable, a composition, which is, in some measure, exempted from all these infirmities."[57] This invention is that in these tasks, in which positive aims and therefore expediency rule, government was given no power of coercion and was subject to the same general and inflexible rules which aim at an overall order by creating its negative conditions: peace, liberty, and justice.[58]

[56] III, 118.
[57] II, 304.
[58] Since the first publication of this essay a number of Continental studies of Hume's legal philosophy have come to my notice, of which the most important is Georges Vlachos, *Essai sur la politique de Hume* (Paris, 1955). Others are: G. Laviosa, *La filosofia scientifica del diritto Inghilterra, Parte I, Da Bacone a Hume* (Torino, 1897), pp. 697–850; W. Wallenfels, *Die Rechtsphilosophie David Humes*, Doctoral Dissertation at the University of Göttingen (1938); L. Bagolini, *Esperienza giuridica e politica nel pensiero di David Hume* (Siena, 1947); and Silvana Castiglione, "La Dottrina della justizia in D. Hume," *Rivista Internationale di Filosofia di Diritto*, XXXVIII (1960), and "Diritto naturale e diritto positivo in David Hume," *ibid.*, XXXIX (1962).

HUME'S AGNOSTICISM

JAMES NOXON

I

David Hume has left his readers to wonder about his personal convictions on the great questions of religion. James Boswell thought that he detected such a discordance between the man and the philosopher that he could not credit Hume with sincerely holding to the skeptical views which he publicly professed. Even when Hume during a deathbed interview assured the biographer that "He had never entertained any belief in Religion since he began to read Locke and Clarke," referred to a future state as "a most unreasonable fancy," and described the morality of every religion as bad, Boswell was not persuaded of the philosopher's sincerity, nor was Samuel Johnson, to whom, inevitably, these remarks were quoted.[1] Even

From *The Philosophical Review*, Vol. LXXIII (1964). Reprinted by permission of the author and *The Philosophical Review*.

[1] James Boswell, "An Account of My Last Interview With David Hume, Esq.," in *Private Papers of James Boswell*, ed. Geoffrey Scott and Frederick A. Pottle (Mount Vernon, 1931); reprinted as Appendix A to the Introduction to Hume, *Dialogues concerning Natural Religion*, ed. Norman Kemp Smith, 2nd ed. (London, 1947). (All references to Hume's *Dialogues* are to this edition.)

Hume himself confessed that at moments his philosophical speculations seemed quite alien to his own being as a man. And no wonder, since his logic frequently drove him to conclusions which he frankly admitted no man of common sense could believe.

Was Hume a dilettante, motivated by a "lust of paradoxes" and a love of notoriety, as his contemporary James Beattie supposed?[2] Did he care more about making a literary reputation than about discovering philosophical truth, as both John Stuart Mill[3] and T. H. Huxley[4] contended? Is it true that Hume was "wanting in high seriousness," as A. E. Taylor believed, that "he did not 'care' in any vital sense" about the issue "between theism and atheism?"[5]

One of Hume's aims, I think, was to arrive through philosophy at the point where he *needed* no longer to care about that particular issue. He had been made to suffer in his youth from having the religious convictions of others imposed upon him, and he had known others—for example, his friend Francis Hutcheson—who had been made to suffer in a similar way. Hume's reaction to such convictions was not simple lack of concern, as Taylor would have us believe; it was, rather, a need to be liberated from them and a desire

[2] James Beattie, *Essay on the Nature and Immutability of Truth in Opposition to Sophistry and Scepticism* (Edinburgh, 1770).

[3] John Stuart Mill, Review of George Brodie's *History of the British Empire, Westminster Review*, II (1824).

[4] T. H. Huxley, *Hume* (London, 1879).

[5] A. E. Taylor, "Symposium: The Present-Day Relevance of Hume's *Dialogues concerning Natural Religion*," *Proceedings of the Aristotelian Society*, Supp. Vol. XVIII (1939), 179–80. The other symposiasts, to be cited later, are J. Laird and T. E. Jessop.

to liberate others. The *Dialogues concerning Natural Religion*, upon which Hume worked intermittently for a quarter of a century, and which he was still revising in the year of his death, measures the limits of the freedom he achieved.

The *Dialogues*, however, have not proven to be the key to the riddle of David Hume. On the contrary, they have themselves posed a riddle: who speaks for Hume? Unless this question can be answered, Hume's last philosophical testament provides us with no clue to his own religious convictions.

II

Of all the traditional "proofs" of God's existence, the argument from design is the one most likely to make a wide appeal. The universe appears to man as an orderly system. Events recur in regular sequences. The pattern observable in one region of existence is found to be nicely adjusted to that of another, and both to conform to an over-all design. Without this order scientific knowledge would be impossible and human life even more precarious than it is. In familiar objects near at hand, particles of matter too small to be seen move in orbits similar to those traced out by remote planets. It is said that if even one particle of matter were destroyed, the entire universe would be annihilated, so delicate are the adjustments of the infinitely complex universe.

Such considerations lead naturally to the idea of a a designer who must be credited with having planned

the cosmos. As early as the fifth century B.C., Anaxa-
goras attributed the working of the universe to a Mind
or Intelligence. Seventeen hundred years later, St.
Thomas Aquinas offered a typical statement of what
came to be called the argument from design. The
principle of St. Thomas' argument is that things in nature regularly act in certain ways in order to accomplish some useful purpose: they act for the best, both
with respect to their own welfare and to that of other
beings who depend upon them. But in most cases, the
thing concerned is obviously not aware of the purpose
for which it acts: it is not acting intentionally or intelligently at all. "Therefore some intelligent being exists
by whom all natural things are directed to their end;
and this being we call God."[6] Like St. Thomas' other
"proofs" of God's existence, the argument from design
reappeared in new versions in the writings of the early
modern philosophers. And this is the "proof" whose
cogency is debated throughout the *Dialogues*.

In a brief preface, the standpoints of the three participants are described as "the accurate philosophical
turn of Cleanthes," "the careless scepticism of Philo,"
and "the rigid inflexible orthodoxy of Demea." The
question of which character speaks for Hume inevitably arises. So far as I know, it has never been suggested
that Hume should be identified with Demea. Oddly
enough, the character who would most naturally be

[6] St. Thomas Aquinas, *Summa Theologica*, Part I, Ques. 11,
Art. 3 (in *The Basic Writings of Saint Thomas Aquinas*, ed.
Anton C. Pegis, 2 vols. [New York, 1944], I, 23). Cf. *Summa
Contra Gentiles*, Ch. LXIV (Pegis ed., p. 113), where it is
proved that "God, by his Providence, is the governor of all
things."

taken to represent Hume more than once finds himself in agreement with Demea, and on such a fundamental issue as the incomprehensibility of God. And of course the character most likely intended to represent Hume is Philo, the skeptic; or so it might seem. Yet one would not expect Hume to describe his own skepticism as "careless." Would he not be more likely to characterize himself as being of an "accurate philosophical turn"—the phrase applied to Cleanthes? The preface is not, however, presented as expressing Hume's own judgment of the participants, but rather that of a fourth person. It seems that every precaution has been taken to elude readers who want to fix Hume's own position. There is, however, a single paragraph of this work in which Hume quite clearly speaks for himself. We must later ask what reasonable inference concerning Hume's own position can be made from this vital piece of evidence.

III

A reader coming to the *Dialogues* from a study of other works by Hume would most naturally identify the author with Philo. Such was the opinion of one of the first reviewers of the work,[7] and it is also the ably defended judgment of one of Hume's most thorough and appreciative commentators, Norman Kemp Smith: "I shall contend," he says, "that Philo, from start to

---

[7] *Monthly Review*, LXI (1779), 343: "Philo is the hero of the piece" (quoted by Norman Kemp Smith in his Introduction to the *Dialogues*, p. 58, n. 2).

finish, represents Hume."[8] Admittedly the role of
Philo is very like that usually played by Hume himself
—the role of the critic who does not commit himself
to defending his own position but makes the claims of
others disintegrate under analysis, who aims not to
prove a claim but to show that no claim can be rationally justified. And certainly many of Philo's speeches do
read like quotations from Hume's texts. Among the
difficulties of this interpretation is the fact that one of
Hume's most important principles is attributed to
Cleanthes, whose deistic position is found to depend
upon it. The principle is that out of human experience
arise certain irrepressible beliefs which are neither
acquired by rational means nor vulnerable to rational
criticism. Belief in an external world of relatively stable objects existing independently of consciousness is
one example of such a natural belief. Although neither
supported by empirical evidence nor justified by logical
reasoning, this conviction persists in all normal minds.
Is Cleanthes' belief in deity, in an intelligent creator,
meant as an example of such a belief, a natural belief
which no candid mind can reject whatever the difficulties involved in attempting to vindicate it? Hume
has Cleanthes express his conviction in such a way
that anyone who rejected it would seem to be in the
untenable position of the skeptic who publicly denies
the existence of an external world for want of a rational proof, but continues privately to believe in it:

> The declared profession of every reasonable sceptic is
> only to reject abstruse, remote and refined argu-

[8] *Dialogues*, p. 59. In *Hume's Philosophy of Belief* (London,
1961), Antony Flew signifies his agreement with Kemp Smith on
this point. See Ch. IX, esp. p. 216.

ments; . . . and to assent, whenever any reasons strike him with so full a force, that he cannot, without the greatest violence, prevent it. Now the arguments for Natural Religion . . . immediately flow in upon you with a force like that of sensation.[9]

Another of the difficulties involved in identifying Hume with Philo is raised by the complete reversal of standpoint made by Philo in the twelfth and final dialogue. Here Philo throws away all his previous arguments, confesses that "no one has a deeper sense of religion impressed upon his mind, or pays more profound adoration to the Divine Being,"[10] claims that doubt concerning a "Supreme Intelligence" represents the "pitch of pertinacious obstinacy,"[11] and concedes that his skepticism amounts to no more than a "love of singular arguments."[12] Must we conclude that Hume's own skeptical philosophy was so completely lacking in serious intention? One commentator, admitting that he is balked by the twelfth Dialogue, says, "The conclusion being disconnected from the argued content of the *Dialogues*, I shall ignore it."[13] But surely a critic has no right to ignore a twelfth of a book upon which he is commenting most unfavorably. Some attempt must be made to interpret this admittedly unexpected finale. And if one does try to think out the connection of the twelfth Dialogue not only with the other eleven but with Hume's other works, one should find an unambiguous clue to Hume's own position.

[9] Part III, p. 154.
[10] P. 214.
[11] P. 215.
[12] P. 214.
[13] T. E. Jessop, "Symposium: The Present-Day Relevance of Hume's *Dialogues concerning Natural Religion*," *loc. cit.*, p. 220.

IV

Toward the end of the *Enquiry concerning Human
Understanding*, Hume unexpectedly introduced a section (XI) written in dialogue form, "Of a Particular
Providence and of a Future State." Here he either
feigns or, as he says, reports a conversation with a
friend who delivers a lengthy oration such as Epicurus
might have offered in defense of his skeptical philosophy against Athenian critics. The conclusion of
this speech, which reads like a résumé of Philo's
argument, is that "While we argue from the course of
nature, and infer a particular intelligent cause, which
first bestowed, and still preserves order in the universe, we embrace a principle, which is both uncertain
and useless."[14] I think it would not be irresponsible to
conjecture that Hume had the unpublished manuscript
of his *Dialogues* at hand, or at least in mind, when he
was writing this section of the *Enquiry*. What is especially to be noticed is that some of the objections put
forth in his own name against this skeptical conclusion
are very similar to those advanced by Cleanthes
against Philo. Let us compare two passages, one from
the *Enquiry* and one from the *Dialogues*. Here in the
Enquiry, Hume claims to be speaking for himself:

If you saw, for instance, a half-finished building,
surrounded with heaps of brick and stone and mortar,
and all the instruments of masonry; could you not

[14] Hume, *An Enquiry concerning Human Understanding*, ed.
L. A. Selby-Bigge, 2nd ed. (Oxford, 1902), p. 142.

infer from the effect, that it was a work of design and contrivance? . . . Why then do you refuse to admit the same method of reasoning with regard to the order of nature? Consider the world and the present life only as an imperfect building, from which you can infer a superior intelligence.[15]

(This argument, it should be mentioned, is countered by Hume's skeptical friend by the same line of reasoning as that used by Philo.)[16] Now here is Cleanthes' speech:

It would surely be very ill received, replied Cleanthes, . . . did I allow, that the proofs of a Deity amounted to no more than a guess or conjecture. But is the whole adjustment of means to ends in a house and in the universe so slight a resemblance? The economy of final causes? The order, proportion, and arrangement of every part?[17]

It seems that we are tending to confirm the judgment of Dugald Stewart,[18] of Burton, Hume's first biographer,[19] of Pringle-Pattison,[20] and of Laing,[21] that it is Cleanthes who speaks for Hume in the

[15] *Ibid.*, p. 143.

[16] Cf. *Enquiry*, pp. 143–44, with *Dialogues*, Part II, pp. 149–50.

[17] Part II, pp. 144–45.

[18] Dugald Stewart, *Collected Works*, ed. Sir William Hamilton, 11 vols. (Edinburgh, 1854–60), I, 605: "It must always be remembered that Cleanthes is the hero of the Dialogue, and is to be considered as speaking Mr. Hume's real opinions" (quoted in Norman Kemp Smith, *op. cit.*, p. 58).

[19] John Hill Burton, *Life and Correspondence of David Hume*, 2 vols. (Edinburgh, 1846), I, 329.

[20] A. S. Pringle-Pattison, *The Idea of God in the Light of Recent Philosophy* (Oxford, 1917) (cited by Norman Kemp Smith, *op. cit.*, p. 59).

[21] B. M. Laing, *David Hume* (London, 1932), p. 179 (cited by Norman Kemp Smith, *op. cit.*, p. 59).

Dialogues. More evidence is available to support this interpretation, but it is enough for the moment to mention only one other point. In the *Enquiry* Hume argues, against the skeptic, that religious belief has a good moral effect, and thereby again puts himself on the side of Cleanthes against Philo:

> Men . . . draw many consequences from the belief of a divine Existence, and suppose that the Deity will inflict punishments on vice, and bestow rewards on virtue. . . . Whether this reasoning of theirs be just or not, is no matter. Its influence on their life and conduct must still be the same. And, those, who attempt to disabuse them of such prejudices, may . . . be good reasoners, but I cannot allow them to be good citizens.[22]

The comparable passage in the *Dialogues* occurs in the final part and is assigned to Cleanthes:

> Religion, however corrupted, is still better than no religion at all. The doctrine of a future state is so strong and necessary a security to morals, that we never ought to abandon or neglect it. For if finite and temporary rewards and punishments have so great an effect, as we daily find: How much greater must be expected from such as are infinite and eternal?[23]

Must we, then, conclude, on the basis of this comparison of the *Enquiry* with the *Dialogues*, that Hume intended Cleanthes as his representative? The truth of the matter is that the evidence of Section XI of the *Enquiry* is far from decisive. The chapter gives so strong an impression of being contrived that I would

[22] *Op. cit.*, Sect. XI, p. 147.
[23] Pp. 219–20.

hesitate to accept at face value Hume's assignment of certain opinions to an anonymous friend and the reservation of others to himself. When Hume puts forth in his own name a claim for the moral value of religion, any reader acquainted with *The Natural History of Religion* must suspect that his statement is made for the sake of the argument, rather than for expressing his own convictions.[24] And even if one did take this "report" to be disingenuous, the positions of Hume and his friend are not so clearly distinguished as one might like. At the beginning of his reply, Hume remarks that the skeptic embraces "those principles, to which . . . I have always expressed a particular attachment."[25] And at the very end he advances an argument sufficiently skeptical of the argument from design to distinguish his own position from that of Cleanthes:

> In a word, I much doubt whether it be possible for a cause to be known only by its effect (as you have all along supposed) or to be of so singular and particular a nature as to have no parallel and no similarity with any other cause or object, that has ever fallen under our observation. It is only when two *species* of objects are found to be constantly conjoined, that we can infer the one from the other; and were an effect presented, which was entirely singular, and could not

[24] See, e.g., Hume, *The Natural History of Religion*, Ch. XIV, "Bad Influence of Popular Religions on Morality": "Hence the greatest crimes have been found, in many instances, compatible with a superstitious piety and devotion: Hence it is justly regarded as unsafe to draw any certain inference in favour of a man's morals from the fervour or strictness of his religious exercises."

[25] *Ibid.*, p. 142.

be comprehended under any known *species*, I do not
see, that we could form any conjecture or inference at
all concerning its cause.[26]

V

In a very unfavorable discussion of Hume's *Dialogues*, A. E. Taylor remarked that "If Philo is meant
as a representative of Hume's philosophical scepticism,
we have, of course, no right to concede that 'this universe' or anything else *has* such a cause, as Hume must
have known."[27] But can we suppose that Philo is
meant to represent Hume, when we know that Hume
wrote to William Strahan of the skeptic being "indeed
refuted" and of having confessed "that he was only
amusing himself by all his Cavils"?[28] Is it plausible
that Hume composed a set of Dialogues in which the
spokesman for his own views is "indeed refuted" and
"only amusing himself"? If, on the other hand, we
should agree with Norman Kemp Smith that Philo is
not refuted, then we must account for Hume's having
said that he was, and for Philo's finally abandoning as
defenseless the position for which he had contended
throughout.

One of the most illuminating aspects of Kemp
Smith's fine argument for the identification of Philo
with Hume consists in showing how very slight Philo's
final concessions to Cleanthes' rational theology really

[26] See, e.g., Hume, *The Natural History of Religion*, p. 148.
[27] *Op. cit.*, p. 181. (See n. 5 above).
[28] *The Letters of David Hume*, ed. J. Y. T. Greig, 2 vols. (Oxford, 1932), II, 323.

were. Despite his rather florid profession of faith, in his subsequent arguments he commits himself only to "the somewhat ambiguous, at least undefined proposition, *that the cause, or causes of order in the universe probably bear some remote analogy to human intelligence.*"[29] Philo proceeds to argue that to raise the question of just how similar this cause or these causes may be to the human mind can only involve us in a verbal dispute incapable of settlement. He also argues that the decision one makes respecting this issue does or ought to have no bearing whatsoever on one's conduct. Thus when Philo's affirmation that "all the sciences almost lead us insensibly to acknowledge a first intelligent Author"[30] has been duly qualified in the light of his ensuing remarks, his position, Kemp Smith contends, has been brought into line with Hume's own. For Hume, Kemp Smith observes, "has himself no belief in miracles nor consequently in a special Revelation; he has no belief in an after-life or in any type of specifically religious duties; he has no belief in a Divine Being to whom moral attributes can be ascribed and none therefore in 'God' as religiously understood."[31] I believe that this characterization of Hume's position is borne out by statements published in his own name. It fails, however, in at least one vital point to state the convictions which Philo professed as his own:

But believe me, Cleanthes, the most natural sentiment, which a well-disposed mind will feel on this

[29] Part XII, p. 227 (italics in text).
[30] Part XII, pp. 214–15.
[31] *Op. cit.*, p. 20.

occasion, is a longing desire and expectation, that Heaven would be pleased to dissipate, at least alleviate, this profound ignorance, by affording some more particular revelation to mankind, and making discoveries of the nature, attributes, and operations of the divine object of our Faith. A person seasoned with a just sense of the imperfections of natural reason, will fly to revealed truth with the greatest avidity.[32]

Faith, according to Hume and contrary to Philo, depends upon a miracle "which subverts all the principles of his understanding, and gives him a determination to believe what is most contrary to custom and experience."[33] Kemp Smith construes Philo's final flight to "revealed truth" as a "conventionally required proviso,"[34] "the conventionally required concessions in regard to faith and revelation."[35] I am not sure whether Kemp Smith had in mind the Ciceronian convention displayed in *De Natura Deorum,* upon which Hume modeled his *Dialogues,* or the social conventions of Hume's time and place, which would have restrained him from concluding skeptically. If the first sense of "convention" is meant, it must be said, first, that Hume had already departed significantly from the Ciceronian model by not speaking anywhere in his own name, and, secondly, that Cicero's skeptic, Cotta, shows nothing like the reversal of standpoint displayed by Philo. If the second sense of "convention" is intended, it must be asked why Hume would pay such deference to social convention in a work planned for

[32] Part XII, p. 227.
[33] *Enquiry concerning Human Understanding,* Sect. X, Part II, p. 131.
[34] *Op. cit.,* p. 74.
[35] *Ibid.,* p. 63.

posthumous publication when he had shown so little in books published during his lifetime. No doubt Cicero recognized a civic obligation to defer to the state religion, but Hume's own persistent disparagement of religious institutions, his vitriolic attacks upon intolerance, and his explicit insistence that philosophy "requires entire liberty above all other privileges"[36] counts heavily against Kemp Smith's claim that for Hume "the Reformed Church teaching stood officially for religion, and that the good citizen was therefore in duty bound to pay it outward deference."[37]

VI

It seems to be no easy matter to decide just which of the positions represented in the *Dialogues concerning Natural Religion* was the one held by Hume. Charles Hendel has suggested that he held all three of them,[38] and John Laird that he held none.[39] Doesn't this settle the issue? In one way, Hume was all or two of his characters; in another way, he was none or neither—as is the case with any literary artist who invents characters. Personally, I am not satisfied, for the question of what Hume *himself* had decided about the doctrine discussed is not answered.

[36] *Enquiry concerning Human Understanding,* Sect. XI, p. 132.

[37] *Op. cit.,* p. 10.

[38] Hume, *Selections,* ed. Charles W. Hendel (New York, 1927), p. xxii.

[39] J. Laird, "Symposium: The Present-Day Relevance of Hume's *Dialogues concerning Natural Religion,*" *loc. cit.,* pp. 206–7.

In the *Enquiry concerning Human Understanding* Hume makes quite plain that the question discussed in the *Dialogues* is in principle unanswerable. All our knowledge of causal connections is a product "of observation and experience," a consequence of remarking constant conjunction between two events. Our knowledge of a causal agent, however thorough, would never permit us to predict its effects on a purely *a priori* basis; and our knowledge of an effect—in the present case, of the universe—would never warrant any inference concerning the nature of the causal agent. The furthest one can go in explaining natural phenomena is to reduce them to order by formulating the general causes and principles according to which different types of events occur. But we can never explain by reference to an ultimate cause or principle why just these particular causes and principles rather than others operate in the world:

> No philosopher, who is rational and modest, has ever pretended to assign the ultimate cause of any natural operation, or to show distinctly the action of that power, which produces any single effect in the universe . . . as to the causes of these general causes, we should in vain attempt their discovery. . . . These ultimate springs and principles are totally shut up from human curiosity and inquiry. . . . Thus the observation of human blindness and weakness is the result of all philosophy.[40]

It is on the basis of this fundamental skepticism that Hume concludes that the only tenable position on the question discussed in the *Dialogues concerning*

[40] *Enquiry concerning Human Understanding*, Sect. IV, Part I, pp. 30–31.

Natural Religion is agnosticism. The trouble with such reasonings as take place in the *Dialogues* is that they go beyond the point where observation and inference can provide any test of the conclusions reached:

> First, it seems to me that this theory of the universal energy and operation of the Supreme Being is too bold ever to carry conviction with it to a man, sufficiently apprised of the weakness of human reason. . . . We are got into fairy land, long ere we have reached the last steps of our theory; and *there* we have no reason to trust our common methods of argument. . . . And however we may flatter ourselves that we are guided, in every step which we take, by a kind of verisimilitude and experience, we may be assured that this fancied experience has no authority when we thus apply it to subjects that lie entirely out of the sphere of experience.[41]

Hume's second argument contests the legitimacy of taking our inability to give final explanations of natural forces as grounds for referring the laws of nature to a divine intelligence. Our idea of a supreme mind must be modeled on our idea of the human mind, and we have no better understanding of mental forces than of physical:

> We are ignorant, it is true, of the manner in which bodies operate on each other: their force or energy is entirely incomprehensible: but are we not equally ignorant of the manner or force by which a mind, even the supreme mind, operates either on itself or on body?[42]

Christian faith involves the subversion of reason,

[41] *Ibid.*, Sect. VII, Part 1, p. 72.
[42] *Ibid.*, pp. 72–73.

and the acceptance of Christian religion entails denying what observation and experience render most
probable:

> The Christian Religion not only was at first attended
> with miracles, but even at this day cannot be believed
> by any reasonable person without one. Mere reason
> is insufficient to convince us of its veracity: and who-
> ever is moved by *faith* to assent to it, is conscious of a
> continued miracle in his own person, which subverts
> all the principles of his understanding, and gives him
> a determination to believe what is most contrary to
> custom and experience.[43]

If, then, on Humean principles, the question of
natural theology is unanswerable, and if religious agnosticism is the only tenable position, is not the discussion of the *Dialogues* futile? I am sure that this was
Hume's opinion:

> If men attempt the discussion of questions which lie
> entirely beyond the reach of human capacity, such as
> those concerning the origin of worlds, or the economy
> of the intellectual system or region of spirits, they may
> long beat the air in their fruitless contests, and never
> arrive at any determinate conclusion.[44]

If, then, Hume's opinion was that theological argument is futile, why did he write the *Dialogues*, keep
them by him for twenty-five years, revise them in the
year of his death, and take such anxious precautions to
ensure their publication?

I am sure that Hume wrote the *Dialogues* precisely
in order to reveal the futility of such theological argu-

[43] *Enquiry concerning Human Understanding*, Sect. X, Part
II, p. 131.
[44] *Ibid.*, Sect. VIII, Part I, p. 81.

ment, and to show that the only sensible course is to abandon such topics for what he calls "the examination of common life."[45] It is obviously not futile to show that a certain kind of argument is futile, and I daresay that Hume himself thought it was very useful.

Thus when Hume on a single occasion speaks for himself in the twelfth Dialogue, he characterizes the entire argument as "verbal" and not admitting "of any precise determination." He makes very clear that this judgment of the dispute between Philo and Cleanthes is his own by stating it in a footnote—the only place available in such a composition for making his own voice heard. It is true that at this very point Philo has also been arguing "That the dispute concerning Theism is . . . merely verbal,"[46] but Philo's argument is of a different order from Hume's. Philo argues that the skeptic and the dogmatist can no more settle the question of the degree of similarity between the divine mind and the human than they could decide a controversy about the degree of Hannibal's greatness or of Cleopatra's beauty. This problem is a particular one encountered *within* the context of the argument set forth in the *Dialogues*. Hume, on the other hand, makes a judgment *of* that argument, specifying the fatal difficulty which vitiates the entire discussion:

> It seems evident, that the dispute between the scep-
> tics and dogmatists is entirely verbal, or at least re-
> gards only the degrees of doubt and assurance which
> we ought to indulge with regard to all reasoning: And
> such disputes are commonly at the bottom, verbal,

[45] *Ibid.*, Sect. VIII, Part ii, p. 103.
[46] P. 218.

and admit not of any precise determination. No philosophical dogmatist denies, that there are difficulties both with regard to the senses and to all science: and that these difficulties are in a regular, logical method, absolutely insolvable. No sceptic denies, that we lie under an absolute necessity, notwithstanding these difficulties, of thinking, and believing, and reasoning with regard to all kind of subjects, and even of frequently assenting with confidence and security. The only difference, then, between these sects, if they merit that name, is, that the sceptic, from habit, caprice, or inclination, insists most on the difficulties; the dogmatist, for like reasons, on the necessity.[47]

On this interpretation, which distinguishes the author from his character, the significance of Philo's recantation in the final Dialogue is quite plain and in perfect accordance with Hume's usual strictures on a certain type of skeptic. Philo was a skeptic and Hume was a skeptic, but Philo's skepticism was of a different type from Hume's, and of a type that Hume consistently repudiated and condemned: Philo's skepticism is excessive skepticism, or Pyrrhonism, a position which it is impossible to maintain consistently:

And though a Pyrrhonian may throw himself or others into a momentary amazement and confusion by his profound reasonings; the first and most trivial event in life will put to flight all his doubts and scruples, and leave him the same, in every point of action and speculation, with the philosophers of every other sect, or with those who never concerned themselves in any philosophical researches. When he awakes from his dream, he will be the first to join in the laugh against

[47] P. 219, n. 1.

himself, and to confess, that all his objections are mere amusement.[48]

What, then, was the nature of Hume's own skepticism? He called it a *mitigated* skepticism, and in the last section of his *Enquiry concerning Human Understanding* he credited it with

> The limitation of our inquiries to such subjects as are best adapted to the narrow capacity of human understanding. . . . A correct judgement . . . , avoiding all distant and high inquiries, confines itself to common life, and to such objects as fall under daily practice and experience. . . . While we cannot give a satisfactory reason, why we believe, after a thousand experiments, that a stone will fall, or fire burn; can we ever satisfy ourselves concerning any determination, which we may form, with regard to the origin of worlds, and the situation of nature, from, and to eternity?[49]

VII

When Hume set himself to become "thoroughly acquainted with the extent and force of human understanding,"[50] he began to work upon a conventional philosophical problem of the eighteenth century. But Hume, it seems, had personal reasons for engaging himself with this question of the scope and limits of the human mind. He wanted to discover whether or

[48] *Enquiry concerning Human Understanding*, Sect. XII, Part II, p. 160.

[49] *Ibid.*, Sect. XII, Part III, p. 162.

[50] Hume, *A Treatise of Human Nature*, ed. L. A. Selby-Bigge (Oxford, 1888), p. xix.

not those who made bold assertions about God, the
immortality of the soul, eternal rewards and punishments, the origin of the universe, and other such matters could really know that what they said was true.
He concluded very early in his career that they could
not know and, further, that there was no way open to
the human mind to discover truth in the realm of
theological speculation.

It appears that this conclusion liberated Hume from
the guilt and anxiety he experienced in his youth
about his inability to believe the religious teachings
which prevailed in his own time and place, and from
the dread of a "future state" in which an unbeliever
like himself would suffer eternal punishment. This
state of cultivated indifference toward the unknow-
able, which allows one "to live at ease ever after,"[51]
is the consummation of a skeptical procedure which
draws the limits of human knowledge short of certain unanswerable questions which have for so long
plagued the human mind.

Having realized for himself the blessed state of *ata-
raxia* (to use the term borrowed by A. H. Basson[52]
from Sextus Empiricus to describe the ultimate goal of
mitigated skepticism), Hume was left with a perplexing question: how did it happen that countless numbers of people, even intelligent ones, held religious
beliefs which were neither rationally justifiable nor
practically useful, and which many others, some of

[51] *Enquiry concerning Human Understanding*, Sect. XII, Part
II, p. 160.
[52] A. H. Basson, *David Hume* (London, 1958). See esp.
Ch. 7.

them also intelligent, rejected? Hume finally satisfied himself about the answer to this question, and said his last word on it in the note he added to the twelfth Dialogue: it is a matter of "habit, caprice, or inclination." According to Hume, it seems, a man is fated to be either a believer or a nonbeliever; his religious standpoint is predestined before his mind is ready or even disposed to consider the arguments. Thus the thorny path of skepticism led Hume back to the domain of Calvinism from which he had exiled himself long before. But it is unlikely that he recognized that country upon his return.

PART X OF HUME'S *DIALOGUES*

WILLIAM H. CAPITAN

In Part X of Hume's *Dialogues concerning Natural Religion*, Philo presents the famous trilemma attributed to Epicurus: "Is God willing to prevent evil, but not able? Is he able, but not willing? Is he both willing and able? Whence then is evil?" Some critics say Philo is trying to disprove God's existence.[1] Some say he is not.[2] Actually, he is demolishing natural religion, not by disproving God's existence, but by invalidating the argument to God's moral attributes. I would like to show how he does this.

Natural religion, in the *Dialogues* and commonly in the eighteenth century, is the set of beliefs about God allegedly derivable from reason and experience unaided by revelation. Natural theologians claimed to

From *American Philosophical Quarterly*, Vol. III (1966). Reprinted by permission of the author and the Editor of *American Philosophical Quarterly*.

[1] Among these are: T. H. Huxley, *Hume* (London, 1879), pp. 146–52; A. H. Basson, *David Hume* (London, 1958), pp. 105–6; Nelson Pike, "Hume on Evil," *Philosophical Review*, LXXII (1963), 180–97; *idem* in his introduction to *God and Evil* (Englewood Cliffs, N. J., 1964).

[2] Among these are: N. Kemp Smith in the Introduction to his edition of Hume, *Dialogues concerning Natural Religion*, 2nd ed. (London, 1947), pp. 67–69; F. Copleston, *A History of Philosophy*, 7 vols. (London, 1946–62), V, 307–9; R. J. Butler, "Natural Belief and the Enigma of Hume," *Archiv für Geschichte der Philosophie*, XLII (1960), 73–100.

know, not only that God exists, but also enough about God's nature to infer that men ought to worship him by being pious and virtuous, that men must repent of their sins, and that there are present and future rewards and punishments.[3]

The position Philo takes against natural religion is, as he says, "moderate scepticism." He questions only the adequacy of the evidence offered by natural theologians for their claims about God's nature. He does not, as would a Pyrrhonist, reject the common sense idea of evidence; for he believes arguments derived from common life can dispel the subtle arguments of the sceptics. "But," he adds, "it is evident whenever our arguments lose this advantage and run wide of common life, that the most refined scepticism comes to be upon a footing with them, and is able to oppose and counterbalance them. The mind must remain in suspense between them; and it is that very suspense or balance which is the triumph of scepticism."[4] Philo maintains this position throughout the *Dialogues*, and this is the key to his argument in Part X.

Demea opens Part II by saying: "The question is not concerning the *being* but the *nature* of God. This, I affirm, from the infirmities of human understanding, to be altogether incomprensible and un-

[3] For example, see: Charles Blount, *The Oracles of Reason* (London, 1693); Mathew Tindal, *Christianity as Old as the Creation, or the Gospel a Republication of the Religion of Nature* (London, 1730).

[4] Hume, *Dialogues concerning Natural Religion*, ed. N. Kemp Smith, *op. cit.*, pp. 135–36. All subsequent references to this work are to this edition and will appear in the text as "Hume." I shall not ask whether Philo speaks for Hume. On this point see Copleston, *op. cit.*, pp. 308–9.

known to us" (Hume, p. 141). And, whatever was said earlier or will be said later, Philo agrees with him here and many times after: "the question can never be concerning the *being* but only the *nature* of the Deity. The former truth . . . is unquestionable and self-evident. Nothing exists without a cause; and the original cause of this universe (whatever it be) we call God . . ." (Hume, p. 142). Philo does not depart from his moderate scepticism here; for, unlike the natural theologians' abstruse reasonings about God's nature, this reasoning about God's existence rests on the solid ground of common sense.

Basson says this agreement is not meant seriously.[5] He believes a substantial part of the *Dialogues* is concerned with the question of existence, and the question of God's existence and the question of God's nature could hardly be discussed independently because the former cannot be other than a question of something's having certain antecedently specified characteristics. But Philo has already said there is an original cause of the universe and we call it God.[6] This is to say

[5] Basson, *op. cit.*, pp. 105–6.

[6] Huxley (*op. cit.*) says this makes us doubt whether Philo ought to be taken as Hume's mouthpiece because in the *Treatise of Human Nature*, Book I, Part III, Sect. 3 and 14, Hume affirms that "there is no absolute nor metaphysical necessity that every beginning of existence should be attended with such an object" [as a cause]; and again, that it is "easy for us to conceive any object to be non-existent this moment and existent the next, without conjoining to it the distinct idea of a cause or productive principle." But Hume explains his meaning in his letter to John Stewart: "I never asserted so absurd a Proposition as *that any thing might arise without a Cause*: I only maintain'd, that our Certainty of the Falshood of that Proposition proceeded neither from Intuition or Demonstration; but from another Source. *That Caesar existed, that there is such an Island as Sicily*; for these

something exists with the attribute of being cause of the universe, an attribute commonly associated with the name of "God."[7] So the disputants are asking whether the cause of the universe has other attributes commonly associated with the name "God." Responding to this question, then, Philo makes two assertions which determine the course of the entire discussion.

First, he gives his view of how we associate certain expressions with the name "God." "Wisdom, thought, design, knowledge; these we justly ascribe to him because these words are honourable among men, and we have no other language or other conceptions by which we can express our adoration of him. But let us beware lest we think that our ideas anywise correspond to his perfections, or that his attributes have any resemblance to these qualities among men. He is infinitely superior to our limited view and comprehension, and is more the object of worship in the temple than of disputation in the schools" (Hume, p. 142).

Second, Philo challenges Cleanthes by saying: "Our ideas reach no farther than our experience: We have no experience of divine attributes and operations: I need not conclude my syllogism: You can draw the inference yourself" (Hume, pp. 142–43). If Philo

---

propositions, I affirm, we have no demonstrative nor intuitive Proof. Woud you infer that I deny their Truth, or even their Certainty? There are many different kinds of Certainty; and some of them as satisfactory to the Mind, tho perhaps not so regular, as the demonstrative kind" (*The Letters of David Hume*, ed. J. Y. T. Greig [Oxford, 1932], I, 187).

[7] For a clear statement of this point and a helpful examination of the question "Does God exist?" see Paul Ziff, "About God," in *Religious Experience and Truth*, ed. Sidney Hook (New York, 1961), pp. 195–202.

wants Cleanthes to infer that God does not exist, he should not have conceded earlier that there must be an original cause of the universe. He wants Cleanthes to infer that we cannot prove anything about God which would make natural religion seem reasonable.[8]

Cleanthes responds to Philo's challenge with the argument from design:

> The curious adapting of means to ends, throughout all nature, resembles exactly, though it much exceeds, the productions of human contrivance; of human design, thought, wisdom, and intelligence. Since therefore the effects resemble each other, we are led to infer, by all the rules of analogy, that the causes also resemble, and that the Author of nature is somewhat similar to the mind of man, though possessed of much larger faculties, proportioned to the grandeur of the work which he has executed (Hume, p. 143).

He wants to prove God is, not just cause of the universe, but also "similar to the mind of man"; for, as we shall see, he thinks it essential for all religion that God be anthropomorphic at least in being benevolent.

Now the battle line between Philo and Cleanthes is drawn. Cleanthes tries to infer what he can about God while Philo deftly and Demea unwittingly keep cutting the ground from under him.

Part X is another stage, and a crucial one, in a series

[8] I agree generally with Professor Butler (*op. cit.*) when he says, "Philo's entire criticism of the argument from design should be viewed as an attempt, not to deny that God exists, but to break down Cleanthes' initial opinion that theological beliefs may find rational support in the recognition of evidence" (p. 87); and when he says, "The *Dialogues* are an attempt to work out precisely how much or how little is involved in this concession" [that God exists] (p. 92). But I prefer my formulations of these two points as more specific for Part X.

of Cleanthes' attempts to infer what he can about God. At this stage Cleanthes is trying to establish God's benevolence; God's existence has not been questioned, nor will it be. We must notice where Philo enters the discussion and where he aims:

> And is it possible, Cleanthes, that after all these reflections, and infinitely more, which might be suggested, you can still persevere in your anthropomorphism, and assert the moral attributes of the Deity, his justice, benevolence, mercy, and rectitude, to be of the same nature with these virtues in human creatures? His power we allow infinite: Whatever he wills is executed: But neither man nor any other animal are happy: Therefore he does not will their happiness. His wisdom is infinite: He is never mistaken in choosing the means to any end: But the course of nature tends not to human or animal felicity: Therefore it is not established for that purpose. Through the course of human knowledge, there are no inferences more certain and infallible than these (Hume, p. 198).

Hume has been criticized for not seeing that God may have had to allow suffering for some reason or other; and, this being so, Philo's reasoning disproves neither God's existence, nor God's benevolence, nor God's omnipotence.[9] But Philo asks this: "In what respect, then, do his benevolence and mercy resemble the benevolence and mercy of men?" (Hume, p. 198). There is no reason to suppose Hume thought Philo's reasoning disproved anything except that the course of nature was an adequate basis for saying the moral attributes of God are the same as those of humans.

[9] Nelson Pike, *op. cit.*

Philo admits to Cleanthes the reasonableness of ascribing a purpose to nature, but he denies that the purpose is to benefit either man or beast:

> You ascribe, Cleanthes (and I believe justly), a purpose . . . to nature. But what . . . is the object of that curious artifice and machinery, which she has displayed in all animals? The preservation alone of individuals and propagation of the species. It seems enough for her purpose, if such a rank be barely upheld in the universe, without any care or concern for the happiness of the members that compose it (Hume, p. 198).

Cleanthes sees the seriousness of Philo's attack, and he sees it for what it is—neither an assertion that God does not exist, nor an assertion that God is not benevolent, but an attack upon the idea that the course of nature is a basis for asserting God's benevolence.[10] So Cleanthes tells Philo: "If you can . . . prove mankind to be unhappy or corrupted, there is an end at once of all religion. For to what purpose establish the natural attributes of the Deity, while the moral are still doubtful and uncertain?" (Hume, p. 199).

Now Philo is in a position not entirely satisfactory to a sceptic; he is asked to prove something and, scepticism aside, something difficult, if not impossible to prove. His next move is important, in fact, the crux of this dialogue, but before he can make it, Demea interrupts to state his theodicy. The interruption helps Philo strategically, and it is a chance for Hume to

---

[10] This strictly parallels the argument Hume puts forth in the *Enquiry concerning Human Understanding*, Sect. XI. See the explication of it by Antony Flew in *Hume's Philosophy of Belief* (London, 1961), pp. 222–23.

interject a representative line of thinking which he thinks must be cut down before the full impact of Philo's scepticism can be appreciated.

Demea's theodicy is the so-called "porch view":

> This life [is] but a moment in comparison of eternity. The present evil phenomena, therefore, are rectified in other regions, and in some future period of existence. And the eyes of men, being then opened to larger views of things, see the whole connexion of general laws, and trace, with adoration, the benevolence and rectitude of the Deity . . . (Hume, p. 199).

This theodicy directs attention to the broad and eternal view of existence, and it is general enough to represent most theodicies. It makes either of two assumptions. One characterizes our view as being so limited that, even though we think we suffer, we really do not. Presumably, a broader or longer view of things would disclose our error. The other is that our view is so limited that, even though we really suffer when we think we do, we do not see that we must suffer for the sake of a greater good, either for ourselves or for the whole world. On the one hand, there really is no evil; on the other, evil is necessary.[11]

Whichever assumption Demea makes, his theodicy will not withstand Cleanthes' blow against it:

11 The distinction between these two assumptions is seldom made. Berkeley seems to think evil is an illusion, but he uses the second notion, that evil is necessary, to explain the illusion (*Principles of Human Knowledge*, Part I, Sect. 153). Berkeley's view resembles Demea's in form and in lack of form. Leibniz, of course, uses the second, more common notion (*Theodicy*, Summary of the Controversy Reduced to Formal Arguments, Objection I, Answer).

"Whence can any cause be known but from its known effects? . . . To establish one hypothesis upon another is building entirely in the air: and the utmost we can ever attain, by these conjectures and fictions, is to ascertain the bare possibility of our opinion; but never can we, upon such terms, establish its reality" (Hume, pp. 199–200). So this theodicy and all others like it cannot interfere with Philo's line of argument. Demea has no naturalistic evidence to claim that there are regions and a period of future existence where the present evil phenomena are rectified.

And, while Cleanthes admits that these conjectures and fictions ascertain the bare possibility of our opinion, thus recognizing that Philo's trilemma does not logically exclude the possibility of a benevolent God, still these conjectures presuppose that God is a moral agent—that he will, because of his nature, rectify the present evils of man—when this is precisely the point at issue. Cleanthes knows Demea cannot argue that God will, in some unknown way and for some unknown reason, validate man's suffering; nor can he base his argument on God's benevolence when he does not know that God is benevolent—when, in fact, he is trying to prove that benevolence, and when the presence of suffering makes it doubtful. So he says to Demea, "The only method of supporting divine benevolence (and it is what I willingly embrace) is to deny absolutely the misery and wickedness of man" (Hume, p. 200).

And now Philo is ready for his crucial move. He says:

I . . . must admonish you, Cleanthes, that you have put this controversy upon a most dangerous issue, and are unawares introducing a total scepticism into the most essential articles of natural and revealed theology. What! no method of fixing a just foundation for religion unless we allow the happiness of human life, and maintain a continued existence even in this world, with all our present pains, infirmities, vexations, and follies, to be eligible and desirable! But this is contrary to everyone's feeling and experience; it is contrary to an authority so established as nothing can subvert. No decisive proofs can ever be produced against this authority; nor is it possible for you to compute, estimate, and compare all the pains and all the pleasures in the lives of all men and of all animals; and thus, by your resting the whole system of religion on a point which, from its very nature, must for ever be uncertain, you tacitly confess that that system is equally uncertain (Hume, pp. 200–1).

Philo has turned the trick without proving or disproving anything, not even that mankind is unhappy. Cleanthes, himself, has shown that the only way to establish the divine benevolence and, consequently, natural religion itself is to stand in a quagmire.

Philo then takes the argument to a second stage and even allows "what can never possibly be proved"—that human happiness exceeds its misery. This takes Cleanthes nowhere because from infinite power, wisdom, and goodness we should reasonably expect no misery in the world at all. The only escape from logic so solid and decisive is to deny that we know anything about these matters. This, says Philo, he has maintained from the beginning of the discussion (Hume, p. 201).

Philo next takes the argument to a third stage and

even grants that pain or misery in man is compatible with infinite power and goodness, even in the ordinary sense of these attributes. Even this takes Cleanthes nowhere, for he must prove that the Deity has these attributes from the present mixed and confused phenomena, and from these alone. Even if there were no evil, Cleanthes would confront sufficient difficulties because the phenomena are finite. Actually, there is evil and the phenomena are mixed (Hume, p. 201). Clearly, Philo is not arguing against God's existence, for then allowing the compatibility of evil and the divine attributes would amount to capitulation.

In Part XI Cleanthes tries to avoid Philo's conclusion and preserve the human analogy: "Supposing the author of nature to be finitely perfect, though far exceeding mankind, a satisfactory account may then be given of natural and moral evil . . . benevolence, regulated by wisdom and limited by necessity, may produce just such a world as the present" (Hume, p. 203). But this supposition allows merely the compatibility of evil and divine benevolence. Philo has already in effect shown it of no avail in Part X, where, for the sake of argument, he allows the compatibility of evil with *infinite* power and goodness. In Part XI he has merely to say, "Conjectures, especially where infinity is excluded from the divine attributes, may perhaps be sufficient to prove a consistency, but can never be foundations for any inference" (Hume, p. 205). And inference has been the matter all along.

So with God's moral character at stake, with Cleanthes' attachment of the fate of natural religion to the fate of God's benevolence, with Cleanthes' demolishing blow against Demea's theodicy and all others like it ("to establish one hypothesis upon another is building entirely in the air"), and with the necessary foundation of natural religion shown to be in principle unprovable, even allowing the compatibility of evil and divine benevolence, Philo justly considers his case logically tight. While this is not a demonstration that God does not exist, nor that God is not benevolent, it is a perfect triumph for the sceptic on perhaps the crucial issue for natural religion.

HUME'S IMMANENT GOD

GEORGE J. NATHAN

The general tendency in Hume scholarship to focus on the negative, critical, and skeptical side of Hume's work has been especially true of the *Dialogues concerning Natural Religion.*[1] A consideration of the roles of Philo, Cleanthes, and Demea in the development of Hume's thought is necessary to remedy the imbalance and to bring out Hume's positive contribution in these dialogues.

The point at issue is initially expounded by the most orthodox disputant, Demea: "The question is not concerning the *being* but the *nature* of God" (D141). This position is also assented to by the most skeptical member, Philo, and Cleanthes at no time disputes it. Demea, however, goes on to qualify his statement as follows: "This [the nature of God] I affirm, from the infirmities of human understanding to be altogether incomprehensible and unknown to us. The essence of that supreme mind, his attributes, the man-

---

[1] The following abbreviations will be used for the works of Hume: D = *Dialogues concerning Natural Religion*, ed. Norman Kemp Smith, 2nd ed. (London, 1947); T = *A Treatise of Human Nature*, ed. L. A. Selby-Bigge (Oxford, 1888); E = *An Enquiry concerning Human Understanding*, ed. L. A. Selby-Bigge, 2nd ed. (Oxford, 1902). The letter is followed in the text by the page number.

ner of his existence, the very nature of his duration; these and every particular, which regards so divine a Being, are mysterious to men" (D141). Philo takes the same line of thought himself and agrees, with Demea's assistance, to "defend the adorable mysteriousness of the divine nature" (D146). Likewise Philo, as allied in this cause with Demea, asks Cleanthes to "adopt our mysticism, as you call it, and admit of the absolute incomprehensibility of the divine nature" (D172). The position of Demea and Philo is in direct accord with principles which Hume has presented in the *Treatise*. There he says "the ultimate force and efficacy of nature is perfectly unknown to us" (T159), and the "ultimate cause [of impressions] is . . . perfectly inexplicable by human reason" (T84). This is a consequence of his discussion of causes in which he tries to show that no examination of the cause ever leads us to an understanding of the way its component parts serve to produce a particular effect. Every event prior to its occurrence is absolutely mysterious and, Hume might have added, is still mysterious to a certain degree afterward. Yet we can explain certain effects by appealing to more general principles. But once we reach the ultimate cause in the series, there is nothing to be done but to say that nature happens to be constructed in that particular way. Philo's remarks here indicate a peculiarly Humean stamp: "These words, *generation, reason*, mark only certain powers and energies in nature, whose effects are known, but whose essence is incomprehensible" (D178). Such powers in nature are what Hume calls "springs or principles." Reason, instinct, generation and vegetation are seen to be prin-

ciples because we observe the regular production of
their typical effects. However, in no case can we know
the principle itself or how it operates. We are only
able to know that such principles exist and that they
are causes of certain effects. The extension of the notion of incomprehensibility to God is a corollary of
Hume's general position that knowledge of the essence, but not of the existence, of ultimate principles
is impossible. Such a notion, however, is not as important as others which are developed in the *Dialogues*.
Just as Demea's role in the dialogue is a minor one, so
the concept of incomprehensibility plays a relatively
minor role in the total conclusion of Hume's argument. The major roles are reserved for positions introduced and developed by Philo and Cleanthes. Let
us examine Cleanthes' arguments first.

Cleanthes makes his most vital point early in Part II.
He presents what has traditionally been regarded as
the argument from design.

> Look around the world: Contemplate the whole and
> every part of it: You will find it to be nothing but
> one great machine, subdivided into an infinite num-
> ber of lesser machines, which again admit of sub-
> divisions, to a degree beyond what human senses and
> faculties can trace and explain. All these various ma-
> chines, and even their most minute parts, are adjusted
> to each other with an accuracy, which ravishes into
> admiration all men, who have ever contemplated
> them. The curious adapting of means to ends,
> throughout all nature, resembles exactly, though it
> much exceeds, the productions of human contrivance;
> of human design, thought, wisdom, and intelligence.
> Since therefore the effects resemble each other, we
> are led to infer, by all the rules of analogy, that the

causes also resemble; and that the Author of nature is somewhat similar to the mind of man; though possessed of much larger faculties, proportioned to the grandeur of the work, which he has executed (D143).

Cleanthes' comparison here rests on certain supposed analogies between machines and the universe. In order for something to be a machine, it must have these characteristics cited by Cleanthes:

(1) an accurate adjustment of the parts to each other.

(2) an adaptation of means to ends.

There is also a third characteristic which is not explicitly mentioned above but which is equally necessary if a thing is to be called a machine, viz., that the cause of its particular ordering of parts must be external to the effect. Cleanthes takes this third aspect of a machine for granted, but it is a key point in his argument. In arguing that the universe resembles a machine, Cleanthes has ensured the conclusion that it must have an external cause. It is possible for there to be an object whose parts are adjusted to one another and which exhibits an adaptation of means to ends without any external cause for this condition. But we cannot call it a machine and then deny the propriety of a question about what external thing is the cause of its order.

Cleanthes is making two points with his analogy. The first is that the means-end relationship and the coherence of parts typify a product of design, thought, wisdom and intelligence. Since both human artifacts and the universe are characterized by such properties, their causes must be intelligent as well. The second point is that because both artifacts and the universe are machines they both have external causes. However, the second point does not hold since we never observe directly that something is a machine. This is an inference from the experience of agents producing artifacts. In the present instance, it would be begging the question to call the universe a machine because the inference from the particular order of the universe to an external orderer is precisely the issue in dispute. The inference, if valid, would justify calling the world a machine, but calling it a machine does not justify the inference.

Philo replies to the two points which Cleanthes has made in Part II. He attacks the first point by indicating that the thought and intelligence of men and animals is but one of the many springs and principles of the universe. There is no obvious reason to give it preference over all these other principles. But even if we did give it preference, there is no justification for regarding it as a standard for the whole. To the best of our knowledge, its influence is confined to one small part of the universe. Philo argues against the second point by asking Cleanthes if he has ever seen worlds being ordered. As was shown above, in order for Cleanthes to call the universe a machine it is necessary that he have experience of worlds being ordered by an external agent. Philo is hammering home the same point. It does not follow that because watches and houses are never experienced to come into existence without a maker that the universe could not have attained its order without one. Experience must be the judge of whether the universe had an external agent as cause and obviously experience can tell us nothing of the origin of the universe.]

Cleanthes not only does not answer Philo's objections to the idea of an external cause, but even says things which are inconsistent with that view. Cleanthes devotes his attention in Part III to showing that the cause of order is rational. He says: ". . . it is by no means necessary that theists should prove the similarity of the works of nature to those of art; because the similarity is self-evident and undeniable[.] The same matter, a like form: What more is requisite to show an analogy between their causes, and to ascertain the origin of all things from a divine purpose and intention?" (D152). Since the alleged similarity is self-evident, Cleanthes resorts to examples to illustrate, rather than strictly to prove, the resemblance.

The first example in Part III deals with an articulate voice heard in the clouds. This voice speaks at the same time to all nations in the appropriate language and dialect and conveys a "just sense and meaning" and "some instruction altogether worthy of a benevolent Being, superior to mankind" (D152). Cleanthes questions whether we can doubt the cause of such a voice or the design and purpose of such a cause. He goes on to say that if this voice because of its power and versatility in languages much exceeds any human voice, it would be foolish to suppose on account of the great disanalogy between the effects that this "rational, wise, coherent speech" proceeded from some accidental circumstance and not from divine reason and intelligence (D152–53).

This example indicates an interesting emphasis. The

words spoken by the voice are characterized by *sense* and *meaning*. They convey an *instruction*. Futhermore the speech is *rational, wise* and *coherent*. The words which are italicized are applicable only to things which display intelligence. The rationality of the voice is self-evident, as Cleanthes has maintained. To someone who cannot understand the voice there can be no rationality to it. But if he does understand it, the very fact of his understanding is sufficient for him to pronounce it the product of intelligence. Rationality appears on the very face of it, although obviously it cannot be directly perceived by the senses as the loudness can. However, along with the rationality of the voice goes the requirement that if we call it a voice, there must be a speaker. We are still involved in this example with the idea of an external contriver. It might be that the works of nature are possessed of a form resembling that of artifacts; that they bear the stamp of rationality upon them. But it is arbitrary to compare them to machines and voices since these types of things are not merely rational but ordered by an external cause. Such a comparison precludes a priori the possibility that natural objects might evidence intelligence without being designed by some agent. Because two objects have a rational form, this does not entail that they both have an external cause.

Cleanthes' second example is intended to bring out in a more obvious way the relation of the universe to a designer. His illustration requires two suppositions: (1) "that there is a natural, universal, invariable language common to every individual of the human race" and (2) "that books are natural productions, which perpetuate themselves in the same manner with animals and vegetables by descent and propagation" (D153). Both of these suppositions do not seem unreasonable to Cleanthes since, as regards (1), some expressions of emotion constitute a universal language, and animals possess a rudimentary but natural speech which is understood by their own species. As regards (2), because there are fewer parts and less evidence of design in a book like the *Iliad* than in an organized body, it is easier to imagine the propagation of such a book than that of any plant or animal.

Having made these assumptions, Cleanthes invites examination of these natural volumes. He asks: "Could you possibly open one of them, and doubt, that its original cause bore the strongest analogy to mind and intelligence? When it reasons and discourses; when it expostulates, argues, and enforces its views and topics . . . could you persist in asserting, that all this at the bottom, had really no meaning, and that the first formation of this volume in the loins of its original parent proceeded not from thought and design?" (D153). Cleanthes continues his argument by suggesting to Philo that any discrepancy between this invented example and the universe is to the advantage of the latter. An animal displays many more instances of design than does any book. Furthermore Cleanthes asserts that the hypothesis of a living library is equally susceptible to the objection Philo put forward earlier, viz., that to uphold a theory of an external cause, one would need to have experience of the formation of the object, in this case the natural volume. The final ultimatum for Philo is: "Assert either that a rational volume is no proof of a rational cause, or admit of a similar cause to all the works of nature" (D154).

Cleanthes' example is curiously inconsistent with his general thesis. He is maintaining here that we call something a book without requiring that such an artifact have an external artificer. The natural volume has a rational order without being produced by a designer who is external to the effect. As Kemp Smith explains the difference: "The adult organism comes into being through the *differentiation* of the previously homogeneous; artificial objects come into being through the *external fitting together* of bodies antecedently shaped and formed" (D102). If the book is an organism it was not externally fitted together. Yet if it was not externally put together, it does not seem proper to call it a book. This example also introduces an essential ambiguity into the word "design" which lingers throughout the *Dialogues*. At some stages the meaning of "design" is taken to be that of the rational or intelligent order which is produced by an external agent or the intentions and plans of that agent. However, "design" can also mean only the rational order itself without any further assumptions about external causes. Thus the book when it reproduces is not conscious of directing its actions to any particular end since it is not conscious at all. Yet this does not prevent us from saying that the book is rational, or that what is contained therein is meaningful, significant and intelligently arranged and argued. Despite the fact that the living library is, as Kemp Smith puts it, "self-developing, self-maintaining, self-regulating, self-propagating" (D102), the particular order does require a rational principle for its explanation.

At this juncture, it would be useful to see just how far Hume is prepared to extend the concepts of reason and rationality. For one thing, he does not require that the rational orderer perceive the order which it produces. In response to a question by Demea as to whether anything can produce order without perceiving it, Philo makes this reply: "A tree bestows order and organization on that tree which springs from it, without knowing the order: an animal in the same manner on its offspring: a bird, on its nest: And instances of this kind are even more frequent in the world, than those of order, which arise from reason and contrivance" (D179). By the reason in this quotation, Hume means the ability shared by men and animals to exercise control over actions by a conscious foresight of the effects which our actions will produce. But in both the *Treatise* and the *Enquiry*, when Hume discusses the reason of animals, he distinguishes two kinds of reason. He makes the following statement in the *Enquiry:*

> But though animals learn many parts of their knowledge from observation, there are also many parts of it, which they derive from the original hand of nature; which much exceed the share of capacity they possess on ordinary occasions; and in which they improve, little or nothing, by the longest practice and experience. These we denominate Instincts, and are so apt to admire as something very extraordinary, and inexplicable by all the disquisitions of human understanding (E108).

Hume goes on to say that

the experimental reasoning, which we possess in common with beasts, and on which the whole conduct of life depends, is nothing but a species of instinct or mechanical power, that acts in us unknown to ourselves; and in its chief operations, is not directed by any such relations or comparisons of ideas, as are the proper objects of our intellectual faculties. Though the instinct be different, yet it is still an instinct, which teaches a man to avoid the fire; as much as that, which teaches a bird, with such exactness, the art of incubation, and the whole economy and order of its nursery (E108).

Reason emerges as an instinctive type of reaction. The knowledge which we have of certain effects is either built-in as in the case of the bird, or else acquired as is the case with men. The bird which builds its nest is adapting means to ends in the same way as a man does in building a house. However, the man acquired his knowledge of house-building from experience whereas the bird was born with his knowledge of nest-building. Hume is pointing out that the instinctive disposition or habit of the mind which is present in passing from the idea of the means to the idea of the end is "built-in" for both the bird and the man. The bird, however, has the content of the causal inference given with the habit. Man in almost all cases must acquire the habit and the content of cause and effect from repeated experience. Reason for Hume, i.e., the ability to make inferences about matters of fact and existence, is ultimately a practical faculty. It is designed to insure the preservation of the individual and of the species and to enable them to obtain pleasure and to avoid pain. If the attainment of these ends were to depend on a process of argumentation or deduction most men and animals would perish. Fortunately, this is not the case.

The argument here is an analogical one. Judging from the marvelous adaptation of means to ends which men evidence we must equally acknowledge a similar process on the part of animals. If man exhibits rationality, then so do other creatures. The fact of rationality is not diminished by the revelation that instinct is the cause of this amazing adaptive process. Rather, we are led to the conclusion that instinct possesses a rationality of its own.

To return to Cleanthes' example, we see that even though the propagation of the natural volumes does not depend on conscious design, nevertheless the volumes are rational and are due to a rational cause. The character of the volumes remains unchanged, even if they did not have an external cause. Whether rational organization is due to a designing intellect or to a built-in disposition or to generation, the organization is still rational. Cleanthes' illustration is important because it brings out this essential point: just as we call a mind rational because of its particular order, and not because of its cause, likewise we determine whether any other thing has an intelligent order by examining its structure and not by looking for the cause. For Hume the way of determining such order is by comparing something to objects which are acknowledged to be rationally ordered and then ascertaining what points of analogy are present in both. If the aspects which are found in the ordered product are also found in the item in question, then we can pronounce that item rational. Of course, human artifacts suggest themselves as the obvious paradigm for such comparisons. For this reason Cleanthes' illustrations are especially apt. His comparison of the universe to machines, houses and books is useful because they all exhibit an intelligent structure. Yet in making the analogy he confuses the evident points of resemblance with the question to be proved. The universe and a book resemble in their structure, but that they have the same type of cause, an external one, is inferred, not observed.

However, there is still some question as to whether Philo accepts the rationality of the universe as depicted by Cleanthes. It is interesting to note that after Cleanthes' lengthy expositing of the self-evident resemblance of the works of nature to human productions, Philo is described by Pamphilus, the narrator, as being "a little embarrassed and confounded" (D155). Demea then interrupts to save face for Philo. This, however, is, I submit, a stylistic trick executed by Hume. Philo is in substantial agreement with Cleanthes but does not reveal it until he has developed his own position. The first hint of such agreement occurs in Part X where Philo says: "You ascribe, Cleanthes (and I believe justly) a purpose and intention to nature" (D198). Likewise later in the same section Philo replies: "In many views of the universe, and of its parts, particularly the latter, the beauty and fitness of final causes strike us with such irresistible force that all objections appear (what I believe they really are) mere cavils and sophisms; nor can we then imagine how it was ever possible for us to repose any weight on them" (D202). Philo has thus become a reasonable skeptic according to the definition laid down by Cleanthes in Part III: A reasonable skeptic rejects only abstruse arguments but sticks to common sense and the "plain instincts of nature" (D154). He gives his assent whenever reasons strike him with such a force that only the greatest resistance can overcome it. In Part XII, the concluding section, Philo's assent to what may be called the rationality of the universe is even more pronounced, but discussion of that section must wait upon an examination of Philo's arguments prior to that point in the *Dialogues*.

As Part IV opens, Cleanthes concedes that if we are to call the Deity intelligent, then he must have a mind "whose acts and sentiments and ideas are . . . distinct and successive" (D159). Philo argues that recourse to a world of arranged ideas does not explain the arrangement of the material world since this ideal world must also have a cause. As he says: "Have we not the same reason to trace that ideal world into another ideal world, or new intelligent principle? But if we stop and go no farther; why go so far? Why not stop at the material world? How can we satisfy ourselves without going on *in infinitum?*" (D161). The best solution is never to go beyond the material world. "By supposing it to contain the principle of its order within itself, we really assert it to be God; and the sooner we arrive at that divine Being so much the better" (D162). Philo then examines two possible ways of accounting for the order of God's ideas. The one is that they fall into order of themselves. But this explanation would also hold for the material world

and, as a matter of fact, occurs in all cases of generation and vegetation. Also we see from experience that
there are cases where order does not obtain among
ideas, as in madness, nor in matter, as in cases of cor-
ruption. The other way of accounting for the order of
ideas is to suppose that God's mind is a rational faculty
and that this is the cause of order. But again if this
were a valid explanation for God's mind it is also valid
for the material universe. We could say that order per-
tained to its very nature. The use of such explanations
remains a sure sign of our ignorance of ultimate causes.
Cleanthes fails to perceive that the focal point of
Philo's attack is on the question of the externality of
the cause for he says: "The order and arrangement of
nature, the curious adjustment of final causes, the
plain use and intention of every part and organ; all
these bespeak in the clearest language an intelligent
cause or Author" (D163). Cleanthes is unaware that
Philo is trying to eliminate only the externality of the
cause. He is not trying to deny its intelligence. However, Cleanthes has made the point which he intended
to make in the argument: the world is rational; it evi-
dences design, intention, intelligence; the parts cohere
together in the adjustment of means to ends. Except
for his criticism of Demea's a priori arguments
Cleanthes has played out his role. The rest of the
argument is Philo's.

In Part V, Philo uses Cleanthes' principle that like
effects prove like causes to reduce the anthropomorphic conception of God to absurdity. Since God's mind
is very much like the human mind it must be finite
and make mistakes. Also we need not assume that

there is one God since all great human productions ordinarily require more than one person. Likewise, human beings have bodies and reproduce. Could this not be true of God as well? Cleanthes' only reply is that these imaginative suggestions not only leave untouched the "hypothesis of design in the universe" (D169), but even tend to confirm it.

The argument developed in Part V is continued in Part VI. Philo adds a new principle, which he claims derives from experience: "that where several known circumstances are *observed* to be similar, the unknown will also be *found* similar" (D170). This new principle supports the argument which Cleanthes had made earlier, viz., that if part of the world is observed to be rational, then the rest should be found to be so also. Philo does not mention this possibility but rather makes a new analogy:

> Now if we survey the universe, so far as it falls under our knowledge, it bears a great resemblance to an animal or organized body, and seems actuated with a like principle of life and motion. A continual circulation of matter in it produces no disorder: A continual waste in every part is incessantly repaired: The closest sympathy is perceived throughout the entire system: And each part or member, in performing its proper offices, operates both to its own preservation and to that of the whole. The world, therefore, I infer, is an animal and the Deity is the SOUL of the world, actuating it, and actuated by it (D170–71).

Likewise it makes sense to regard the universe as a mind joined with a body because we never observe mind without body. It is not unreasonable to "suppose the divine mind and body to be also coeval, and to have both of them, order and arrangement naturally inherent in them, and inseparable from them" (D171). Cleanthes' reply is that there is some plausibility to such a theory, but since there are no sense organs and no "seat of thought or reason" (D172), a more likely analogue would be a vegetable. However, he is still granting Philo that the universe has an internal principle of order and that such a principle is a sufficient explanation for the order. But Philo wants to make a stronger claim for this internal principle. He is saying that not only is it a sufficient explanation, it is a necessary one. He expands on this on p. 174:

> And were I obliged to defend any particular system of this nature . . . I esteem none more plausible than that which ascribes an internal, inherent principle of order to the world; though attended with great and continual revolutions and alterations. This at once solves all difficulties; and if the solution, by being so general, is not entirely complete and satisfactory, it is, at least, a theory, that we must sooner or later, have recourse to whatever system we embrace. How could things have been as they are, were there not an original, inherent principle of order somewhere in thought or in matter? (D174).

Philo is defending the principle of an internal cause of order in the universe. Cleanthes is positing an external cause which is itself internally ordered. Both seek to avoid the infinite regress. To prevent the regress in which the order of the universe is explained by an external cause and the order of that external cause is explained by another external cause, etc. ad infinitum, it is necessary that there be an internal principle of order somewhere in the series. If the internal principle is necessary, then an external principle is impossible. Since the internal principle is necessary for explanation, it is also sufficient. Philo and Cleanthes agree that experience reveals an internal principle of order in the universe in planets, animals, and minds. Such things as watches and houses are observed to be the result of human minds which are themselves internally ordered. Therefore because this internal principle exists in the universe, the universe has within it a necessary and sufficient explanation for its order. As a result an external principle of order for the universe is impossible. Furthermore, if one external principle is impossible, an infinite series of such principles is equally impossible.

The same point can be expressed in another way. The order of a thing can be explained either by a principle within itself or by a principle external to it. It is impossible that an object's order be explained both ways since this would entail that a principle both did and did not explain the order. (It is true that the order of one part of a thing can be explained by the one principle and the order of another part by the other principle. However, the order of the same part cannot be explained by both principles.) We see from experience that the universe has internal principles of order. Therefore, it is impossible that it can also have an external principle of order.

Similarly, the order of any object either springs from within it because of an internal principle, or is imposed on it from without by an external principle. If the order springs from within, it cannot be imposed and vice versa. From experience we see that the order in the universe (at least in plants, animals and minds) springs from an internal principle within the objects of the universe. Therefore, it is impossible that this order was imposed on the objects by an external cause.

⌈Hume is, I believe, the first to notice that the argument from design must prove not one but two propositions: (1) that the universe has an intelligent order and requires an intelligent cause, and (2) that this cause must be external to the universe.⌉ It is not sufficient to prove (1). It is also necessary to prove (2) to save the argument from design. As Philo has shown by his arguments, this task is impossible. However, perhaps it is possible for Cleanthes to deny that internal principles of order are necessary. If he makes this move he is open to the infinite regress counterargument. Cleanthes' only remaining out is to deny that there are such things in the universe as internal principles of order. To this Philo could retort that if experience informs us only of external principles of order, there is no reason to assume that there exists anywhere else an internal principle of order. Thus, Cleanthes is back into the infinite regress. As a matter of fact, though, both Cleanthes and Philo agree that there are internal principles of order. Consequently Philo's points hold.

It is interesting to note that only the cosmological argument could prove Cleanthes' thesis that an external cause of the universe exists necessarily. But it is a touch of irony on Hume's part that the task of destroying the a priori cosmological proof is reserved for Cleanthes. With the destruction of this argument the last hope for preserving Cleanthes' position disappears. Philo's comments in Part IX seem particularly appropriate: "So dangerous is it to introduce this idea of necessity into the present question! And so naturally does it afford an inference directly opposite to the religious hypothesis!" (D191).

In Part VII, Philo continues the analogy developed in the previous section. If the universe resembles animals and vegetables, is it not likely that its cause bears a greater resemblance to the causes of animals and vegetables, viz., generation and vegetation, than it does to reason and design? Philo then goes off to expound outlandish theories of cosmogony to show to what limits principles like generation and vegetation can be pushed, just as he previously reduced to absurdity Cleanthes' rather naïve conception of the divine mind. But Philo readily admits that we have no data for any system of cosmogony whatsoever. We cannot tell how things came into being since experience tells us nothing of the origin of the universe. We can, however, learn a great deal about the present order of the world from experience. We observe that in our corner of the world there are four principles which continually produce rational effects. Wherever reason, instinct, generation and vegetation are present, there we find an adjustment of the parts to each other and to a common end. Rational effects can be produced as easily by internal causes as by external. But whether the cause is internal or external, it still remains rational.

In Part VIII, Philo attempts to revive the Epicurean hypothesis. He states that in an infinite amount of time a finite number of particles of matter in motion will produce the present order. However, this system is not completely random, for as Philo says: "But wherever matter is so poised, arranged and adjusted so as to continue in perpetual motion, and yet preserve a constancy in the forms, its situation must of necessity, have all the same appearance of art and contrivance which we observe at present" (D183). Philo is simply saying that if matter has a particular order inherent in it, it will produce a definite order which would resemble that produced by reason. Again Philo, under the guise of presenting a particular system of cosmogony, is merely repeating the principle of internal causes of order. However, since Philo must always appear the careless skeptic, he must run even his own principles wide of the mark on occasion so that the balance between Philo and Cleanthes can be maintained in the dialogues.

It is Part XII, long considered to be the most puzzling dialogue in the sequence, which clinches the interpretation here offered. In his florid profession of faith, Philo says, "No one has a deeper sense of religion impressed on his mind, or pays more profound adoration to the divine Being, as he discovers himself to reason, in the inexplicable contrivance and artifice of nature. A purpose, an intention or design strikes everywhere the most careless, the most stupid thinker" (D214). He continues by quoting in support of his position the two maxims *"that nature does nothing in vain"* and *"that nature acts by the simplest methods, and chooses the most proper means to any end"* (D214, Hume's italics). He marvels over Galen's account of the numerous circumstances which nature must have adjusted in order to attain the proper end in the anatomy of man.

Philo's position would only seem strange if he had ever denied that there was a marvelous order in nature or that this was a rational order. However, he has gone to great lengths not to deny such organization, but only to explain it by an internal principle. Philo's statement gives Cleanthes the opportunity to renew the comparison of the universe to a machine of human contrivance. He says that the best a skeptic could do is to present such a remote view of things as to produce a suspension of judgment. Philo replies that he considers such a suspension of judgment so little possible that the issue must revolve about a dispute of words.

> That the works of nature bear a great analogy to the productions of art is evident; and according to all the rules of good reasoning, we ought to infer, if we argue at all concerning them, that their causes have a proportional analogy. But as there are also considerable differences, we have reason to suppose a proportional difference in the causes; and in particular ought to attribute a much higher degree of power and energy to the supreme cause than any we have ever observed in mankind (D216–17).

The first question we must ask is, "How do works of nature resemble productions of art?" We have already given part of the answer in discussing Cleanthes' comparison of the universe to a machine. Philo, echoing Cleanthes, describes works of human contrivance as those things "which, along with a symmetry of parts, discover an adjustment of means to ends and a tendency to self-preservation" (D184). As to works of nature, animals and vegetables are typical examples. In the *Treatise* Hume describes animals and vegetables as having "a *sympathy* of parts to their *common end*" and asserts that these parts "bear to each other, the reciprocal relation of cause and effect in all their actions and operations. . . . [T]he several parts not only have a reference to some general purpose, but also a mutual dependence on, and connexion with each other" (T257). There is then an exact similarity between natural objects and human contrivances. In both the parts are related to each other by cause and effect, as well as relating to a general purpose in the whole object. If one is intelligently ordered, then so is the other. This is the point on which Cleanthes has all along insisted and with which Philo has secretly agreed. But the points of resemblance mentioned do not include having a cause. This is something which is independent of the resemblance on the grounds of intelligent order.

The second question which comes to mind is, "What are the considerable differences between the works of nature and productions of art?" The answer is obvious again. Works of nature, such as animals and vegetables, have an internal cause of order while productions of art have an external cause. Philo is not unaware of this fact for he wonders whether it is proper to call this cause of order "*a mind or intelligence,* notwithstanding the vast difference, which may reasonably be supposed between him and human minds." He asks, "What is this but a mere verbal controversy?" (D217). Moreover, if we do not feel that the terms "God" or "Deity" are entirely fitting, Philo invites us to call him

MIND or THOUGHT. Why are the terms "a mind or intelligence" inappropriate while "MIND or THOUGHT" is
deemed fitting? The answer would seem to be based
on Hume's conception of the mind, as given by Demea
in the *Dialogues:* "a composition of various faculties,
passions, sentiments, ideas; united, indeed into one
self or person, but still distinct from each other"
(D159). Such a system of ideas and passions must
necessarily be external to any effect it produces as the
human mind is external to all its productions. However, MIND or THOUGHT could be construed to be the
rational organizing factor which might order either
ideas or matter. In fact, something like this must be
true in Hume's system to account for the extraordinary resemblance between artifacts and natural objects which he points out.

Philo follows up this so-called verbal dispute by
attempting to reconcile the disagreement between the
theist and the atheist. The theist will attempt to emphasize the great difference between the human and
the divine mind. However, if Philo were to ask the
atheist

> whether, from the coherence and apparent sympathy
> in all the parts of this world, there be not a certain
> degree of analogy among all the operations of nature
> in every situation and in every age; whether the rot-
> ting of a turnip, the generation of an animal and the
> structure of human thought be not energies that prob-
> ably bear some remote analogy to each other: It is
> impossible he can deny it: He will readily acknowl-
> edge it. Having obtained this concession, I push him
> still farther in his retreat: and I ask him, if it be not
> probable, that the principle which first arranged, and

still maintains, order in this universe, bears not also some remote inconceivable analogy to the other operations of nature and among the rest to the economy of human mind and thought (D218).

To this the atheist must assent. As a result the atheist acknowledges some resemblance, and the theist a great difference, between the order of the universe and its cause. Therefore it is a merely verbal dispute. But actually Philo has slipped in a very significant notion under the guise of amicably settling a verbal disagreement. First of all, the suggested analogy is made between the rotting of a turnip, the generation of an animal, the structure of human thought and the cause of order in the universe. The turnip, the animal, and human thought all have in common an internal principle of order. The turnip is ordered by the rotting, the animal by generation, and human thought by its structure. Also they all have in common a rational principle of order because there is a relation of the parts to each other and to a general purpose. Just as the turnip, the animal, and the human mind are ordered from within by a rational principle, so the universe is internally structured by a rational cause. It is especially noteworthy that the original principle of order in the universe is compared not to the human mind itself but rather to its economy or order. The use of the two entities "structure of human thought" and "economy of human mind and thought" as bases of comparison is not accidental. It provides direct support for the interpretation of the passage above in which the phrase "MIND OR THOUGHT" is preferred to "a mind or intelligence." The same internal cause which forms the structure of the human mind also forms the structure of all other natural organisms. Hume picked the term "mind" to designate this cause since any other term would only have tended to obscure the fact which he was trying to point out. However, since this internal, rational cause is the ultimate explanation for all order in the universe, it is, in a sense, also entitled to be called God. This God has only the remotest connection with the one traditionally conceived. Hume's God is immanent in the world as its structuring force and not transcendent to it as a designer.

The immanent principle which is responsible for the order in the universe has already been characterized as rational. It is rational or intelligent because its effects resemble the intelligently ordered objects of human artifice. Both natural and artificial objects have parts which are related to each other by the reciprocal relation of cause and effect and which also contribute to some general purpose of the object as a whole. All those objects of this type which are not ordered by men or animals are designed by Nature. By Nature we mean not the sum total of things in the world but rather the dynamic, internal structuring principle in the universe. Since Philo's God or "Mind" is such a force, the identification of God with Nature is certainly intended by Hume.

As thus conceived, God is not conscious or personal. According to Hume there can be a self or person only if a mind is present and a mind consists of a number of ideas or perceptions united together by certain relations. But Nature is the principle which arranges and structures the ideas. It is not the ideas or perceptions themselves. The same principle which orders ideas in the mind also orders matter in the universe. Only in the case of the operations of men and animals is the ordering of means to ends due to an awareness of causal connections. In the operations of the other principles of Nature, like instinct, vegetation and generation, the order is produced without conscious direction. God or Nature emerges as the impersonal, immanent and rational orderer of the universe.

Philo is not certain whether the ultimate cause, Nature, is one principle or a plurality of causes referred to collectively, for he says that there exists a "cause or causes" of the particular design in the universe. However, no matter how one might hesitate about the number of principles or the degree of rationality of Nature, that it is rational and internal to the universe is well established. Dispute about a name is possible, but the facts are plain for all to see.

The purpose of the *Dialogues* is not exclusively negative and critical. Although the argument from design is demolished, it is done only because Hume is developing a concept of the principle of order as incomprehensible, rational and internal. This task is performed by the three characters of the *Dialogues:* Demea, who expounds the doctrine of the incomprehensibility of God; Cleanthes, who develops the concept of the rationality of the Ultimate Cause; and Philo, who proves that a principle internal to the universe is the required explanation of the order because it alone is a necessary and sufficient condition of order.[2]

This incomprehensible, rational and internal principle is identified as Nature. The *Dialogues* are important to an understanding of Hume's system first in emphasizing the influence of Nature over human lives and secondly in their refusal to identify Nature with blind irrationality.

[2] Ronald J. Butler in "Natural Belief and the Enigma of Hume," *Archiv für Geschichte der Philosophie*, XLII (1960), 73–100, agrees that all three characters act as spokesmen for Hume's ideas. However, Professor Butler contends that natural belief in design and in a designing God is what is assented to by the three. On my interpretation Philo's arguments directly oppose this contention.

BIBLIOGRAPHY

This is a list of some of the editions of Hume's works, and of some of the works on Hume in addition to those included in this volume, that have been published since 1938, the date of T. E. Jessop's *Bibliography of David Hume and of Scottish Philosophy from Francis Hutcheson to Lord Balfour* (London and Hull).

EDITIONS OF HUME'S WORKS

INDIVIDUAL WORKS

A Treatise of Human Nature, ed. L. A. Selby-Bigge (originally published 1888), repr. Oxford, 1941, 1946, 1949, 1951, 1955.

An Abstract of a Treatise of Human Nature, ed. J. M. Keynes and P. Sraffa. Cambridge, 1938.

Enquiries concerning the Human Understanding and concerning the Principles of Morals, ed. L. A. Selby-Bigge, 2nd ed. (originally published 1902), repr. Oxford, 1946, 1955.

An Inquiry concerning Human Understanding, ed. Charles W. Hendel. Indianapolis, Ind., 1955.

An Inquiry concerning the Principles of Morals, ed. Charles W. Hendel. Indianapolis, Ind., 1957.

The Natural History of Religion, ed. H. E. Root. London, 1956.

Hume's Dialogues concerning Natural Religion, ed. Norman Kemp Smith, 2nd ed. London, 1947; repr. Indianapolis, Ind., 1962.

Dialogues concerning Natural Religion, ed. Henry D. Aiken. New York, 1948.

Collections and Selections

The Philosophical Works of David Hume, ed. T. H. Green and T. H. Grose, 4 vols. (originally published 1874–75), repr. London, 1964.

Essays Moral, Political and Literary (originally published 1903), repr. London, 1963.

New Letters of David Hume, ed. Raymond Klibansky and Ernest C. Mossner. Oxford, 1954.

David Hume's Political Essays, ed. Charles W. Hendel. Indianapolis, Ind., 1953.

An Enquiry concerning Human Understanding, and Other Essays, ed. Ernest C. Mossner. New York, 1963.

Hume on Human Nature and the Understanding, ed. Antony Flew. New York, 1962.

Hume on Religion, ed. Richard Wollheim. Cleveland, O., 1964.

Hume's Ethical Writings, ed. Alasdair MacIntyre. New York, 1965.

Hume's Moral and Political Philosophy, ed. Henry D. Aiken. New York, 1948.

Of the Standard of Taste and Other Essays, ed. John W. Lenz. Indianapolis, Ind., 1965.

The Philosophy of David Hume, ed. V. C. Chappell. New York, 1963.

Selections, ed. Charles W. Hendel (originally published 1927), repr. New York, 1955.

Theory of Knowledge, ed. D. C. Yalden-Thomson. London, 1951.

Theory of Politics, ed. Frederick Watkins. London, 1951.

A Treatise of Human Nature [in part], ed. D. G. C. Macnabb. Cleveland, O., 1962.

Writings on Economics, ed. Eugene Rotwein. London, 1955.

WORKS ON HUME

BOOKS

Basson, A. H. *David Hume*. London, 1958.

Bongie, Lawrence L. *David Hume: Prophet of the Counter-revolution*. London, 1965.

Broiles, R. D. *The Moral Philosophy of David Hume*. The Hague, 1964.

Brunius, Teddy. *David Hume on Criticism*. Stockholm, 1952.

Flew, Antony. *Hume's Philosophy of Belief*. London, 1961.

Heinemann, F. H. *David Hume: The Man and His Science of Man*. Paris, 1940.

Hendel, Charles W. *Studies in the Philosophy of David Hume* (originally published 1925), new ed. Indianapolis, Ind., 1963.

Kydd, Rachael M. *Reason and Conduct in Hume's Treatise*. London, 1946.

Leroy, André. *David Hume*. Paris, 1953.

Macnabb, D. G. C. *David Hume: His Theory of Knowledge and Morality*. London, 1951.

Mossner, Ernest Campbell. *The Forgotten Hume: le bon David*. New York, 1943.

———. *The Life of David Hume*. London, 1954.

Passmore, J. A. *Hume's Intentions*. Cambridge, 1952.

Price, H. H. *Hume's Theory of the External World*. Oxford, 1940.

Price, John Valdimir. *The Ironic Hume*. Austin, Tex., 1965.

Smith, Norman Kemp. *The Philosophy of David Hume*. London, 1941.

Stewart, J. B. *The Moral and Political Philosophy of David Hume*. New York, 1963.

Zabeeh, Farhang. *Hume: Precursor of Modern Empiricism.* The Hague, 1960.

David Hume: A Symposium, ed. D. F. Pears (original articles by Stuart Hampshire, D. F. Pears, P. L. Gardiner, G. J. Warnock, Philippa Foot, B. A. O. Williams, and H. R. Trevor-Roper). London, 1963.

Human Understanding: Studies in the Philosophy of David Hume, ed. Alexander Sesonske and Noel Fleming (previously published articles by H. H. Price, Antony Flew, Douglas Gasking, Karl R. Popper, P. F. Strawson, C. D. Broad, and Terence Penelhum). Belmont, Calif., 1965.

ARTICLES

Aschenbrenner, Karl. "Psychologism in Hume," *Philosophical Quarterly,* XI (1961), 28–38.

Atkinson, R. F. "Hume on Mathematics," *Philosophical Quarterly,* X (1960), 127–37.

Broad, C. D. "Hume's Doctrine of Space," *Proceedings of the British Academy,* XLVII (1962), 161–76.

Butchvarov, Panayot. "The Self and Perceptions: A Study in Humean Philosophy," *Philosophical Quarterly,* IX (1959), 97–115.

Butler, Ronald J. "Natural Belief and the Enigma of Hume," *Archiv für Geschichte der Philosophie,* XLII (1960), 73–100.

Capaldi, Nicholas. "Hume's Rejection of 'Ought' as a Moral Category," *Journal of Philosophy,* LXIII (1966), 126–37.

Day, John. "Hume on Justice and Allegiance," *Philosophy,* XL (1965), 35–56.

Furlong, E. J. "Imagination in Hume's Treatise and Enquiry," *Philosophy,* XXXVI (1961), 62–70.

Leroy, André. "La liberté de spontanéité chez David Hume," *La Liberté: Actes du IVᵉ Congrès des Sociétés de Philosophie de Langue Française* (Neuchâtel, 1949), pp. 363–67.

————. "Statut de l'objet extérieure dans la philosophie de Hume," *Revue Internationale de Philosophie*, VI (1952), 199–212.

Markus, R. I. "Hume: Reason and Moral Sense," *Philosophy and Phenomenological Research*, XIII (1952–53), 139–58.

Marshall, Geoffrey. "David Hume and Political Scepticism," *Philosophical Quarterly*, IV (1954), 247–57.

Mossner, Ernest Campbell. "The Enlightenment of David Hume," *Introduction to Modernity* (Austin, Tex., 1965), pp. 43–62.

Noxon, James. "Hume's Opinion of Critics," *Journal of Aesthetics and Art Criticism*, XX (1961), 157–62.

Pike, Nelson. "Hume on Evil," *Philosophical Review*, LXXII (1963), 180–97.

Pomeroy, Ralph S. "Hume on the Testimony for Miracles," *Speech Monographs*, XXIX (1962), 1–12.

Price, H. H. "The Permanent Significance of Hume's Philosophy," *Philosophy*, XV (1940), 10–36.

Price, Kingsley Blake. "Does Hume's Theory of Knowledge Determine his Ethical Theory?" *Journal of Philosophy*, XLVII (1950), 425–34.

————. "Hume's Analysis of Generality," *Philosophical Review*, LIX (1950), 58–76.

Randall, John H., Jr. "David Hume: Radical Empiricist and Pragmatist," *Freedom and Experience: Essays Presented to Horace M. Kallen*, ed. Sidney Hook and Milton R. Konvitz (Ithaca and New York, 1947), pp. 289–312.

Smith, James Ward. "Concerning Hume's Intentions," *Philosophical Review*, LXIX (1960), 63–77.

Sweigart, John. "The Distance between Hume and Emotivism," *Philosophical Quarterly*, XIV (1964), 229–36.

Taylor, A. E., John Laird, and T. E. Jessop. "The Present-Day Relevance of Hume's *Dialogues concerning Natural Religion*," *Aristotelian Society Supplementary Volume*, XVIII (1939), 179–228.

Tranoy, Knut Erik. "Hume on Morals, Animals, and Men," *Journal of Philosophy*, LVI (1959), 94–103.

Wand, Bernard. "Hume's Non-Utilitarianism," *Ethics*, LXXII (1961–62), 193–96.

———. "A Note on Sympathy in Hume's Moral Theory," *Philosophical Review*, LXIV (1955), 275–79.

Weinberg, Julius R. "The Novelty of Hume's Philosophy," *Proceedings of the American Philosophical Association*, XXXVIII (1964–65), 17–35.

Will, Frederick L. "Will the Future Be Like the Past?" *Mind*, LVI (1947), 332–47.